Islam and Feminism:

Theory, Modelling and Applications

In the Name of Allah,

the Beneficent, the Merciful

Islam and Feminism:

Theory, Modelling and Applications

Edited
by
Ali H. Al-Hakim

Institute of Islamic Studies – London
2005

Islam and Feminism: Theory, Modelling and Applications

First published in the UK by the Institute of Islamic Studies
Affiliated to the Islamic Centre of England
140 Maida Vale, London W9 1QB, UK
Tel: 020-7604 5544
Fax: 020-7604 5545
Email: iis@islamic-studies.org
Homepage: www.islamic-studies.org

ISBN: 1-904934-04-8

Collected papers from a Conference held on 9th September 2001 by the Institute of Islamic Studies at the Islamic Centre of England. Responsibility rests with the authors of the articles presented in this book to have obtained permission to use any material from various sources and to have acknowledged them in the text. The publisher will not take any responsibility in this regard.

Contents

PART TWO- ISLAM AND FEMINISM: APPLICATIONS.. 179

ARTICLE 7: A GLANCE AT WOMEN'S SOCIO-POLITICAL ROLES IN ISLAMIC GOVERNMENT 181

ARTICLE 8: THE SHARI'AH LAW AND EDUCATION FOR WOMEN 191

Contributors

Al-Hakim, Ali H. – Institute of Islamic Studies - London
Ali H. Al-Hakim studied Arabic literature in Iraq - his homeland - and completed his studies up to the level of *Ijtihad* at the theological seminary of Qum in 1997. He has delivered many lectures at the University of Oslo, the Islamic College for Advanced Studies, London, and at Croydon CETS in South East London. He is currently a researcher at the IIS in London. He has written extensively on Islamic law, history and ethics. He has recently finished two researches: *'The Martyr of Freedom'* about Al-Husayn (as), and *'The Awaited Saviour'*, about Al-Mahdi (as) with a comparison of the concepts of mysticism, occultation and salvation in different religions.

Ameli Renani, Saied Reza – Faculty of Sociology, Tehran University
Saied Reza Ameli holds a Ph.D. in the Sociology of Culture and Mass Media from the Royal Holloway University of London. His conference papers include: "Eurocentrism and Islamophobia". He has written many books, the most recent being: "Globalization, Americanization and British Muslim Identity", 2002. He is currently an Associate Professor at the University of Tehran.

Araki, Mohsin - Islamic Centre of England - London
Mohsin Araki studied in the seminary of Najaf from 1968 until 1975, and then continued his advanced studies at the seminary of Qum up to the level of *Ijtihad*. His publications include amongst others: *The Bases of the Global Islamic Vision* (Persian), *The Authority of Allah and the Authority of the Jurists* (Arabic), *The Ownership of Mines in Islamic Jurisprudence* (Arabic), *Causality and Human Intention* (Arabic), *The Contemporary Islamic Awakening, Phases and Pioneers* (English), *Ideological and Jurisprudential Frontiers of Islam* (English), and *The True Meaning of Intedhar* (Persian). He is currently a lecturer at the Imam Hussain Institute – London, and a member of the Academic Board of the Institute of Islamic Studies.

Borujerdi, Ashraf – Iranian Ministry of the Interior
Ashraf Borudjerdi is an Advisor to the Minister and Head of the Women's Affairs Department in Iran's Ministry of the Interior. She is also a member of the Central Council of the Islamic Republic of Iran's Women's Society, and the Editorial Board of *Neda* quarterly magazine. She holds an MSc in theology and Islamic culture. Her publications include contributions to *An Overview of Women's Status in the Order of Creation.* Her research activities include studies on the status of man from the approach of the Holy Qur'an, woman in *Nahj-ul-Balagah*, and piety in the Holy Qur'an.

Cantone, Kafia – SOAS – University of London
Kafia Cantone holds an MA in Islamic Art and Architecture from SOAS, University of London, where she is currently a PhD candidate in the department of Archaeology and Africa.

Iravani, Shahin - Faculty of Psychology and Education - Tehran University
Shahin Iravani has studied Education and the Philosophy of Education at the University of Tehran. Her MA thesis dealt with the subject of women in Islam, and she is currently a lecturer at the Faculty of Education, University of Tehran.

Jamshidian, Turan – Mahjubah Magazine – Tehran, I. R. Iran
Turan Jamshidian holds a MA in Teaching ESL, and has studied for eleven years in the Islamic seminary. She is currently editor-in-chief of the magazine *Mahjubah* – Tehran.

Krausen, Halimah – Imam Ali Mosque – F. R. Germany
Halimah Krausen has studied Islamic Studies, Protestant theology, and Comparative Religions at the University of Hamburg. She has published a German translation of the Qur'an. She is currently co-operating with the Imam Ali Mosque in Hamburg – Germany.

Seraj, Saedah - University Malaya – Malaysia
Saedah Seraj holds a PhD and is currently head of the Department of Educational Development, Faculty of Education at the University of Malaysia.

Shabazz, Adeela - Muslim Women's Helpline - England
Adeela Shabazz is trained in counselling and community development. She is an advisory member to MIND, a mental health charity, as well as a member of the management board for the Muslim Women's Helpline.

Introduction

Through history, women's issues have been repeatedly dealt with by both secular and religious thinkers alike. The Islamic period, medieval times, and the modern eras have all produced different ideas and theories relating to the role of women in society. We are not here to criticise the Jewish Orthodox view regarding the female nature, nor the view of women as perceived by the Christian philosophers, or any other religious groups, but to examine more closely the opinions prevalent during the medieval ages.

We will commence by considering the roots of these opinions. Unfortunately, the medieval age based its concept of women on the Ancient Greek understanding of women's natures. According to Plato (427 - 347 BC), women came about through a physical degeneration of the human being. "It is only males who are created directly by the gods and are given souls. Those who live rightly return to the stars, but those who are 'cowards' or [lead unrighteous lives] may with reason be supposed to have changed into the nature of women in the second generation."

Aristotle (384 - 322 BC) considered women 'defective' human beings. Women were 'infertile males'. "The female, since she is deficient in natural heat, is unable to 'cook' her menstrual fluid to the point of refinement, at which it would become semen (i.e. 'seed'). Therefore her only contribution to the embryo is its matter and a 'field' in which it can grow." Her inability to produce semen is her deficiency. The reason why the man dominates in society is his superior intelligence. Only the man is a full human being. "The relationship between the male and the female is by nature such that the male is higher, the female lower, that the male rules and the female is ruled."

According to Roman family law, the husband was the absolute lord and master. In Roman civil law women's rights were very limited. The reasons given in Roman law for restraining women's rights are variously described as 'the weakness of her sex' or 'the stupidity of her sex'. The context clarifies that the problem did not lie in women's physical weakness, but in what was perceived as her lack of sound judgement and her inability to think logically.

The prevailing tradition of Romans and Hellenists saw society as segmented in higher and lower forms of the human being. Women were inferior to men by nature. Thus Roman law, which became the basis for the Church's laws, gave women a low status in society. Women did not enjoy equal rights in their homes, nor in the civic society. Some Fathers of the Church linked women's presumed inferior status to scriptural texts: only the man, they said, was created in God's image. Moreover, Paul had forbidden women to teach in church.

'Church Orders' of the first millennium also demonstrate traces of the belief in women's inferiority. Theologians, too, copied this line of thinking, integrating the anti-women views of Ancient Greeks and Romans into their theological reasoning. Let us read through the following points:

> Both nature and the law place the woman in a subordinate condition to the man.[1]

> It is the natural order among people that women serve their husbands and children and their parents, because the justice of this lies in (the principle that) the lesser serves the greater . . . This is the natural justice that the weaker brain serve the stronger. This, therefore, is the evident justice in the relationships between slaves and their masters that they who excel in reason, excel in power.[2]

> Nor can it be doubted, that it is more consonant with the order of nature that men should bear rule over women, than women over men.

---

[1] Irenaeus, Fragment no 32.
[2] Augustine, Questions on the Heptateuch, Book I, § 153.

It is with this principle in view that the apostle says, "The head of the woman is the man"; and "Wives, submit yourselves unto your own husbands". So also the Apostle Peter writes: "Even as Sara obeyed Abraham, calling him lord.[3]

The Apostle wants women, who are manifestly inferior, to be without fault, in order that the Church of God be pure.[4]

Who are there that teach such things apart from women? In very truth, women are a feeble race, untrustworthy and of mediocre intelligence. Once again we see that the Devil knows how to make women spew forth ridiculous teachings, as he has just succeeded in doing in the case of Quintilla, Maxima and Priscilla.[5]

In conclusion, many Fathers, canon lawyers, theologians and Church leaders were of the opinion that a woman could not be equal to a man, and many thinkers from the Dark Ages argued that a woman's soul was something animalistic, and completely distinct from that of the superior male soul. Medieval European literature generally portrayed women as second-class citizens. Nevertheless, historical sources from medieval times confirm that intellectual women abounded, and contributed profusely to the cultural life, enriching the intellectual milieu. Due to the various contradicting notions concerning women, one is at a loss to explain how such humiliating opinions were held by humanist thinkers and historians.

Historical sources confirm that a lower criminality rate existed amongst women as compared to men during the medieval period. However, one of the first works on female antisocial behaviour, *Melleus Maleficarum*, written in 1487, has a readymade explanation for both the methods and types of offences committed

---

[3] Augustine, On Concupiscence, Book I, chap. 10.
[4] Ambrosiaster, On 1 Timothy 3,11.
[5] Epiphanius, Panarion 79, §1.

by women against society. Women, according to the authors, were prone to deceit, lies, and concealment because: 'There was a defect in the formation of the first woman since she was formed from a bent rib, that is, a rib from the breast, which is bent, as it were, in the contrary direction to a man.' Through this defect she is an imperfect animal, and thus she always deceives. However, the apparently low criminality among women led to much speculation among criminologists, especially concerning the nature of the female offender, when dealt with from a societal angle.

There are several theories in this matter explaining this low criminality rate. Are women, indeed, the gentle creatures which the chivalric literature of all centuries assumed them to be, or do they commit just as many crimes as men but get caught less frequently?

The first group claims that women are less criminally inclined than men, and they base their arguments either on the assumption that a woman's psychological drive makes her gentle and motherly or that, culturally, women are taught to take a less aggressive and more subordinate role in society. In terms of their crime pattern, the first argument suggests that women are, by their instinctual makeup, not prone to violence and antisocial behaviour. Coupled with this mild-mannered psychological portrait is that of comparative physical weakness which, before the days of the gun, limited the crimes women could commit. On the other side are those who claim that in crime, as in all other aspects of life, women have been forced into a submissive, non-aggressive role. Women, therefore, commit fewer crimes than men because it is less culturally acceptable for them to do so.

A group with opposing views claim that there is another common explanation for the paucity of female offenders, which is that women are more capable of concealing their crimes than men are. For instance, very few cases of women killing newborn children appear in either the coroners' rolls or in gaol delivery, and yet one assumes that unwanted babies were sometimes killed. We cannot know how many mothers, like the peasant woman in Pearl Buck's *The Good Earth*, suffocated their children at birth and then claimed that the child was stillborn. Manorial records indicate that many of the lesser antisocial acts were concealed. Petty thefts were called trespass, assaults on children were regarded as disciplinary, and even the prostitute could claim to be the housekeeper.

However, there is another explanation for the lower incidence of women than men in criminal records, which can be documented in both medieval and modern statistics, and that is that the courts treated women more leniently. Fewer women than men are arrested and, even when they are brought into courts, they are more likely to be acquitted. Medieval English judges and juries were no exception to this rule: of the women tried in gaol delivery 83.7 percent were acquitted compared to 70.3 percent of men.

Whether the first theory or one of the other two is correct, two important facts are certain; women were unjustly blamed for the wicked society that they had to endure during the medieval period. They also possess - in general - more sociable attitudes – or at least various statistics and historical facts support this claim.

Religious texts have furthermore boosted this old conflict, because these texts – with sometimes extremely distorted versions – were misused to justify unfounded andocentric theories. Consequently the Church and religion - often mixed together as if Christianity was the sole and unique manifestation of all religions - were made responsible for the stagnation of miserable conditions of women. It is even observed that many contemporary feminists blame the Church for standing against women's emancipation.

One may partly agree with such allegations; however we do not consider it wise to generalise the view of criticizing religious texts by classifying them under one category.

However, Western thinkers changed gear, and after a long period of discrimination against women, shifted from these backward concepts to the other extreme. It reached a stage where women were treated like masters and an Egyptian visitor to Paris about two hundred years ago, comparing French and Egyptian women wrote the following comment:

> Men among them are slaves of women and subject to their commands whether they be beautiful or not... women among the people of the East are like household possessions while among the Franks they are like spoiled children.

Although one may set aside the excesses of both extremes, the issue is now seen from another perspective within the Western intellectual milieu. The Czech author, Milan Kundera (1929-), has introduced the theme as one solution to the problems of the 20th century; to let ourselves be led by the woman:

> Woman is the future of man. That means that the world which was once formed in man's image will now be transformed to the image of woman. The more technical and mechanical, cold and metallic it becomes, the more it will need the kind of warmth that only the woman can give it. If we want to save the world, we must adapt to the woman, let ourselves be led by the woman, let ourselves be penetrated by the (Ewigweiblich) the eternally feminine![6]

Thus Western thinkers began to extensively argue for the most extreme standpoints, which are now being firmly criticized by some feminist activists.

Muslims Standpoint

All of this wavering has occurred while Islamic ideology has continuously put emphasis on the neutral nature of the human soul, and maintained that any form of andocentric position is to be rejected, and argued that any sort of unfounded gender-based favouritism was futile. This is the objective worldview propounded by Islamic sources, of which the Qur'an represents the perennial inspiration for human thinking and will continue to play a central role while introducing a unique principle of equality. It says:

---

[6] Cybernation Quotation Library

Never will I [God] allow to be lost the work of any of you, be he male or female.[7]

It also says:

O mankind! Be dutiful to your Lord, Who created you from a single person, from whom He created his partner, and from them both He created many men and women; and fear Allah through whom you demand (your mutual rights), and (do not cut the relations of) the wombs (kinship). Surely, Allah is Ever Watchful over you.[8]

The Qur'an addresses humanity in this way in order to remind us that we are created from the same nature, which is here identified as "a single person". This single person reflects the Islamic theory that, in the primordial period, there were only two human beings (Adam and Eve), but whether they existed in a state differentiated by gender is questionable.

Sadly, many Muslims have also been manipulated by inauthentic narrations, or have misunderstood canonical texts, in such a way as to create the same sort of primitive mentality found in Medieval Europe. The same misguided souls are now presenting this distorted image as a picture of the true Islam.

It is for the above reason as well as the distorted image of women in Islam created by the manipulative world mass media, that it was felt necessary to launch an intellectual and balanced movement for the English speaking community. The aim is to present the natural Islamic views regarding gender issues, and the Islamic response to unfounded accusations, as well as to address the problems and concerns faced by Muslim women. This is the intellectual background behind the one-day Conference on "Woman in Islam" arranged by the Institute of Islamic Studies at the Islamic Centre of England in London on Sunday 9th September 2001. The

---

[7] *Qur'an*, 5:196
[8] *Qur'an*, 4:1

Conference was convened by S. G. Safavi, who was at that time Director of Institute if Islamic Studies – London, and myself. During this Conference some of these papers were presented, from which this book is collected and published. There were lively discussions following each of the papers, and active contributors took account of many of the points raised when revising their papers for publication. The chapters below, with one exception ('Flexible Marriage' by A. H. Al-Hakim), originated either as presentations or as papers sent to the organisers of the Conference. The 'Flexible Marriage' paper was produced later, when the author became aware of the confusion revolving around this kind of marriage, and the need to clarify a couple of vague points.

The Papers in Brief

Part One - Islam and Feminism: Theory and Modelling

The book is divided into two parts, the first entitled: "Islam and Feminism: Theory and Modelling" and the second part: "Islam and Feminism: Applications".

Ameli's paper: "Feminist Expectations and the Response of Muslim Women", is the first paper presented in the book. He examines the feminist expectations of Muslim women according to the various perspectives of feminism. He has classified the feminist groups into five categories. The first is Amazon feminism, which is concerned with "physical gender equality". It rejects the idea that certain characteristics or interests are inherently masculine (or feminine), and upholds and explores a vision of heroic womanhood. This is a sort of radical feminism, which questions women's adoption of certain roles, just as it questions why men adopt certain roles. Radical feminism attempts to draw lines between biologically determined behaviour and culturally determined behaviour.

The second category is Anarcho-Feminism, which seeks the fragmentation of all the norms, values and customs related to women. This includes those values of both today's and yesterday's generations. It is concerned with the deconstruction of all traditional principles without establishing any systematic principle for the position of women within the modern or post-modern society.

The third is Liberal Feminism, which may be manifested in a variety of feminism that works within the structure of mainstream society in order to integrate women into that structure. Its roots stretch back to the social contract theory of government instituted by the American Revolution. The liberalisation of women according to the liberal democratic political system is their main slogan for women all over the world.

The fourth is Marxist or "Socialist Feminism". Marxism recognises that women are oppressed, and attributes this oppression to the capitalist/private property system. Thus, it insists that the only way to end the oppression of women is to overthrow the capitalist system.

The fifth category is Material Feminism, a movement in the late 19th century, which aimed to liberate women by improving their material condition. It focused on releasing women from the burden of housework and cooking, which were the exclusive chores of women in the household.

Ameli added that Islam established a movement for the revitalisation of women's rights, and it may be argued that social, cultural and political circumstances have created differences in the perception of Muslim women in society. Towards that he examined the response of Muslim women to Western feminism, from three perspectives:

The first was "Apologetic Feminism" - as he described it - a kind of liberal feminism for Muslim women. The second was "Reactionary Feminism", which is a movement that argues that Muslim women have already obtained an equal and respectable position within the Islamic tradition, without the need for further reform, and the third, was the Holistic Approach, which is presented by those activists and theoreticians who do not seek to isolate women from the whole of society. They see women's rights and position in terms of the whole structure of society, and avoid the segregation of society in terms of "feminism" or "masculinism".

This paper has undeniably provided a scholarly piece of work examining many, but not all, of the different tendencies of the feminist movement. This assessment was followed by a wise analysis of the Muslim woman's response. On the whole, the paper is a concise and an epigrammatic presentation, which is considerably useful for a wide readership.

The paper of Araki, entitled "The Status of Women in Islamic Thought", has explained the status of woman in Islam, in terms of the following principles: 1) Men and women are equal before God. They possess an equal potential for achieving perfection. 2) Men and women have equal rights and responsibilities towards nature. Both have an equal share in the benefits of nature. Conversely, they both share the same responsibility for guarding it. 3) Men and women have an equal position within the social structure. One focus of this paper is to explore the equal rights and responsibilities held by men and women, in relation to the society that they live in. 4) There is "unity in diversity". Even though there are many things in the world that exist in contradiction to each other, there is an underlying unity throughout all of creation. This is one of the sublime characteristics of the Islamic worldview. 5) The universe is created in a form where everything is linked. Everything is in need of another in order to be integrated and complete. Woman exists in order to complete man, and man exists in order to complete woman.

This paper offers in brief a sharp implementation of the approach of Islamic mysticism whilst dealing with issues relating to gender. Therefore it provides a useful presentation of Qur'anic models with a comparison between the virtuous and corrupt female exemplars.

At first glance one could claim that there are many fragmentary, repetitious passages in the text; however, a second reading may help to distinguish the difference. It is apparent that there is no attempt to deal with potential counter-arguments which may be directed from people who believe that women really are second-class citizens when it comes to their rights within the Shari'ah Law. The arguments, nevertheless, are formed in a systematic manner and the coherence between the argument's premises is apparent.

In his paper "The Status and Complementarity of the Two Genders" Al-Hakim confirmed that the relationship between men and women, in terms of their positions, roles and interrelationship with each other, has been a controversial topic throughout history. There are many theories and ideas dealing with this issue. Some have claimed support from revelation, while others have based themselves on traditional social structures. Few of these theories have proven to be satisfactory in creating a harmonious relationship between men and women. First depriving women of some of their civil rights, and then later giving them extra bonus or remuneration in compensation, has not provided the appropriate solution for the problems existing in their interrelationship. He established that the Islamic theory is that in the beginning, there were only two human beings. Unique to the Islamic position is the idea that they were undifferentiated by sex, with no gender differences. He claimed that it is the Qur'an which presents this position. Thus they were friends or partners, but not husband and wife. Prompted by satanic machinations, they were seduced into committing the first disobedience, after which their shame appeared before them. The author emphasised that Muslim philosophers have claimed that women and men are not just superficially similar to each other. They argue that the soul does not recognise any sexual differences. If we remove their material bodies from consideration, the argument goes, we will then find that women and men are actually identical. But we can argue even beyond this, saying that since their initial physical state was gender-neutral, even their bodies are basically identical as well. It is humanity's own actions that have divided them into two genders; therefore, gender is a human production, rather than a Divine distinction. He argued that there are historical and psychological factors, which prevent the two genders Divine and mutual integration, and he has attempted to answer this question, while simultaneously trying to uncover the Islamic view of gender relations and gender complementarity.

This paper certainly constitutes a scholarly piece of innovative research, providing an extensive study of women and gender issues from varying angles. The author draws on a wide range of quotations from both Western and Islamic sources, and he supplies adequate support from Qur'anic exegesis for his interpretation of the Qur'anic verses in the backing his of theory. An interesting comparison of differing theories is made, despite the absence of a thorough study regarding the elucidation of equality. In conclusion the paper is extensive in its scope and new in its ideas.

Iravani, in her paper titled "Exemplary Women in Islam and the Holy Qur'an", discussed the concept of feminine spiritual perfection as it is presented in the Qur'an. Islam is a religion based on emulation. As such, the Holy Qur'an demands that people pursue a spiritual path based upon the careful imitation of those individuals most beloved by Allah (swt). In order to make this possible, the Qur'an presents small spiritual biographies of numerous prophets, martyrs, and sages. Most of those examples given are of men; but there are, nonetheless, many detailed descriptions of perfect and exalted women given in the Qur'an. Most prominent of these is Mary, mother of Jesus (as), although others, such as Asiya (as), are presented as well. The books of history and Islamic narrations also give us many examples of holy and pious women, such as Khadijah, Fatima, and Zainab (as).

Firstly, she discussed the images presented of these women in great detail. Through a careful study of the Qur'anic text, she attempted to elucidate precisely what virtues these women possessed, and what it was about them that made them so beloved by Allah (swt). The virtues of chastity, patience, self-abnegation, and asceticism are discussed in this regard.

After this detailed discussion of the Qur'an, she then moved on to a discussion of those women who are praised in history and in Islamic narrations. This is necessary as the Qur'an only speaks of those women who lived before the Prophet (saws). In this section she focused on the exalted life of Prophet Muhammad's (saws) daughter, Fatima Zahra (as). There are numerous reports praising her as an embodiment of all virtue so a careful study of her life will shed light on exactly how virtue is defined in Islam. After this discussion, she demonstrated that, throughout history, women have achieved an elevated status in Islam.

This paper highlights, positively, the attributes of exemplary women incorporating a wide-ranging use of Qur'anic verses. The paradigm of virtue embodied in women mentioned in the Qur'an is examined and thereafter the author sets forth the criteria necessary for attaining perfection. Most of the references are taken from scholars of a Shi'ah-Muslim background. The claims put forward in this research are supported by a statistical survey regarding the role of women in Iranian society.

Krausen's paper "Personalities of Women in the Qur'an and their Reflection on Women in Islamic History" is written with a systematic presentation of topics, which manifests her ideas in a coherently argued paper. She has claimed that the position of women in Islam is currently one of the most popular topics amongst Muslims and in inter-cultural dialogue. The discussion is often triggered by burning questions resulting from the encounter with non-Muslim value systems, and a re-evaluation of past experiences within the Islamic community (ummah). The background for this is a need for orientation concerning the implementation of Islamic values in the modern world. In this context she said that one is often presented with descriptions of "the ideal Muslim woman" in an attempt to oppose the stereotypes one is confronted with from outside, ranging from critical sociological studies of the actual situation of our sisters, in the world between Indonesia and Morocco, to romantic images lifted from the 'Arabian Nights'. She concluded that what is often sadly missing is an idea of how women have actually endeavoured to realise their ideals, to overcome obstacles, and to contribute to the development of the community side by side with men, so that they can motivate our present and future generations in developing visions of their own.

Her paper begins by analysing those women mentioned in the Qur'an (for example, Mary (as), or Pharaoh's wife) in order to illustrate the ontological position, religious and social responsibilities, and ethical framework of women that was implemented amongst the Prophet's (saws) contemporaries. The paper then proceeds to show how women in Muslim history received and reflected these impulses, becoming active and even famous in various fields. However, she courageously declares that there are, unfortunately, only a few examples of women scholars, mystics, scientists, and politicians, and forms the question that although names like Umm Salama, Fatima, and Zainab (as) might be part of common vocabulary, in what way can they inspire us in our own age and time? What can we learn from examples like Nafisa, Rabi'ah al-'Adawiyah, Fakhr an-Nisa' and many others throughout the centuries? What other role models can be found for present-day Muslim girls and women to encourage them to unfold their potential and to use their abilities in meaningful ways? In her final step, she asks how and why Muslim women in recent centuries suffered the setback that has created their present situation in many Muslim countries, and what strategies can be developed to overcome this situation. This was associated with the hope that it would open ways for women to live a rich and dignified life, leading to the greater benefit of society as a whole.

It is a brief but interesting presentation of Muslim exemplars provided with their achievements throughout history. Additionally, the author offers many ideas. Therefore, this paper is a refreshingly neutral work, above sectarian disagreements and into which many Muslim women from other factions have been introduced, which has, therefore, paved a common ground for an inter-faith dialogue between various Muslim factions.

Saedah Seraj, in her paper "Women and Intellectualism", attempts to discuss the unique spiritual status of women in Islam. She claims that it is the goal of Islam to elevate all human beings, man or woman, to a state of perfection before their Creator. This potential for spiritual elevation is something all human beings have in common. However, there is no doubt that women have been given a unique quality and nature by Allah (swt), and it is this quality that needs to be addressed if we are to attempt to chart a spiritual path for women.

The paper begins with an analysis of the four holy women who are considered perfect by Islam: Asiya (as), wife of Pharaoh; Mary (as), mother of Jesus (as), Khadija (as), wife of Prophet Muhammad (saws), and Fatima Az-Zahra (as), daughter of Prophet Muhammad (saws). These women, being infallible, serve as a perfect guide for emulation. When a woman seeks nearness to Allah (swt), the obligation upon her is to emulate these four women in every way. The first step, then, is to chart out the lives and characters of these perfect souls.

She concludes that the way to emulate them is to try to achieve the high and perfect state of knowledge that they were endowed with. Spiritual wayfaring is ultimately an intellectual endeavour, and a struggle for knowledge. But it is a special kind of knowledge, one that can only be achieved through hard spiritual struggle. It is something quite above and beyond any form of worldly knowledge. As such, we can refer to spiritual wayfaring as an attempt to achieve high intellectualism. Beyond discussing the spiritual status of the perfect women, she attempts to chart out what is required in terms of belief and actions in order to reach this stage of high intellectualism. This has shed light on the spiritual path of women.

This research presents an academic analysis of the subject, with a study based on the work of religious scholars. The author introduces a new implementation of the term 'Intellectualism' with a brief clarification of the reasons behind this adoption. This also results in some confusion between 'intellectualism' and (*Shuhud*) the knowledge due to the soul's purity or Gnostic knowledge, which is entirely different. Nonetheless, this work is enriched with a wide range of references from both Muslim scholars and Western intellectuals.

Part Two - Islam and Feminism: Applications

In part two, where the book deals with applications of Islamic theory, Borujerdi - in her paper "Muslim Women's Participation in the Political Arena"- argues that there is disagreement amongst the scholars of Islamic jurisprudence regarding the competency of women for political activity. Much of this revolves around the potential held by women for political leadership. She insisted that it is especially acute in light of the fact that men have total guardianship over women - the father before marriage and the husband afterwards. In this paper, she attempts to discover the boundaries and limitations of women's rights and duties while extending the discussion into the political realm. In the beginning, she defines the meaning of political participation, as it is the endeavour of a person or persons to win political authority through the establishment of legislative and executive powers, or by taking hold of high-ranking positions in the administrative and legislative sectors. She argues that women are quite capable of contributing to the needs of their society through this form of political participation, especially when they are able to assess the achievements and approaches of the government and its political leaders. The late Imam Khomeini strongly emphasised this point, arguing that women should have a key role in the steering and guidance of society. Based on this, she seeks to vindicate the position of women within Islamic government.

It is obvious that the author approaches a sensitive issue in an ambitious manner. Qur'anic verses and narrations are interpreted, appropriately. Despite the absence of quotations and ideas from various Western intellectuals, the author manages a clever implementation of quotations from prominent Muslim scholars.

In her other paper "*Shari'ah* Legal Education for Women", Siraj attempts to establish first the meaning of *Shari'ah* Law, and claims that Islam came to save women from the dark oppression they suffered during the period of *jahilliyah,* the period of ignorance before Islam. One of the basic ways in which Islam strives to save people, men or women, from spiritual darkness, is education. Islam is a religion based on education, and one of the most important facets of education is proper instruction in *Shari'ah*, or Islamic law. She highlighted the role women have had in the history of *Shari'ah* Law, as well as discussing the position of women before the law itself.

The author emphasised that there are some apparent restrictions on the position of women within the *Shari'ah*, one such renown distinction made between men and women in the *Shari'ah* being that a women's testimony is worth only half of a man's, during a court proceeding. These issues were discussed, and it is shown that, contrary to many unfounded opinions, Islam gives women an important spiritual and leadership role.

Finally, the practical requirements for proper Islamic legal education for women was addressed, and a broad plan for Islamic education, with emphasis on the traditional study of the *Shari'ah* Law, was presented. She argues that it is of crucial importance that a system be established for giving Muslim women proper knowledge concerning their religious obligations, and the source of those obligations.

If one reads the paper with a second view, one may reach the opinion that it is an academic research. Her paper states that the *Shari'ah* Law is derived from the Qur'an, Islamic narrations and *Ijtihad,* whereas the latter is, in fact, the name of the act itself, which could be based on the two formerly mentioned, or on the other two sources, i.e. consensus and reason. Nevertheless, the paper provides a coherently linked and systematic presentation of the issues covered. Extensive ranges of material from both Islamic and Western intellectuals were implemented and Qur'anic verses and narrations were widely and appropriately used throughout.

As a Ph.D. student (of SOAS, University of London), Kafia Cantone has produced an academic piece of outstanding research supported by fieldwork, including a visual presentation (slides shown at the conference). She believes that owing to a scarcity of documentation and archaeological evidence that would shed light on the place allocated to women in the mosque at the time of the Prophet, the issue of women in the mosque can be discussed from two perspectives:

Firstly, historically, by using early sources, such as the authentic narrations and the accounts of travellers or historians; and secondly by looking at contemporary mosques and their use of space, along with their justifications for the use of such space.

She has investigated the question from the second perspective, i.e. by looking at contemporary mosques, their uses as well as their users, in order to present living case studies, rather than simply admiring empty spaces or monuments. Questions about the nature of the mosque were raised and the material presented drew attention to the non-monumental aspect of the mosque, whose origins may be traced back to the primordial concept of "mosque" at the time of the Prophet (saws).

She explored this question from an architectural perspective, bringing in examples of contemporary mosque architecture from an area that has been largely neglected, Senegal. The paper discussed the physical nature of mosque buildings, including their material and stylistic forms. Her aim was to put forward some theoretical approaches derived from the methodology used in the field. She briefly referred to the works of phenomenologists such as Michael Jackson and Paul Stoller, as well as those of Muslim anthropologists such as Merryl Davies, all of whom were found to have adopted suitable theoretical and methodological frameworks with which to analyse the material. The ultimate aim of this part of the paper was to open the discourse between Western academia and Muslim scholarship and to show the possible dialogue, and even the potential marriage, between the two discourses. That has very much helped to prove that there is not necessarily a contradiction between being an "academic" in the Western sense and being a Muslim.

Due to the fact that the greatest majority of those women who frequented the mosque were young and "orthodox" Sunni, her study focused on them. In the traditional establishments dominated by the *Sufi turuq*, only old women are tolerated in the mosque (most of the time in a separate building or relegated to the courtyard). The paper has therefore considered the implications of the rise in female mosque attendance - particularly amongst the young - in the chosen region in order to answer the broader question of whether women can or cannot frequent the mosque, from both a practical and legal perspective.

Both in her interviews with women and with Imams of mosques, it transpired that the space formerly allocated to women by men was being appropriated by women. This was reflected in their desire to have more space, to decorate it according to their taste, to have more facilities in their prayer areas, and so forth. It was felt that this type of female appropriation of space – both public and sacred – reflects, on a microcosmic scale, the increasing role women are starting to play in society.

Cantone also introduced some historical background to her research, saying that Islam penetrated Senegal from North Africa, in the form of Sufi brotherhoods who claim to follow the Maliki school of thought like most of North and West Africa. Traditional society and its interpretation of Maliki jurisprudence discourages women from going to the mosque maintaining that (a) it is not obligatory for them to do so and (b) it is preferable for them to pray at home. For this reason, up to the present day most Tijani, Khadr and Murid mosques (with the exception of the Layenne brotherhood) usually include a separate, small "outbuilding" for the only women who are tolerated within the sacred precinct, i.e. post-menopausal women. As the study focused on women who attend the mosque and the reasons for their attendance, she has chosen to concentrate on a relatively recent phenomenon dating from the last 10-15 years. She claimed that an increasing number of young women are breaking with tradition and are turning to Sunni Islam, which does not hold the same cultural taboo against pre-menopausal women attending the mosque. Such women quote the same narrations but with different interpretations. The Sunni movement, also known as the revivalist movement or "Mouvement Islamique", started gaining ground in the late '70's - 1980's by promoting a return to the Qur'an and the Sunnah. This phenomenon is what is referred to in the paper as "sunnification" and has primarily affected the young through the means of education (also known as da'awah).

Regarding the role of the mosque in the propagation of Sunni Islam, and due to the fact that the inspiration of the "Mouvement Islamique" is the Prophet Muhammad (saws) and his practice or Sunnah, efforts were made to recreate the environment of his time. The mosque of the Prophet played a vital spiritual role, but equal to this was its social, communal and educational role. It was a space that grouped and catered for the sacred as well as the secular. Similarly, a Sunni mosque wishes to extend its function beyond that of worship alone, and indeed Sunni mosques are open almost 24 hours a day; giving lessons, organising meals during the Holy month of Ramadhan, and, of course, offering communal prayers five times a day as well as providing a sermon in a local language alongside the Friday prayer. All these functions are in contrast to the practice of the Sufi brotherhoods.

The paper has concentrated on the correlation between the phenomenon of the Hijab and the frequenting of public places of worship, which were previously male-dominated spaces. Of particular interest is the issue of visibility: women who were previously invisible and secluded (praying in separate buildings), are now either plainly visible (i.e. praying behind men) or partially visible (by means of transparent curtains or windows). In a sense, they are metaphorically "invading" previously banned public/ sacred space.

Due to the shortage of equipment – during the Conference – not all the pictures provided with this paper could be presented, however her contribution was widely welcomed by various scholars. A few narrations were included in the paper. Nevertheless, the research provided a broad presentation of comparative religious practices, with a mixture of culture, archaeology and analysis of traditions.

In the synopsis "Polygamy" from Martyr Mutahari's work "Woman's Right in Islam" the custom of polygamy was examined in comparison with other forms of sexual institutions such as polyandry and sexual communism. The causes, which gave rise to polygamy, were discussed and the opinions of some Western intellectuals were criticised, and he concluded that polygamy, where a man can marry more than one wife, is the only form that is acceptable and beneficial to all parties involved. It is a custom which has been practiced since ancient times and by civilised societies, and is grossly misunderstood and hypocritically condemned by the West.

He clarified the reasons why Islam did not abolish the practice of polygamy showing that under certain circumstances it is, in fact, the right of women and it is for their benefit. He provided a detailed analysis into the main contributory factor to this, i.e. the outnumbering of men by women, showing that this law in fact is a safeguard for women and the society, as opposed to some chauvinistic establishment. He ultimately discussed the reasons, which have impelled men and women to stand abjectly against this custom, despite the fact that polygamy serves society in terms of protecting the moral structure as compared to the West where, in reality, polygamy is apparent, but practised through deception and without moral or legal responsibility.

This work supplies an extensive and academic research, which details a thorough comparison between the ideas of Muslims and non-Muslims, including the viewpoints of leading Western intellectuals such as Bertrand Russell. However, the author has overlooked the use of physiological facts in arguing the case for the validity of polygamy. Some claims concerning the engagement of the emotional side in such a marriage were generalised and may not reflect the reality in all cases. Nonetheless, all the possible conditions pertaining to polygamy were discussed in a shrewd way, and an astute analysis of ideas regarding polygamy and their comparison with some misuse in everyday life was provided.

This synopsis is ensued by an extensive paper regarding the "Flexible Marriage" written by A. H. Al-Hakim. The author asserts that Mut'ah, or flexible marriage has always been a controversial issue both within the differing schools of Islamic Jurisprudence and amongst the laity. He argued firstly through an examination of Qur'anic verses and historical narrations that the legitimacy of this marriage is well founded. He then demonstrated the reason why it is considered as an institutional marriage while presenting a comparison between both the flexible and permanent marriages. This was followed by a justification for his adoption of a new technical term for this type of marriage, i.e. "the Flexible Marriage". A brief elaboration of the family life and sexual satisfaction in the West was then introduced, as this helps to manifest the parallel ideas of both cultures. He highlighted the purpose this law serves within the community and how it can be viewed as a wise solution for mankind's need for sexual satisfaction. He argued how people's disapproval of this institution is, in fact, based on the way it is abused within different societies.

This research represents an academic research of a jurisprudential topic providing a novel review of a grossly misunderstood issue. An innovative technical term is introduced for the Mut'ah marriage. There is a comparison made between Western companionate marriage and the Muta'ah marriage, which is further supported and illustrated with a wide range of quotes from both Western intellectuals and Islamic sources.

Further, the style in which the paper is written is somewhat hard at the beginning, but flows more lucidly towards the end. On the other hand, it coherently articulates and establishes the legality of this marriage and provides a wise argument for society's need of such an institution. In conclusion, it is a beneficial paper and many considered its arguments as innovative and convincing.

The author of "Divorce as an Islamic Institution", Shahbaz, whose work involves working with women, sets out to discuss divorce as an Islamic institution given to mankind as a Mercy from Allah (swt). She has stated that although it is permitted, it is one of the most disliked actions. This is in contrast to many popular but unfounded beliefs. Divorce is not intended to be an irrational quick fix left to the whims and fancies of men. As with marriage, there are set rules and guidelines for divorce. According to the teachings of Islam, there is equality among the sexes as to who may institute divorce proceedings. The process is something clearly delineated, involving attempts at mediation and reconciliation, arranging separation, establishing financial arrangements, and arranging for care and development of children. In her paper she explored the reasons and consequences of divorce. Comparisons were made with other systems where divorce is not permitted due to a system defined by an ecclesiastical hierarchy, where unhappy couples are forced to either survive in a melancholy marriage, or opt out for an alternative, but immoral, relationship with others.

Evaluating this paper after a second reading one assumes a practical introduction and direction throughout the paper. The ideas are presented in a systematic way. The demonstration of the differing solutions that a woman seeking divorce can obtain is based on the alternatives provided within the *Shari'ah* Law.

In her paper "The Right of Custody in Islam" Jamshidian has emphasised that there is a lack of material on the right of custody in Islamic *Shari'ah* Law, especially in terms of the mother's roles and responsibilities. But throughout the paper one may discover that the author adopts a classical approach to an extremely sensitive issue. Whilst a wide range of Qur'anic verses and narrations are used to support the author's ideas, many of the issues in question are not thoroughly dealt with.

She starts with asserting that mankind in the Holy Qur'an was called by three names: man (*Adam*), human being *(insan)* and the masses *(nas)*. Humanity, according to the logic of the Qur'an, is a sacred entity. Whenever people are praised and supported, it is humanity as a whole that is praised, regardless of gender.

Although this introduction is irrelevant to the subject presented, her aim from this general perspective was, nevertheless, to conclude that men and women share something in common, as all human beings are subject to Divine Law. She added that this means that men and women are treated identically throughout the text because, if one examines the literal meaning of Holy Qur'an, it can be perceived that Allah (swt) has created man in two different forms: as an independent creation, and as a creation that exists to perpetuate itself. It is from this standpoint that gender differences begin to play a definite role.

Analysing custody from this angle, she declared that custody means supporting and treating the child in a humane manner or taking care of him or her in terms of food, shelter, and education. The principle of custody originates from human nature and is based on a close relation between the child and his or her parents. Custody is a natural phenomenon. It will appear where there is a need for it, and as soon as the child reaches adulthood, custody will be removed.

The right to child custody is given to women in the case of divorce or the father's death. If the child is a boy, the mother is responsible until the age of two. If the child is a girl, the mother has to care for her up to the age of seven. Allah (swt) has planned for the young girl that she be a mother of the coming generation. As such, she must absorb her mother's training, behaviour and manners. The boy's two years with his mother is established so that he may enjoy the mother's compassion, love, and be raised according to Islamic standards. It is the child's need for love and compassion that is the most important factor in custody. According to Islamic *Shari'ah* Law, a child needs both parents' love in order to grow up positively. The basis for custody is that the child should not be in distress or under constraint. It is this reason that underlies the uniform custody regulations for boys or girls under the age of two. Both need breastfeeding, so both are left with the mother. There is a close relationship between custody and breastfeeding (*rida'ah*). There are different aspects and views about breastfeeding (with regard to custody issues) discussed in this paper. The Muslim scholars' opinions, which are presented, are done so in a clear manner.

It has been felt that a shortened version of Martyr Mutahari's book "Islamic Modest Dress" would be very beneficial, therefore we have included it in this book after having shortened and edited it. Mutahari aims first to define the limits within which sexual relations must remain, and explains how the Islamic dress code is a means for preserving and protecting society from corruption and expended energies. This paper presents a philosophical and socio-historic discussion analysing the reasons that resulted in the appearance of the modest dress (*Hijab*), which was a practice prevalent throughout the non-Arab world prior to the advent of Islam. It then examined as to whether such reasons conform to the Islamic philosophy of *Hijab*. Qur'anic texts and Islamic narrations were explored to deduce the precepts and conditions of the Islamic modest dress, and it is shown that this particular form of restriction pertaining to a woman's attire does not symbolise her exclusion from playing an active role in society. Mutahari argued, contrary to popular Western perception, that the modest dress (*Hijab*) in actuality adorns a woman with dignity and respect, and elevates her in the eyes of men far above her Western counterpart.

Reading through the paper with an evaluating intention in mind, one may conclude that it presents a scholarly research. As the book was written for Iranian women five decades ago, it therefore did not address the contemporary issues and problems encountered by women wearing the hijab in the Western world, which have recently became internationally controversial subjects. However a wise implementation of Qur'anic quotes, Islamic narrations and Western references are incorporated into the discussion to support and illustrate the author's insightful opinions. The paper could have benefited from a study of and comparison between the practice of modest dress (*Hijab*) in other religions, such as Christianity and Judaism that also adopt the practice of chastity, and whose religious texts prescribe women to also cover their heads. Nevertheless, an interesting socio-historical analysis is provided, detailing the reasons behind the emergence of the modest dress in society. The Islamic philosophy which lies behind the adoption and adaptation of this custom (*Hijab*) is then astutely contrasted and affirmed as being incontrovertibly capable of benefiting a wide range of readership.

I hope that this brief reading of the papers will give an insight into the various ideas explored, and that the critical evaluation will contribute to a further investigation of the different subjects. It is also worth emphasising that these papers represent solely the authors' ideas as to how to perceive the Islamic views, and do not necessarily reflect the actual views of the organizer, i.e. Institute of Islamic Studies, London. Although the Conference was held on 9th September 2001, we have not been able to publish the book until now. The reasons for this are many and varied. Furthermore, we encountered various technical problems, and certain papers required rewriting, or supplementation. Therefore the finalised papers were only received two years after their having been delivered at the Conference. Due to this extreme lapse of time, the editor was faced with no alternative other than to edit those available papers, add an extra article about 'Flexible marriage' and the book was ready for publication after nearly three years.

It is our heartfelt concern and intention that this academic work shall endeavour to serve all the truth seekers - in general - and in particular the English speaking Muslim Community around the globe, and contribute to an enlightened and improved understanding of the various aspects of gender issues in Islamic thought.

A. H. Al-Hakim

Institute of Islamic Studies

November 2004

Part One

Islam and Feminism:
Theory and Modelling

Article 1

Feminist Expectations and the Response of Muslim Women

Saied Reza Ameli

Abstract

The feminist movement is considered by most to be a movement for the liberation and protection of women's rights in society. In this paper, we will examine the feminist expectations of Muslim women according to five different perspectives of feminism: Amazon Feminism, Anarcho-Feminism, Liberal Feminism, Marxist/ Socialist Feminism and Material Feminism.

Although Islam established a movement for the revitalisation of women's rights, it may be argued that social, cultural and political circumstances have created differences in the perception of Muslim women in society. In this paper, we will also examine the response of Muslim women to Western feminism, from three perspectives: Apologetic Feminism, Reactionary Feminism and the Holistic Approach.

Introduction

There are a variety of theories and movements in feminism which present a diversity of ideas, values and perspectives. In general, the feminist movement is considered as a movement for the liberation and protection of women's rights in the society. Such a movement has been diversified due to the differences of cultural and ideological contexts. This is why Islamic feminism, Social feminism and Western feminism have meaning today.

Due to historical changes and the multi-disciplinary orientations of feminism, it is indeed problematic to define the concept. However one can define 'feminism' in terms of its historical origins and development and its fragmentation into many differing forms. The term 'feminism' was first used in 1871 AD, in a French medical text, to describe a cessation in the development of sexual organs and characteristics in male patients, who were believed to be suffering from the feminisation of their bodies. From the mid 19th century, the term gradually started to be used when women questioned their inferior status and demanded amelioration in their social position (Freedman, 2001). Among many feminist movements, Material feminism emerged as a movement in the late 19th century, which aimed at liberating women by improving their material condition. It focused on releasing women from the burden of housework and cooking duties, which was a weight on their shoulders in the home.

For the last hundred years, many forms of feminism have appeared, but feminism in the general term can be defined as an 'advocacy of rights for women to equality with men in all spheres of life'.[1]

To understand Islamic feminism and the consequences of the feminist movement in the liberation of Muslim women, or the movement which tries to provide women with a greater role in the public sphere, it is necessary to review the diversity of theories of feminism throughout history; in particular liberal feminism, in the West. In this paper, we will briefly examine the feminist theories, and then discuss the different responses from Muslim women.

1.1   Western Feminism

Western feminist researchers in general, hold the belief that once men dominate a society in certain spheres, women will become a suppressed and passive group.[2] Western feminism is the continuation of a historical process. One can argue that the basis of Western feminism is the product of sole gender domination by the Church and the crude discrimination between men and women and the denial of women in terms of Western social rights. Theirs was a period when the male of the species governed, culminating in exclusive power and ownership in all aspects of socio-economic life. Women were regarded as a subservient species and denied any kind of right, from expressing their views to any social

---

[1] A. Giddens, *Sociology*, Cambridge: Polity Press, 1989, p.727.
[2] S. Duval, "New Veils and New Voices: Islamist Women's Groups in Egypt", in *Women and Islamization: Contemporary Dimensions of Discourse on Gender Relations*, Karin Ask and Marit Tjornsland (eds.), Oxford and New York: Berg, 1998, p. 46.

participation. Today feminism pursues the emancipation of women from any kind of bondage, or whereby she is segregated from the caravan of male supremacy; occupational equality, equality in social and political status, male and female equality in social rights and their rights in regard to children. From their perspective there is no disparity between a man and woman in relation to the private and public sphere. Feminism is merely a secular ideology. Fundamentally feminism does not only have no concept of Divine principles, but to the contrary, religion is often regarded to be the main source of inequality between men and women. In other words, like other principles of secular liberalism, the main theories and principal values of feminism arise from the mental creation of human desires.

According to the principle that the majority of feminists share with regards to the subjective equality between men and women in terms of social and individual ability and right, feminist theorists argue that most of the organised religious belief systems, which dominate the historical and modern world, are profoundly sexist. There are three major feminist theories about religion - the radical, the liberal and the reformist critique of existing practice and the utopian creation of a new counter culture practice.

The racial theory of feminism with regards to religion represents the Marxist and Social theory. They believe, in principle, that 'Religion' is the opium of the masses, and consider it to be the main reason for the inequality of men and women in society. The liberal theorists also share the same idea that religion, and in particular Christianity, is a major source for the typical presentation of the gender issue. Elizabeth Cady Stanton in her book *The Woman's Bible* made the first major feminist contribution to changes in the Christian religion. Stanton believed that the language and interpretation of passages dealing with women in the Bible were a major source for the inferior status given to women. The central message of Christianity, Daly (1975, 1978) claims, is sadomasochism legitimised in torture. Susan Griffin (1981) also agrees that a fundamental theme of the Western Christian tradition is its hatred of the flesh, which is based on an idea that a woman's body calls man back to his animalistic nature.

From the reformist perspective, religion should be reformulated in a way whereby it can create equality between men and women in all aspects of human life. From their perspective, religion has legitimised misogyny throughout history; therefore they see a serious need for rewriting the religious doctrine based on feminist principles. Indeed not all feminists think alike, and they can be categorised as follows:

1.1.1 Amazon Feminism

Amazon feminism is concerned with 'physical gender equality'. It rejects the idea that certain characteristics or interests are inherently masculine (or feminine), and upholds and explores a vision of heroic womanhood. This is a sort of radical feminism, which questions why women must adopt certain roles based on their biology, just as it questions why men adopt certain other roles based on theirs. Radical feminism claims to draw lines between biologically determined behaviour, and culturally determined behaviour, in order to free both men and women, as much as possible, from their previous gender roles.

Firestone argues that the origin of the dualism lays in 'biology itself – procreation', a natural or original inequality that is the basis for the oppression of women and the source of male power. Men, by confining women to their reproductive nature, have freed themselves for the business of the world and have so created and controlled culture. The proposed solution is to eliminate natural differences between the sexes by introducing artificial reproduction. Nature and the private sphere of the family will then be abolished and individuals, of all ages, will interact as equals in an undifferentiated cultural or public order.[3]

Mary Daly (1978) makes Amazon feminism into a metaphor for

---

[3] C. Pateman, "Feminist Critiques of the Public/Private Dichotomy", in *Feminism and Equality*, Anne Phillips (ed.), Oxford: Basil Blackwell, 1987, p. 111.

describing women who are fighting to affirm the true identity of our foremothers. This accepts that women, to develop an entirely separate and self-contained women's culture, can use aggression. This perspective went as far as to influence their interpretation of God. For example, Merlin Stone suggests that the term was used to describe goddess worshippers who fought to protect their temples.

1.1.2 Liberal Feminism

This is the variety of feminism which works to integrate women into the structure of mainstream society. Its roots stretch back to the social contract theory of government instituted by the American Revolution. They look to focus their energies on establishing and protecting equal opportunities for women through legislation and other democratic means. They tend to establish equal opportunities for women in the public sphere in terms of payment and work opportunities. According to Giddens[4], while liberal feminists have contributed to the advancement of women over the past century, critics charge that they are unsuccessful in dealing with the root causes of gender inequality and do not acknowledge the systematic nature of women's oppression in society. By focusing on independent deprivations which women suffer - sexism, discrimination, unequal pay - liberal feminists draw only a partial picture of gender inequality.

1.1.3 Socialist Feminism

Marxism recognises that women are oppressed, and attributes the oppression to the capitalist/private property system. Thus they insist that the only way to end the oppression of women is to overthrow the capitalist system.

Like one of the main theories of western feminism, socialist feminism believes that women are second-class citizens in patriarchal capitalism, which depends on its survival of the exploitation of working people, and on the special exploitation of

---

[4] A. Giddens, *Sociology* (4th Edition), Cambridge: Polity Press, 2001, pp. 115-116.

women. Socialist feminism argues that we need to transform not only the ownership of the means of production, but also social experience, because the roots of women's oppression lie in the total economic system of capitalism (see Reed, 1975).

Socialist feminism argues that men have a specific material interest in the domination of women and that men construct a variety of institutional arrangements to perpetuate this domination. Socialist feminism goes beyond the conventional definition of economy to consider activity that does not involve the exchange of money, for example by including the procreative and sexual work done by women in the home. Socialist feminism has a theory of epistemology, which takes the view that all knowledge represents the interests and values of a specific social group, by describing historical variations in practices and in the categories by which values are understood (Eisenstein, 1986).

Socialist feminism is now engaged in a more adequate explanation of women's subordination in order to show how types of production, not ordinarily considered economic, can be understood in economic terms. The ideal is that women and men might disappear as socially constituted categories. Socialist feminism is attacked by radical feminism because it obscures and occludes an understanding of how central the institution of heterosexuality is to women's oppression (Ferguson, 1992).

The analytical observation based on social class structure, merely stems from the materialistic perspective based upon the capacity and the aptitude of the members of the society. In this respect, a person who enjoys greater economic prosperity is considered as belonging to the cream of that society, labelled as upper class citizens. On the said ratio, persons with a lesser degree of financial gain are categorised as being at a lower level on the social ladder. In this respect, women as second-class citizens, from a materialistic perspective, require a detailed analysis in such social milieu. From Divine observation, the aim of a pious and healthy society is to utilise the opportunity of life given by the Creator.

To utilise the equal opportunity of life, it cannot be limited to economic opportunities. Henceforth, the spiritual opportunities play an important role in directing the society towards peace and tranquillity. From this point of view, humanity is based on the foundation of utilising human virtuosity for the purpose of individual classification. In this regard, there exists no difference between the male and the female. The existence of male and female inequality is the product of a cultural, social and political situation in a society which tolerates such a specified criteria as a result of unequal material opportunities, and the superimposed distinction upon the male and female gender.

1.1.4   Radical Feminism

Radical feminism argues that women's oppression comes from their categorisation as an inferior class to the class 'men' on the basis of their gender. Radical feminism aims to destroy this sex-class system. What makes this feminism radical is that it focuses on the roots of male domination and claims that all forms of oppression are extensions of male supremacy. The central thesis of radical feminism is the belief that the personal is political and that woman-centeredness can be the basis for a future society (Eisenstein, 1986).

Certain issues put radical feminism at odds with other feminist perspectives, specifically a socialist view of the centrality of class and a black view of the centrality of race. Juliet Mitchell criticised Firestone in particular and radical feminism in general for not speaking of women's oppression in a historically specific way (Mitchell, 1971). Radical feminism believes that women cannot be liberated from sexual oppression through reforms of gradual change. This is due to the fact that patriarchy is a systematic phenomenon, and they argue that gender equality can only be attained by overthrowing the patriarchal order (Giddens, 2001).

In the 1970s radical feminism gradually abandoned the 'linear', macho style of traditional political theory and moved into a poetic and metaphorical mode. A radical feminist paradigm is still emerging. Radical feminists differ in how they name reality because they use a limited range of concepts, such as rape or slavery, to bring together apparently disparate phenomena such as marriage and prostitution.

What we have explained here so far are the different approaches of western feminism. Within the diversity of the theories of feminism, one fundamental conclusion can be established: feminism, no matter whether Liberal, Radical, Amazon or Socialist, all share one common idea; which is that religion is one of the major impediments to the revitalisation of women's rights in society. Hence their approach is either secular or in some cases anti-religious. The second common idea among all feminists is the mono-sexism inclination, which causes the scarification of one sex for the other.

1.2   Muslim Responses to Feminism

Although, one can argue that the movement for the revitalisation of women's rights in the Muslim world has been established based on the Western form of feminism, it may be argued that social, cultural and political circumstances have resulted in a different perception of women's rights in the history of Muslim society. Therefore we are observing a variety of responses from Muslim scholars and Muslim women to the social phenomenon of feminism. The position of Muslim women within the family and society has been a central concern of many scholars in the modern approach. The process of modernisation and movements of feminists in the West have accelerated women's discourses in the Muslim world [see Mernissi (1993), Nasir (1994), Basit (1997), Moghissi (1999) and Smith (2001)].

We can categorise the theories and orientations on the position of Muslim women within the society into three different approaches:

1.2.1   Apologetic Feminism

Apologetic Feminism is basically embodied in the liberal feminism of Muslim women. Liberal and secular perspectives of Muslim activists and Muslim scholars have led them towards an apologetic reaction.[5] This group either tries to adapt religion to fit in with feminist principles or accept feminism as an inevitable way of life for Muslim women, whether religious principles can be established accordingly or not.

This group of feminists re-reads the *Shari'ah* texts in order to introduce women's rights according to Islamic values.[6] It is important to find out whether their aim is reformation or reconstruction of the woman's position in the family, society and the whole social structure and public sphere.

In the Christian and Judaic feminist narrations, the Holy texts were regarded as being limited by historical context. They were thus divided, and the fragments classified according to whether they were regarded as universal and essential, or culturally relative.[7] According to Duval:

> Islam is viewed as the main origin for the prevalence of sexual inequality in the Middle East.[8]

From the Western feminist point of view, Islam, and in particular veiling, are the main barriers preventing Muslim women and, in general, Muslim society from becoming civilised.

---

[5] Z. Mir-Husseini, "Stretching the Limits: A feminist Reading of the Shari'a Post-Khomeini Iran" in *Feminism and Islam: Legal and Literary Perspectives*, Mai Yamani (ed.), London: Ithaca Press, 1996, p. 285.

[6] *Ibid.*, p. 286.

[7] A. S. Roald, "Feminist Reinterpretation of Islamic Sources: Muslim Feminist Theology in the Light of the Christian Tradition of Feminist Thought", in *Women and Islamization: Contemporary Dimensions of Discourse on Gender relations*, Karin Ask and Marit Tjomsland (eds.), Oxford and New York: Berg, 1998, p. 18.

[8] S. Duval, "New Veils and New Voices: Islamist Women's Groups in Egypt", in *Women and Islamization: Contemporary Dimensions of Discourse on Gender Relations*, Karin Ask and Marit Tjornsland (eds.), Oxford and New York: Berg, 1998, p. 46.

In Western eyes, only by giving up these "peculiar" and "intrinsic" practices, would Muslim societies move forward on the path of civilisation. The veil, for the colonisers but also in the vision of contemporary Western political culture is the most visible marker of the 'otherness' and 'inferiority' of Islamic societies.[9]

Early Arab feminists, such as the Lebanese Nazira Zayn ad-Din, incorporated feminist ideas into an Islamic frame of reference. In 1928 she published a book called *Removing the Veil and Veiling*, which aroused the anger of Muslim scholars.[10] Amin's book, *Women's Liberation* (1989) marks the entry for the debate around the veil, in which the veil epitomised Islamic inferiority. The veil is an example; other principles and Islamic values may also introduce a sort of gender otherness, and be considered as inferior for Muslim women in an apologetic manner to Western feminism.

The apologetic approach is very secular. According to Jayawardena, the emergence of feminist movements is basically a general movement towards secularism, a new concern with social reform and modernity, and the ascendance of an enlightened indigenous middle class. Their main concern with women's rights includes the issues of education, seclusion, veiling and polygamy, coinciding with a broader agenda about progress and the compatibility between Islam and modernity.[11]

1.2.2   Reactionary or Defensive Feminism

This form of feminism is a movement which lays emphasis on the idea that Muslim women have already obtained an equal and respectful position (based on Islamic tradition) without the need for

---

[9] *Ibid.*, p. 48.
[10] A. S. Roald, "Feminist Reinterpretation of Islamic Sources: Muslim Feminist Theology in the Light of the Christian Tradition of Feminist Thought", in *Women and Islamization: Contemporary Dimensions of Discourse on Gender Relations*, Karin Ask and Marit Tjomsland (eds.), Oxford and New York: Berg, 1998, p. 18.
[11] D. Kandiyoti, "Introduction" in *Women, Islam & the State*, Deniz Kaniyoti (ed.), London: Macmillan, 1991, p. 3.

further reform. From their perspective, Western oriented Muslim women have highlighted the status of women in Muslim societies but Islamists, male and female, have also joined the debate, stressing the liberating potential Islam has for women (Roald, 1998).

1.2.3   Structuralist Approach

These activists and theoreticians do not isolate women from absolute society. They see women's rights and positions within the whole structure of the society and avoid the segregation of society in terms of 'Feminism' or 'Masculinism' or any sort of mono-centric approach. In opposition to feminism, masculinism for the last decades has become a popular topic across the advanced capitalist world.

According to Structuralism, society as a whole, including men and women, is addressed by individual and social responsibilities without any mono-sexual inclinations. The major differences between the Structuralist viewpoints of Muslims and Western feminism is referred to by the methodology of understanding and establishing the rights and responsibility of women. The feminists of the Western hemisphere, regardless of religious teaching, insist upon women's rights and her role in society. They hold a mono-sexist perspective and neglect the valuable place of man and woman side by side as a unifying force in family and society. Structuralism looks at one comprehensive position for women and men in public and private, in society and in politics.

One of distinguished scholars who upholds Structuralism is Mutahari. He explained the reasons and the necessity for the different treatment of women in Islam according to biological and psychological differences between men and women, while the apologists try to re-read the Holy texts in line with the changing conditions of the current society.[12]

1.3   Summary

In a nutshell the approaches of Western social scientists reflect a high degree of ethnocentrism in assuming that liberation for Muslim women has to follow the same mono-centric line as the American and European women's movements. It is expected that these goals are universal and that they should more or less be followed in the same order (Ahmed, 1992 and Joseph, 1994).

For the last three hundred years Western alien thought has influenced Islamic thought in different spheres. The common denominators of all imported ideas were in the direct relationship with centres of political power. Powerful domination of the West was the result of the demonstration of wealth and capital against poverty and powerlessness. The transformation period of the industrial revolution, the renaissance in thinking in the West and the formation of the basis of ideological modernism were the most important vacuums in the Islamic world for the past three centuries. The 19th and 20th centuries witnessed the defensive response or ideological and religious resistance or absolute assimilation into Western modernism. Western modernism belongs to Western history, Western religion and changes in Western intellectual secular liberalism.

At the end of the 20th century more than six hundred million Muslim populations were subjected to the system of political democracy. Yet Western politics still blame Islam for a non-democratic doctrine and labels Muslims as fundamentalists and terrorists.

According to Brian Turner:

---

[12] Z. Mir-Husseini, "Stretching the Limits: A Feminist Reading of the Shari'a Post-Khomeini Iran" in *Feminism and Islam: Legal and Literary Perspectives*, Mai Yamani (ed.), London: Ithaca Press, 1996, p. 316.

Islam was perfectly compatible with the modernisation project involving, as it did, a high degree of secularisation of traditional religious cultures,

But from his perspective

Islam cannot deal satisfactorily with post-modernity which threatens to deconstruct religious messages into more fairy tales and to destroy the everyday world by the challenge of cultural diversity. The problem of cultural perspective is an effect of the pluralisation of life-words brought about by the spread of a diversified, global system of consumption. See Brian Turner (1994: 78)

This is due to the fact that in the post-modern era, the subject matter of human life is in ongoing change therefore no definite verdict can be issued.

Western feminism is also the product of modernism and postmodernism. This movement and school of thought is fundamentally and principally in serious conflict with Islamic tenets. However, in many instances subject matter propounded by feminism is in uniformity with the Islamic views on women, but from the Islamic perspective entering into this domain, provides another background for loosing the principles and values given by the Islamic divinity.

It is certain that throughout history women have been suppressed and deprived from their fundamental rights. It is also without a shadow of a doubt, that women's natural dispositions and their talents and strengths in many fields are far superior to that of men, but unfortunately they have been unjustly damaged. The vanquishing of women's talents and potential resulted in non-entity, and they were unable to manifest their natural dispositions. Throughout history, men took such advantage that the inability of a woman's true potential and her gifted abilities were totally ignored. History witnesses the bitter truth of unjustifiable male supremacy.

This is a fundamental theory in sociology that

> ...you cannot have modernization technology, urbanization and bureaucratization without the cultural baggage that goes with it and this baggage is essentially a post-Enlightenment system of thought. (See Turner 1994: 8)

According to structuralism, the oppression of women in the past should not result in institutionalised oppression based on secular feminism. The Islamic world and societies of Muslim women must observe their duties and rights from a Divine perspective. The principle must be accepted, that the wisdom of Almighty God (swt) is the absolute benefactor for any society at large and He knows the best deliberation for social happiness or aberration of a society. Consequently, the policies of our social and individual rights must be based upon such wisdom. Salvation of the Muslim world depends emphatically upon independent observation for the need and the interest of society facing the Western vacuum. This depends on returning to the pure message of religion and the revival of the Muslim woman's integrity, and emphasis must be on manifesting the rights of Islam. Total submission to holistic Islam indicates that man and woman are two fundamental members of the society. Islam has provided independent and co-operative roles for them. This will be the revival of the Muslim woman's individual and social rights.

While feminism will lead to social deviance, masculinism will unbalance the coherence of individual members of the society, creating deviance and an unhealthy social setting. Mono-sexism creates social deviation and social fragmentation.

From the holistic perspective the direction of Western feminism, in essence, is a negative and secular outlook on religion. In reality, the foundation of feminist thought is a serious confrontation to Divine observation, and therefore cannot be a reference to the revival of Muslim women's rights and neither can it guarantee the happiness and health of the Muslim society at large.

Conclusion

There are a variety of theories and movements in feminism that present a diversity of ideas, values and perspectives. However, the feminist movements – taking into consideration the various perspectives of these groups - are different, but in conclusion after being examined by Muslim women they cannot be considered as a liberation or a protection of women's rights in a human society in general and Muslim women in particular. In this paper *Amazon Feminism, Anarcho-Feminism, Liberal Feminism, Marxist and Socialist Feminism* and *Material Feminism* do not seem to represent a vital or crucial voice for women in our global society. In this paper, we have also examined the response of Muslim women to Western feminism, from three perspectives: *Apologetic Feminism, Reactionary Feminism,* and *the Holistic Approach,* and tried to present a balanced analysis within the Islamic worldview.

Bibliography

Ahmed, L. 1992, *Women and Gender in Islam: Historical Roots of a Modem Debate,* New Haven and London: Yale University Press.

Basit, T. N. 1997, *Eastern Values; Western Milieu: Identities and Aspirations of Adolescent British Muslim Girls,* Aldershot, Brookfield USA, Singapore and Sydney: Ashgate.

Daly, M. 1975, *The Church and The Second Sex: With a New Feminist Postchristian Introduction by the Author,* New York, London: Harper & Row Publishers.

Daly, M. 1978, *The Metaethics of Radical Feminism,* London: Women's Press.

Duval, S. 1998, "New Veils and New Voices: Islamist Women's Groups in Egypt", in *Women and Islamization: Contemporary Dimensions of Discourse on Gender Relations,* Karin Ask and Marit Tjornsland (eds.), Oxford and New York: Berg, pp. 45-72.

Eisenstein, Z. R. 1986, *The Radical Future of Liberal Feminism,*

Boston: Northeastern University Press.

Ferguson, M. 1992, *The Mythology about Globalization*, European Journal of Communication, 7.

Freedman, J. 2001, *Feminism*, Buckingham, Philadelphia: Open University Press.

Giddens, A. 1989, *Sociology*, Cambridge: Polity Press.

Giddens, A. 2001, *Sociology* (4th Edition), Cambridge: Polity Press.

Griffin, S. 1981, *Pornography and Silence: Culture's Revenge against Nature*, London: Women's Press.

Jackson, S. 1993, "Women and the Family" in *Introducing Women's Studies*, Diane Richardson and Victoria Robinson (eds.), Hong Kong: Macmillan, pp. 177-200.

Joseph, S. 1994, *Gender and Family in the Arab World*, Special MERIP Publication.

Kandiyoti, D. 1991, "Introduction" in *Women, Islam & the State*, Deniz Kaniyoti (ed.), London: Macmillan.

Mernissi, F. 1993, *Women and Islam: An Historical and theological Enquiry*, Oxford: Kali for Women.

Mir-Husseini, Z. 1996, "Stretching the Limits: A feminist Reading of the Shari'a Post-Khomeini Iran" in *Feminism and Islam: Legal and Literary Perspectives*, Mai Yamani (ed.), London, Ithaca Press, pp. 285-319.

Mitchell, J. 1971, *Woman's Estate*, Harmondsworth.

Moghissi, H. 1999, *Feminism and Islamic Fundamentalism: The Limits of Postmodern Analysis*, London & New York: Zed Book.

Nasir, J. J. 1994, *The Status of Women Under Islamic Law and Under Modern Islamic Legislation*, London: Graham & Trotman.

Pateman, C. 1987, "Feminist Critiques of the Public/Private Dichotomy" in *Feminism and Equality*, Anne Phillips (ed.), Oxford: Basil Blackwell.

Reed, E. 1975, *Woman's Evolution from Matriarchal Clan to Patriarchal Family*.

Roald, A. S. 1998, "Feminist Reinterpretation of Islamic Sources: Muslim Feminist Theology in the Light of the Christian Tradition of Feminist Thought" in *Women and Islamization: Contemporary Dimensions of Discourse on Gender relations*, Karin Ask and Marit Tjomsland (eds.), Oxford and New York: Berg, pp. 45-72.

Smith, B. G. 2001, *Global Feminisms since 1945*, London and New York: Routledge.

Turner, B. S. 1994, *Orientalism, Postmodernism and Globalism*, London, and New York: Routledge.

Article 2

The Status of Women in Islamic Thought

Mohsin Araki

Abstract

This paper aims to explain the status of women in Islam. We will highlight their equality with men before Almighty God, and their potential for reaching spiritual perfection. Their equal rights and responsibilities towards nature will be discussed, where both sexes share in nature's benefits and together hold the trust to nurture and maintain it. The equal position of both genders within the social structure will be examined. Here this paper will focus on the rights and responsibilities held by both men and women in relation to the society within which they live. We will also elucidate on the underlying unity, which runs throughout creation, despite the apparent diversity, which we witness around us. Finally we will discuss the inter-connection between all things, and how for an object to become actualized, it needs another in order for its own completion. In this way both men and women need each other to become whole and perfect human beings.

Introduction

We can base our explanation and commentary on the status of women in the Islamic world on five principles:

2.1   First Principle: The Equality of Men and Women before God

All human beings are equal before Almighty God (swt) and there is no distinction made between male and female. Mankind by its very nature is able to ascend through the various gradations of spiritual perfection, culminating in the utmost nearness to the Divine Presence.

This process is driven by virtue, and virtue can be found in both men and women in equal capacity. The best human being is the most virtuous, and it is through this virtuousness that one can reach the ultimate spiritual perfection. The potential for spiritual growth has not been bestowed upon any other creature, and it is only human beings that have the ability to attain perfection and become God's (swt) vicegerent (*Caliph*).

2.1.1   Examples of Pious Women

The Holy Qur'an refers to four women as exemplars for all human beings. In a verse of Surah Tahrim, Allah (swt) says:

> Allah sets forth, for an example to the Unbelievers, the wife of Noah and the wife of Lot: they were (respectively) under two of our righteous servants, but they were false to their (husbands), and they profited nothing before Allah on their account, but were told: Enter the Fire along with those who enter.[1]

Allah (swt) continues:

> And Allah sets forth an example to those who believe, the wife of Pharaoh when she said: My Lord! Build for me a house with Thee in the garden and save me from Pharaoh and his doings, and save me from the unjust people.[2]

Elsewhere Allah (swt) says:

> And Mary the daughter of 'Imran, who guarded her chastity; and We breathed into (her body) of Our spirit; and she testified to the truth of the words of her Lord and of His Revelations, and was one of the devout (servants).[3]

In these verses, there are two sets of examples, one representing evil and the other representing goodness. Woman has been addressed in both cases. These verses refer to the wives of Lut (as) and Noah (as) as two archetypes of the evil human being. Despite the fact that these two women were close to two of God's most

---

[1] *Qur'an*, 66: 10.
[2] *Ibid.*, 11.
[3] *Ibid.*, 12.

distinguished servants, they both strayed far from the right path and allowed themselves to fall headlong into a mortal abyss. In comparison to this the Qur'an presents two other women who are referred to as archetypes of virtue: Asiya the wife of Pharaoh and Maryam (as) (Mary) the daughter of Imran. About the latter, God says that she was chaste and that 'We breathed our spirit into her and made it capable and worthy of receiving our soul'. The exalted Maryam (as) and the wife of Pharaoh are two examples for all believers. We can discern from such examples that women as well as men hold the ability to grow spiritually, attain perfection and reach proximity to God.

The fact that men and women have an equal standing before God in terms of spiritual potential is established by other verses in the Qur'an. In verse 189 of Surah Al-e-Imran, Allah (swt) speaks about the position of the believers and their relations to Him:

> Behold! In the creation of the heavens and the earth, and the alternation of night and day - there are indeed Signs for those of understanding. So their Lord accepted their prayer...[and said] 'I will not waste the work of a worker among you, whether male or female, the one of you being from the other'.[4]

What has been emphasised here is that learned and virtuous individuals are all of one breed, and none is superior to the other because of gender.

2.1.2   Nearness to Allah

In a sacred narration (*Hadeeth qudsi*) Almighty Allah (swt) says:

---

[4] *Qur'an*, 3:189.

My servant, obey Me so that you may become similar to Me, so that if you say to a thing 'Be,' then it will be.[5]

Through spiritual struggle, which is something possible for both men and women, individuals may attain such a status that their wish, will, and command become identical to those of God. In this regard, Fatemeh Zahra (as) - the daughter of the Prophet of Islam (saws) - is a typical example and she is one of the supreme individuals, about whom Allah (swt) says in the Qur'an:

Allah only desires to keep away the uncleanness from you, O people of the House! And to purify you a (thorough) purifying.[6]

Similarly, we find in a verified narration that the Prophet (saws) of Allah (swt) says:

The pleasure and satisfaction of Fatemeh is my pleasure. God becomes pleased for her pleasure and becomes angry when she is angry.[7]

The import of this is that Fatima (as) has obtained such a high spiritual status, that God is pleased with whatever pleases Fatemeh (as) and displeased with whatever displeases her. God Almighty, who is the All Just, All True, and All Perfect can elevate the status of His servant so that he becomes identical to the truth; his wish becomes God's wish, and his pleasure and wrath becomes God's pleasure and wrath. This is a very high status indeed.

2.1.3   Obtaining Infinite Perfection

According to what was said before, both men and women have

---

[5] S. H. Sherazi, *Al-Hadith Al-Qudsi*, S. M. Zaki Baqri (tran.), Qum, Iran: Ansarian Publication, 1999, hadith 16, p. 29-30. See also Ahmed Rahmani Al-Hamadni, *Imam Ali* (as), p. 362.

[6] *Qur'an*, 33:33.

[7] Al-Majlesi, *Bihar Al-Anwar*, vol. 27, p. 62, narrated from As-Shaikh Al-Mofid, *Al-'Itiqadat*, p. 105, Najaf/ Iraq

been endowed with the unlimited ability to progress and attain perfection. In the first principle, which portrays the equality of all human beings in their relationship to God Almighty, the ways to progress and perfection have been equally provided for both men and women. Such progress does not halt at a certain stage, but continues into infinity. Men and women can reach a status whereby their satisfaction and pleasure is God's satisfaction and their wrath is God's wrath.

2.2   Second Principle: Equal Rights vis-à-vis Nature

In this principle man's relation to nature is delineated. We read in the Holy Qur'an:

> And Allah has made what is in the heavens and what is in the earth subservient to you.[8]

Elsewhere, it says:

> He it is Who created for you all that is in the earth.[9]

Allah (swt) in the Holy Qur'an has emphasised the fact that the control and conquering of nature must be coupled with a sense of responsibility towards one's physical environment. Human beings have the right to make use of nature but must also be responsible for its completion and growth. Nature is at the service of man; but mankind is responsible for its supervision. In other words, mankind should pave the way for the growth and completion of nature and bring its treasures into actuality. Therefore, man is on a mission to construct and improve the world. Allah (swt) says:

> He brought you forth from the earth and has made you inhabit it.[10]

And if it is our mission in this world to nurture creation, then both

---

[8] *Qur'an*, 45:13.
[9] *Ibid.*, 2:29.
[10] *Ibid.*, 11:61.

genders must play an identical role.

2.3   Third Principle: The Place of Women in the Social Structure

Women as well as men have a responsibility towards the society in which they live. They both have an equal duty to protect it from pollution and contamination. As men take an active role and enjoy their social rights, women share along with them the same rights and responsibilities. The Holy Qur'an says:

> O people! Be careful of (your duty to) your Lord, Who created you
> from a single being and created its mate of the same (kind) and spread
> from these two, many men and women.[11]

Human beings all emanate from the same source and therefore neither man nor woman can claim superiority over the other in nature.

Men hold no superiority over women in social responsibilities and rights. Duties of society should be allocated between the sexes according to capability. On this basis, the Holy Qur'an has spoken of a division of jobs and duties between men and women due to their differing natures. It should be understood that this does not imply discrimination, for discrimination involves usurping the legitimate rights of the other and Islam strongly opposes this. The enjoyment of equal rights does not imply that men and women are indistinguishable from each other. The Holy Qur'an says:

> Surely We have created you of a male and a female.[12]

Meaning: You are all equal and of one stock.

Elsewhere it says:

---

[11] *Ibid.*, 4:1.
[12] *Ibid.*, 49:13.

> We did indeed offer the Trust to the Heavens and the Earth and the
> Mountains; but they refused to undertake it, being afraid of it: but man
> undertook it.[13]

Therefore, man is undertaking the social trust offered to him, and all whether men or women have the same responsibility towards it.

2.4   Fourth Principle: Diversity in Unity

Even though the phenomenal world is a diverse entity, it possesses an underlying unity. This is one of the delicate issues in the Islamic worldview concerning the phenomenal world, which believes in a world of numerous similarities.   In other words, this world-view believes that the world inhabited by human beings is a various and multiple one, which is at the same time single and identical. We read in the Qur'an:

> Surely We have created you of a male and a female, and made you
> into tribes and families that you may know each other.[14]

This variety is not limited to the world of human beings. Rather, it exists throughout the phenomenal world. Allah (swt) says in the Holy Qur'an:

> Do you not see that Allah sends down water from the clouds, then We
> bring forth therewith fruits of various colours; and in the mountains
> are streaks, white and red, of various hues and (others) intensely
> black?[15]

Allah (swt) thus asks: 'do you not consider this multi-coloured world?' This gives a very interesting perception and commentary: We have created a multi-coloured world for you. Think about this variety! At the beginning it says, 'We send the water from heaven

---

[13] Ibid., 33:72.
[14] Ibid., 49:13.
[15] Ibid., 35:27-28.

onto you'. The water sinks into the earth. The water is single and the earth is also single. However, various fruits are derived from it. Its origin is one, but its results are various. The Holy Qur'an conveys this unity-cum-variety in a beautiful way for us. Then it says,

> Look at the mountains and see how we have created rocks and colourful mountains; White Mountains and red mountains and colourful lines and furrows. We have also created various peoples and animals too.

Then it says, 'the erudite among His servants fear Allah alone'. This verse and other similar verses explain the fact that at the same time that the origin of the world is unique, the world is also a multi-coloured and multiple one. The same state exists in the world of human beings. The Holy Qur'an says:

> And so amongst men and crawling creatures and cattle, they are likewise of various colours.

That is to say,

> We have also created a multiple and various human society, which consists of men and women; we have created multi-coloured and various people.

The same principle exists in the relationships among men and women and we must admit and acknowledge this variety. Woman and man are each species from among other divine species, however they both originate from the same source.

2.5   Fifth Principle: The World of Creation is Continuous and Perfect despite Being Various

This multiplicity has a single origin and a single *telos*. In this everlasting struggle all are in a continuous and harmonious movement from the beginning to end, completing each other in the process. All things in the world have two aspects to them: the aspect of presence and the aspect of lack. Everything in this world has a specific perfection, whilst lacking in other perfections, which are found in other things. The things that exist in this world provide for the needs of each other, and every entity makes up for the deficiency of the other entity, helping it to move towards the great goal of the phenomenal world. It is in this way that this numerous and multiple world becomes one unique and entire one. This paves the way for the realisation of the return to God, that is the *telos* of existence. This very movement, in its own turn, is the Divine Will and pleasure.

This dynamic harmony is brought about through the practice of Divine law. If people abide by the rule of Allah (swt), they make up for the deficiencies of other creatures in their move towards perfection. This is a responsibility left on the shoulders of human beings. From the Qur'anic standpoint, man (or woman) has the responsibility of managing the world in order to achieve the final goal: he has the duty of leading the other creatures towards God Almighty. In this way, the variety and multiplicity in the world of creatures turns into unity.

Variety and multiplicity also exist in the world of human beings. Men and women each possess certain perfection, which is unique to its own gender. Therefore, by means of a perfect harmony and continuity, they should create a harmonious society. The relationship between man and woman is defined and formed on the basis of this principle. Woman possesses a special ability and perfection. Of course, one must not think that because they are both human beings, there is no difference between them. It is an undeniable fact that men and women are different. If they were to be exactly the same, then they would not complete each other and family life would be meaningless in terms of the world's existential *telos*. Moreover, families as cordial and interconnected units were not formed in the context of society. If the organisation of society wants to be a single and interconnected one, it should have a unity, which is based on affection, love, assistance, co-operation and altruism.

A society functions happily when the relationship of its members is a representation of unity, complimetarity and interconnection. The cheerfulness and auspiciousness of every society depends on its interconnection, similarity and convergence. That is to say that if each section of the society helps to complete the other section and in that completion exhibits competence and capability, all sections of the society will join together to create a satisfactory, pleasant and rational society. An auspicious society is the one, which is away from divergence and numerousness and is unified. To do this, it seeks the co-operation of its many sections to complete its appropriate internal needs and requirements.

Family is the principal foundation of the society; society comprises of a set of families, which form its interconnected and continuous nucleus. The uniqueness and continuity depends on the continuity and interconnection of its nuclei. The internal association and harmony of the members of the society are the principal conditions for the formation of families, which are active units inside the society. A family becomes a cordial, unified and interconnected one, when its members complete each other under a wise management and leadership.

In Islamic texts, the woman's role inside the family has been clearly defined. Man is a dynamic creature that is in the process of change and evolution. He does not have two identical days. Interconnection in a dynamic group is dependent on two factors: attraction and management. The members of this set must be attracted to each other; this action of attraction must be complementary and in line with the process of achieving the given goals of the family. The realisation of this matter requires management and direction. Therefore, the family requires two principal factors in its dynamic formation; these are attraction and attractiveness and direction and management. According to many Qur'anic verses, narrations and religious rulings, the principal role of woman in the form of the family, is the management of attraction and that of man is the management of planning. When this attraction and planning come together, they form a unified, dynamic and active set that can make progress and live in tranquillity, avoiding conflicts and anxieties. The fact that the woman plays the role of attraction does not mean that she plays no role in the management of planning. Rather, we mean that the superior role of man (as opposed to woman) is that of planning. Likewise man can also take part in the role of attraction but the woman holds the superior position. Therefore, one can see that many of the religious rulings about the family relationships are proportionate to this matter. For example, in a marriage contract, a woman must say, 'I consign myself to you as your wife', and the man must say, 'I accept'. A woman attracts and a man becomes receptive of this attraction.

Allah (swt) Almighty says in the Holy Qur'an:

> It is He Who created you from a single soul, and made his mate of like nature, in order that he might dwell with her (in love).[16]

'ليسكن إليها' in this verse means that woman has this peaceful attractiveness and that man feels peace and tranquillity in her company. Family does not form if this role does not exist. In some Islamic texts, it has been mentioned that the woman is attractive to the man in all senses. A narration says: 'woman is entirely a shame (Owrat)'.[17] An Owrat in this narration means something that deserves to be covered and protected and this is due to its attractiveness. A thing that does not stimulate a person's greed does not need to be covered, but a thing that provokes one's greed and is full of attraction should naturally be kept and protected. If a woman's beauty is exposed to all and not used in its own proper place and correct manner, the key role of a woman in the family is lost. Therefore, the woman cannot fulfil the role of attraction; the possibility of attracting and active pull is denied to her and,

---

[16] *Ibid.*, 7:189.

[17] The author classified this statement as an Islamic narration, which is usually perceived to stem from one of the Infallibles. However as far as I have checked it does not exist in any of the Shi'ah Ahadeeth collections, rather it is a statement from a Shi'ah scholar. His name is Abu As-salah al-halabi. See Bihar Al-anwar of 'Allamah Majlesi, vol. 80, p. 180 (Editor's note)

consequently, one of the most important factors in harmonising and interconnecting the requirements of the family is destroyed. In Islamic culture, the woman must be *Mahjoob* (i.e. veiled) and one reason for this has already been given. The *Hijab* (i.e. veil) is not a limitation; it is immunity, which aims to protect the woman against the factors that destroy her personality. In Western societies, which are dominated by nakedness and nudity, men are not so much interested in women as a family partner, whereas in religious societies in which the *Hijab* culture is prevalent, man's dependence on his family life is usually very strong. In these societies, man is completely attracted to a woman; that is to say, the woman fulfils her role best. There is clear interconnection, cordiality, purity and unity in families where the members of which believe in religious rulings. Man can visibly and clearly feel the wisdom and philosophy behind Islamic rulings concerning the significance of a woman's attraction in the family. It is this very same role that brings the family into existence, turns it into a live and active being, and makes it move towards the principal role of achieving a certain goal in the society. This will occur only if we believe in the principle of training, that is to say, we accept that man is a creature that can have moral and spiritual progress and can be trained and improved. However, if we believe that man is not capable of being trained and improved and that one must surrender to the realities of the society, then the danger of collapse will threaten the society.

Today, the situation in the Western world is sending warning bells so as to be aware of this danger. Sometimes, a person grows up in such a way that he can destroy a society. However, if this person is trained and guided to a correct path, he becomes like the rain, which brings joy and life, and all people are blessed by his existence. Man (or woman) can receive a good education and become the source of happiness and wisdom for himself and others. All human calamities stem from bad and uncultured people, and human calamities like hunger, ignorance, poverty, war, etc. stem from a lack of education and training. With regard to the importance of good training, which has an influence on the fate of the society, we should pay careful attention to the important and fateful role of the family in making the society happy and efficient.

Good training is possible only in an appropriate family atmosphere and is formed in a family structure. Parents want to have well-educated and well-trained children, though they themselves might not have received a good training. Generally, parents who themselves suffered from the lack of a good education do not wish their children the same moral deficiency, but rather encourage their children to learn how to behave with the correct conduct. The majority of people are like this, although of course, there are some exceptions but this is unusual. In human society, nobody is as close and kind to children as their parents. Of course, parents are responsible for the safety and health of their children as they are for their spiritual personality. A family with these positive characteristics trains a person who is at least, on average, good and efficient. The contrary to this rarely happens.

In a society which enjoys the presence of a majority of efficient and decent people, absurd people cannot do anything. The happiness or discontentment of every individual depends on the family as does the correct training and progress of every society. The formation of this family depends on whether the man and woman are at one with each other. The woman is to attract and the man to plan and direct. In his role of management, man must provide for the needs of the family and reciprocate the love and attraction of his wife. What we read in Islamic texts indicates that the family is the very foundation of the society and forms the basis for society's evolutionary movement. The family is formed based on the two factors of love and reason or attraction and management and continues towards its elevated goals. The best role for a woman in the structure of the family is to play the attracting role and keep up the warmth of love. The most important role of a man is to organise and deliver wise management. It is with the warmth of love and a wise management that a family is turned into a dynamic, happy, wise, cheerful, active and constructive unit. As the main formative texture, it can have the most constructive and developing influence on the body of the society.

Conclusion

The position of women within the field of Islamic thought is unique. Man's goal is to strive towards spiritual perfection and virtue is the key factor and driving force necessary for traversing this path. Virtue by its nature knows no gender distinction and is accessible to both men and women alike. We witness such a quality in its highest form in the person of Fatima Zahra (as), who has reached such Divine proximity whereby her satisfaction is God's satisfaction. The journey to perfection is infinite and therefore the path is open to whoever desires to undertake it.

However in order for man to reach perfection, he is in need of completion and such completion is based on unity. We see diversity in all creation around us, but can trace such variety back to an underlying unity and essential source. Creation is interconnected and each part needs the other in order to actualize itself. In the same way this inherent drive, manifests itself on a societal level. A society in order to function in a beneficial way must be unified. This requires the establishment of healthy family units, which are able to interact with each other. Roles within the family structure should be clearly defined to ensure its smooth operation and ability to provide a wholesome environment for the training and bringing up of righteous individuals. They in turn will be able to collectively go on to shoulder the Divine responsibilities bestowed on mankind. Such responsibilities and rights in turn need the co-operation and commitment of men and women together.

Bibliography

The Holy Quran.

Al-Hamadni, Ahmed Rahmani. *Imam Ali (as)*.

Majlesi, Allamah. 1984, *Bihar Al-'anwar*, Beirut.

Sherazi, S. H. 1999, *Al-Hadith Al-Qudsi*, S. M. Zaki Baqri (tran.), Qum: Ansarian Publication.

Article 3

The Status and Complementarity of the Two Genders

Ali Hussain Al-Hakim

Abstract

Many theories and ideas have arisen to deal with the issues concerning the various relationships between the sexes. Islam holds a unique position that initially there was no gender discrimination between the two sexes. We can further argue that, since this initial state, their bodies are primordially identical and that it is man's own actions, which have divided them into the two genders. Therefore, gender is a human production, rather than a Divine distinction.

This paper asks: Is it the natural dialectic of nature that women should array themselves, as if in battle, against men? Or are there historical and psychological factors, which prevent the two genders Divine and mutual integration? To answer this question, we will analyze these historical factors and attempt to understand the actual psychological differences between men and women, while simultaneously trying to uncover the Islamic view of gender relations and gender complementarity.

Introduction

The relationship between men and women, with regards to their status, roles, and mutual interrelationship, has been a controversial topic throughout history. Many ideas have arisen, some of which have claimed support from revelation, others of which have claimed support from traditional social structures. Few of these, however, have proven satisfactory for solving the problems of gender status. Women were firstly deprived of some of their civil rights, and were later given extra rights as remuneration. This attempt at evening the mistakes of history has solved nothing, because most women have continuously felt themselves to be inferior to men, while men on the other hand have seldom been willing to accept women as genuine rivals in social, economic, and political life.

In light of the gender schism that is the result of many modern day feminist movements, we must ask ourselves: Is it a natural dialectic that women should array themselves as if in a battle against men, in order to secure their rights? Or have the problems of the male-female relationship been the result of contingent historical and psychological factors? In order to answer this, one must embark upon a historical study and a psychological analysis. But this analysis must be followed by a dynamic attempt to uncover the Islamic view on the two genders' status and complementarity. Our attempt in this paper is to prove that Islam has made an extraordinary contribution in changing the course of history in favour of gender integration. Islam still has this potential, and it provides the most thorough solution for the world's serious gender problems.

3.1   Historical Factors

We present an analytical observation of two tendencies dealing with women along with their historical roots:

3.1.1   Inhumane Treatment of Women

Amongst the primitive cultures of various regions, such as Africa, Australia, and America, man held a firm belief in his right of exploitation. This right extended to such things as cattle and other domestic animals, which he was entitled to use as he wished. He made use of their hair, wool, meat, bones, blood, hides and milk. Of course, such animals have no say about their own necessities of life and desires, like food and drink, living space, and so forth. It is only their owner who provides them with these according to his own wishes, and his wish is only for his own benefit.

The position of a woman *vis-à-vis* a man in these tribes and societies was exactly the same. According to their belief, woman was created for man. She was man's appendage in existence and in life. It was the father who owned her while she was not married, and the husband assumed that right soon after marriage. The man could sell her, give her away or loan her to some other man for the purpose of cohabitation, procreation, or service, etc. He could mete out to her any punishment he decided upon, even the death penalty. He could abandon her, without concern as to whether she would live or die. In cannibalistic societies he was allowed to kill her in order to feed on her meat, especially in feasts and during famine. All the properties and rights of the woman belonged to the man; only he, and not she, could enter into dealings – selling, buying, accepting, rejecting – on her behalf.

For people of many ancient civilisations such as ancient China, India, Egypt and Iran, woman had no independence or freedom, either in her intentions or her actions; she was totally under the guardianship and control of man. Neither could she decide on anything concerning herself, nor had she any right to interfere in civil areas such as the government and judiciary. It was her duty to participate with man in all the responsibilities of life, such as earning a livelihood. In addition, it was her exclusive duty to look after the domestic affairs and the children. Finally, she had to obey man in all his orders and desires.

The condition of women within the Arab tribes who lived in the Arabian Peninsula was no better. Most of such Arabs belonged to nomadic tribes far removed from any civilisation; they lived on raid and plunder. Their neighbours were Iran on one side, Rome (the Byzantine Empire) on another and Ethiopia and Sudan on the other. As a result of this geography, most of their customs and narrations were barbarous, and traces of Roman and Iranian traditions could be found in them, as well as some Indian and Egyptian customs. The Arabs did not accord any independence to the woman in her life; nor did she have any honour or dignity except that of her family. She was not entitled to inheritance. A man could marry as many wives as he desired; there was no restriction on divorce. Daughters were buried alive, a wicked custom, which was started by Banū Tamim. Gradually other tribes adopted the practice. However, it can be seen that in certain families women possessed some freedom. In particular, we find that daughters were free in matrimonial affairs, and that their consent and choice was respected and accepted. In this they were influenced by Iranian upper class society.[1]

3.1.2   Treatment of Women as Second-class Human Beings

British novelist Iris Murdoch summarized this mentality when she says:

> I think being a woman is like being Irish. Everyone says you're important and nice, but you take second place all the same.

Most societies that give women the status of second-class citizen claim support from revelation. This tendency is mainly rooted in misunderstandings of Biblical texts, or a result of psychological complexes.

This group is well represented in the medieval interpretation of the creation of Adam and Eve as it is narrated in detail in Genesis 2:4-3:24. God prohibited both of them from eating the fruits of the forbidden tree. The serpent seduced Eve to eat from it and Eve, in turn, seduced Adam to eat with her. When God rebuked Adam for what he did, he put all the blame on Eve. Consequently, God said to Eve:

> I will greatly increase your pains in childbearing; with pain you will give birth to children. Your desire will be for your husband and he will rule over you.

To Adam He said:

> Because you listened to your wife and ate from the tree...Cursed is the ground because of you; through painful toil you will eat of it all the days of your life.

The Biblical image of Eve has had an extremely negative impact

---

[1] Sayyid Muhammad Husayn Tabataba'i, *Al-Mizan: An Exegesis of the Qur'an*, S. S. Akhtar Razawi (tran.), vol. 4, pp. 62-70.

on women throughout the Judaic-Christian tradition. All women were believed to have inherited from their mother, the Biblical Eve, both her guilt and her guile. Consequently, they were all untrustworthy, morally inferior, and wicked. Menstruation, pregnancy, and childbearing were considered the just punishment for the eternal guilt of the cursed sex. In order to appreciate how negative the impact of the Biblical Eve was on all her female descendants we only have to look at the writings of some of the most important Jewish and Christian scholars, as well as the Biblical text itself.

The Biblical Eve has played a far greater role in Christianity than in Judaism. Her sin has been pivotal to the whole Christian faith because the Christian conception of the reason for the mission of Jesus Christ (as) on Earth stems from Eve's disobedience to God. She had sinned and then seduced Adam to follow suit. Consequently, God expelled both of them from Heaven to Earth, which had been cursed because of them. They bequeathed their sin, which had not been forgiven by God, to all their descendants and, thus, all humans are born in sin. In order to purify human beings from their 'original sin', God had to sacrifice Jesus, (as) who is considered to be the Son of God, on the cross. Therefore, Eve is responsible for her own mistake, her husband's sin, the original sin of all humanity, and the death of the Son of God. In other words, one woman acting on her own caused the fall of humanity.[2]

Her daughters are sinners like her accordingly and have to be treated as such. St. Augustine, being faithful to the legacy of his predecessors, wrote to a friend:

> What is the difference whether it is in a wife or a mother, it is still Eve the temptress that we must beware of in any woman... I fail to see what use woman can be to man, if one excludes the function of bearing children.

---

[2] Rosemary R. Ruether, "Christianity" in *Women in World Religions*, Arvind Sharma (ed.), Albany: State University of New York Press, 1987, p. 209.

Centuries later, St. Thomas Aquinas still considered women as defective:

> As regards the individual nature, woman is defective and misbegotten, for the active force in the male seed tends to the production of a perfect likeness in the masculine sex; while the production of woman comes from a defect in the active force or from some material indisposition, or even from some external influence.

Again and again all women are denigrated because of the image of Eve the temptress, thanks to the Genesis account. To sum up, the Judaic-Christian concept of women has been poisoned by the belief in the sinful nature of Eve and her female offspring. This, in short, was the condition of woman in human society in various eras before the advent of Islam, or during the medieval ages. This can be summed up as follows:

1- Men thought that women were beings, but on the level of dumb animals, or with very weak and inferior human qualities, who could not be trusted if set free. The first was the view of primitive people, and the second, of more developed societies.

2- Society did not accord her the status of a member; and she was not considered an integral part of humanity. For primitive people, she was one of the necessities of life like a home and accommodation. For civilized people, she was a captive and dependant on her masters who took advantage of her labour and always remained alert lest she escaped or cheated.

3- Both types of society deprived her of all common rights; men gave her only that which was necessary for her exploitation.

4- They treated her as a strong person treats a weakling. In other words, the basis of their dealings with her was exploitation. In addition, civilised nations believed that she was a weak human being, incapable of independently looking after herself, and who could not be trusted in any matter.[3]

As Murtada Mutahari has argued while analysing the historical facts, one cannot deny that men have been cruel to women. One is only against how this cruelty is explained. Throughout history, men have oppressed women, but they maltreated their children as well, despite all the love they had for them, and through ignorance, prejudice and custom, and not by way of exploitation. The roots of these kinds of oppression are those very factors which make man oppress and do injustice even to himself. These are: ignorance, bias, traditions and habits. These play far more of a role than mere selfish cravings.

3.2   Psychological Factors

What a strange thing man is; and what a stranger thing woman.

This is how the British poet, Lord Byron (1788-1824), has described the two genders. For many reasons the psychological effect of gender difference was obvious for all. The term "gender" has played a key role in feminist theory and politics since the late 1960s. Debates over its meaning reflect major turning points within the women's movement of the past thirty years.

Prior to the late 1960s, English language-speakers used the word "gender" in a linguistic sense. The word "ship" has often been thought of as feminine. During the 1960s, English-speaking feminists extended the meaning of "gender" so that it came to describe the understanding of not only words but also types of behaviour as female or male. Feminists wanted to make the point that the association of specific types of behaviour with females or males was as much a social convention as was the association of specific words. Prior to this time, the dominant understanding was that such phenomena were "naturally" linked with males or

---

[3] Sayyid Muhammad Husayn Tabataba'i, *Al-Mizan: An Exegesis of the Qur'an*, S. S. Akhtar Razawi (tran.), vol. 4, pp. 62-70.

females. It was thought that the biological distinction between women and men, often referred to as the difference between "the sexes", caused women to behave one way and men another. Feminists wished to emphasise that such differences in behaviour were not a consequence of biology, but of social convention. By including these under the category of "gender" rather than "sex" they hoped people would come to see such differences as socially rather than biologically caused.

3.2.1   The Differences

Nevertheless there are certain natural differences which divide human beings into two genders: male and female, and there are at least four different factors, which have to be taken into consideration.

3.2.1.1 The Anatomical Differences

In the first place there are anatomical differences:

1- The chromosomal sex. The male body cells contain one X and one Y chromosome, whereas female cells contain two X chromosomes. Recently other combinations have been recorded, at least one of which (XYY) may be linked to severe aggressive tendencies. Nevertheless, chromosomal sex appears to be the most basic distinction between male and female.

2- There is gonadal sex. The male's testicles and the female's ovaries are their primary anatomical sexual characteristics, but in rare cases tissues of both may occur in the same body.

3- The external sex organs. There is evidence that the presence or absence of a penis is the most marked sign upon which sex is assigned to a child, with considerable social consequences.

3.2.1.2 The Physiological Differences

The hormonal sex - the balance of the androgens and oestrogen's - which starts sex differentiation in the second month of foetal life, and continues throughout puberty and adult sexual maturity to old age, affecting all stages of growth and differentiation has a wide range of characteristics of its own. Hormonal balance has considerable affects upon the essential sex-linked physical features during maturation, such as body shape and hair distribution, as well as the control of the reproductive process. This physio-chemical development process is responsible for the male and female sexual organs, usually clearly differentiated by birth, which are the *primary characteristics.* At the same time, hormonal influences produce the *secondary sexual characteristics* of pubertal qualities, confirming the maleness or femaleness of the individual in varying degrees by varying emphasis on anatomical structures.

Thirdly, the individual may assume a gender identity other than the gender role assigned during early development. In cases of trans-sexualism, for instance, the gender identity a person wishes to assume is the opposite of the gender role that has been assigned socially.[4]

Finally, *tertiary sexual characteristics* are those gender role qualities of being masculine and feminine that cultural or sub-cultural conditioning emphasises as appropriate to one sex or the other. It is clearly in the area of tertiary characteristics that there is the most room for change, as the primary and secondary are physiologically determined whereas socio-psychological forces determine the tertiary. Therefore the feminists' claim could be accepted if the *tertiary sexual characteristics* are discussed. However, to generalise to the primary and the secondary sexual characteristics would not be an easy task.

Within the feminists' discourse, a distinction soon developed between "sex" and "gender". It became widely accepted that while "sex" referred to those differences between women and men that were biologically given, that is, grounded on the differences in a

---

[4] R. L. Gregory, *The Oxford Companion to The Mind*, Oxford University Press, 1987, p. 703.

woman's and man's body, "gender" referred to the differences between women and men that were the product of socio-psychological factors.

Distinguished thinkers have laid emphasis on the behaviour and qualities of the two genders. Jean Jacques Rousseau (1712-1778), the Swiss political philosopher, educationist, and essayist claimed that a man says what he knows, while a woman says what will please. Others - like Emma Jung - believed that the real thinking of a woman is pre-eminently practical and applied. It is something we describe as sound common sense, and is usually directed to what is close at hand and personal. Some thinkers – like Adam Smith (1723-1790), the Scottish economist - tried to argue for a difference through values between the two genders; claiming that humanity is the virtue of a woman, while generosity is that of a man. The fact is that one can claim the opposite to be correct as well, because both are virtues given by God to the human beings without consideration of sex. Giving birth to a human being is the most generous act of a human being, while managing a family and working for its members' welfare is a virtue of humanity. These are virtues, which cannot be separated from each other.

3.3   Feminist Reaction

In light of the above-mentioned facts, one can say without a doubt that women have had to endure a state of inferiority for many centuries. Feminist movements have resulted as a reaction to the unjust and miserable circumstances which women have had to encounter throughout history. Feminism is grounded on the belief that women are oppressed or disadvantaged in comparison to men, and that this oppression is illegitimate or unjustified. But under the umbrella of this general conceptual scheme, we find many interpretations of women and their oppression. Therefore, many believe that it is a mistake to consider feminism as a consistent single philosophical worldview, or as a universal unified political program.

I would definitely consider it to have been a natural reaction of feminist activists, when they made the comparison that they were in a battlefront, and were fighting a war for their party's interests. Because of this attitude, feminism was recognised by the average man as a conflict in which it was impossible for a man - as a chivalrous gentleman, as a respecter of the rights of the other part, as a highly evolved citizen of a highly civilised community - to refuse the claim of this better half to self-determination, as the British author and painter, Wyndham Lewis (1882-1957), put it. However, there were failures amongst these activities, which did not seem to be quite usual. Somebody may claim that it is misogyny which lies behind all these failures, but some may declare the reasons for feminism's failure to dislodge deeply-held perceptions of male and female behaviour was its insistence that women were victims, and men powerful patriarchs, which made a travesty of the ordinary people's experience of the mutual interdependence of men and women.

In conclusion, it seems clear that the anti-feminist sentiment is not based on misogyny. It is pessimistic to claim that any opposition to feminism is an expressive of an anti-female stance. The reality is that the most righteous and just leaders and reformers who have striven for the best conditions for women within their societies, have, at the same time, worked hard to create a balanced, moderate and mutual respect between the two genders. They have rejected the theory of struggle between the two genders, and refuted any kind of superiority of man over woman, and vice versa. These efforts were never made in favour of a total feminism, or of masculinist hegemony. In sum, their great endeavour was aimed at the development and integration of the two genders, not a system of gender-based hegemony and conflict.

3.4   The Status of Women

In order to understand the fairest relationship between man and woman, one must first study the status of woman compared to that of man, and explore this relationship in light of it.

3.4.1   Man and Woman - Story of Creation

The reason underlying the Muslim philosophers' claims that men and women possess an intrinsic similarity is that the soul does not recognize any sexual differences. In light of the ensuing verses we would argue further beyond these lines saying that, once we take physicality into consideration, the distinctions of man and woman cease to have relevance. According to the Qur'anic verses, in the beginning there was a single human nature; Adam and Eve were quite identical and neither of them possessed any gender differences. They were pure and neutral human beings without sexual organs. The Qur'anic view presents this position. It explains in two of its verses that when Adam and Eve were created and sent to live in Paradise, they were neither man nor woman. They existed as friends or partners, but not as husband and wife. It was only after the satanic machinations, which seduced them into committing the first sin that their shame appeared before them. In the chapter of Al-'Araaf we read the following verses:

Verse 11- Verily We created you. Then We fashioned you, then We said to the angels: "Prostrate yourselves to Adam." They all fell prostrate except Iblis; he was not of those who make prostration.

Verse 12- (Allah) said: "What prevented you that you did not prostrate yourself when I commanded you?" (Iblis) said: "I am better than he, You created me from fire while You created him from clay."

Verse 13- (Allah) said: "Get you down from this. It is not for you to show pride here, so get out; verily you are of those despised."

Verse 14- (Iblis) said: "Grant me respite till the day they are raised up."

Verse 15- (Allah) said: "Verily you are of those who are respited."

Verse 16- (Iblis) said: "Since You have sent me astray, surely I shall lie in wait for them on your straight path.

Verse 17- Then surely, I will come upon them from the front and behind, right and left, and you will not find most of them thankful."

Verse 18- Allah said: "Get out of this, despised, driven away. Whosoever of them follows you, certainly I will fill hell with you all,"

Verse 19- "O Adam! Dwell you and your partner in the garden, and eat you two wheresoever you like, but go not near this tree, otherwise you two will become of those who are unjust."

Verse 20- Then Shaytan whispered (evil) suggestions to them both in order that he might display to them what was kept hidden from them of their shame, and (Iblis) said: "Your Lord did not forbid you two from this tree but lest you two may become angels or immortals."

Verse 21- And he swore to them both: "Verily I am to you a sincere adviser."

Verse 22- Then he instigated them by deceit. When they tasted of the tree, their shame became exposed to them, and they both began to cover themselves with the leaves of the garden; and their Lord called out to them: "Did I not forbid you two from that tree, and (did I not) tell you both that Shaytan is your declared enemy?"

In another verse we read similar details that confirm the same fact. In the Chapter of Ta Ha, Allah says:

Verse 116- When we said to the angels: "prostrate yourselves before Adam", they prostrated themselves, but Iblis did not, he refused.

Verse 117- Then We said: "O Adam! Verily, this is an enemy to you and your partner therefore let him not drive you two out of the garden, (then) you shall have to toil:

Verse 118- Verily it is ordained that therein you shall not go hungry nor shall you be naked,

Verse 119- Nor shall you be thirsty, nor shall you feel the heat of the sun."

Verse 120- But Shaytan whispered to him, saying: "O Adam, shall I direct you to the tree of eternity and a kingdom that never decays?"

Verse 121- Then the two ate thereof, so their nakedness appeared to them, and they began to cover themselves with the leaves of the garden. And Adam did not act (as advised by) his Lord and (in his search for the pleasure of his Lord) made a mistake.

In conclusion it is humanity's own action during the primordial period that has divided them into the two genders. As such, the gender's distinction is a result of human action, and a natural consequence of a human decision rather than Divine direct intervention.

There are two narrations from Imam Ja'afar Al-Sadiq (as) which support this new theory:

1- From S. Ali b. J. A. Huwayzi's exegesis *"Noor At-Thaqalayn"*, who narrated from some of the companions from Abu Abdullah As-Sadiq (as) regarding the Qur'anic verse 7:22 that he said: *"Their private parts could not be seen, they were hidden inside"*.[5]

2- From S. Faydh Al-Kashani's exegesis *"As-Safi"*, who narrated from Imam Sadiq (as) saying: *"Their private parts were invisible to them, then it appeared, they were hidden inside (their bodies)"*.[6]

One may encounter two contradictory points regarding this new

---

[5] S. Ali B. J. A. Huwayzi, *Noor At-Thaqalayn*, S. A. 'Aashur (ed.), Beirut: Al-Tareekh al-'Arabi, 2001, vol. 2, p. 440.
[6] S. Al-Faydh Al-Kashani, *As-Safi*, S. M. H. Amini (ed.), Tehran: Dar Al-Kutub Al-Islamiyyah, 1419 AH, vol. 3, p. 154.

interpretation:

- Firstly, this theory contradicts the Qur'an when it states that Adam was created and dwelt with his wife in Paradise. (See for example Qur'an 2:35)

- Secondly, where it states in another verse that they were covered by clothes, some form of Paradise clothes, which were removed from them once they disobeyed.[7]

In response to the first point, the Qur'an uses the word *zawj*, which lexicographically can be interpreted to mean 'pair', and thus does not necessarily carry a gender related connotation. Referring to the second point, the word 'clothes', may not literally refer to a material peace of clothes, but rather a natural one, especially if we apply the rules of rhetoric, one may metaphorically perceive it as a form of Divine cover.

3.4.2   The Qur'anic Principle

3.4.2.1   General Equality

This concept of gender equality is best exemplified in the Qur'anic rendition of Adam and Eve. The Qur'an states that both sexes were deliberate and independent, and there is no mention of Eve being created out of Adam's rib.

The issue of which sex was created first is not specified, because we have already explored the fact that that they were identical. After a careful reading of what the Qur'an has to say about women, we are able to realise that the Islamic concept of women is radically different from the medieval Christian one. The Qur'an states:

---

[7] S. N. M. Sherazi, *Tafseer Al-Amthal,* (Arabic version), Qum: Ameer ul-Momineen School, 1412 AH, vol. 4, p. 593.

For Muslim men and women, for believing men and women, for devout men and women, for true men and women, for men and women who are patient, for men and women who humble themselves, for men and women who give in charity, for men and women who fast, for men and women who guard their chastity, and for men and women who engage much in Allah's praise--For them all has Allah prepared forgiveness and great reward.[8]

The believers, men and women, are protectors, one of another: they enjoin what is just, and forbid what is evil, they observe regular prayers, practice regular charity, and obey Allah and His Messenger. On them will Allah pour His Mercy: for Allah is Exalted in power, Wise.[9]

And their Lord answered them: Truly I will never cause to be lost the work of any of you, Be you a male or female, you are members one of another.[10]

Whoever works evil will not be requited but by the like thereof, and whoever works a righteous deed - whether man or woman - and is a believer- such will enter the Garden of bliss.[11]

Whoever works righteousness, man or woman, and has faith, verily to him/her we will give a new life that is good and pure, and we will bestow on such their reward according to the best of their actions.[12]

It is clear that the Qur'anic view of women is no different than that of men. They are both God's creatures whose sublime goal on earth is to worship their Lord, do righteous deeds, and avoid evil and they will both be assessed accordingly.

---

[8] *Qur'an*, 33:35.
[9] *Ibid.*, 9:71.
[10] *Ibid.*, 3:195.
[11] *Ibid.*, 40:40.
[12] *Ibid.*, 16:97.

3.4.2.2 The Elucidation of Equality

What is clearly specified in the Qur'an is that woman is equal to man in religious duties; she has the same obligations and will earn the same rewards or punishments.

Therefore most Muslim women agree that Islam gave them their full rights. However some may disagree over the definition of these rights, while other Muslim women are in the midst of a debate as to whether Islam provides them with "gender equality" or "gender equity". There are certain reservations concerning the former concept because its detractors view it as coming dangerously close to the Western concept of mechanical equality, based on an individualistic view of society. The debate can become very intense, and therefore some may resolve it by adopting the compromising slogan "Equality with Equity".[13]

To frame the debate, we must distinguish properly between the different meanings of equality. An attempt to explore the precise Qur'anic theory first needs a demonstration of the potential probable notion of equality:

Formal Equality - The familiar principle is that individuals who are alike should be treated alike, according to their actual characteristics rather than any stereotyped assumptions made about them. The principle can be applied either to single individuals, whose right to be treated on their own merits can be viewed as a right of individual autonomy, or to groups, whose members seek the same treatment as members of other, similarly situated groups.

The explosion of legal reform on behalf of woman is old, but early in the 1970s was guided by the formal equality model. Landmark Supreme Court decisions, as well as legislation in the areas of employment, education, credit, and the family, presupposed the similarities between men and women and the desirability of

---

[13] Azizah Al-Hibri, "Islamic Law" in *A Companion Feminist Philosophy*, Alison M. Jagger and Iris Marion Young (eds.), Oxford: Blackwell, 1998, p. 545.

treating them by the same rules.

However, an absolute formal equality faces its biggest challenge in rules, legislations and practices based on the differences between men and women. Some scholars, as discussed in brief before, urge measures and methods - as revealed in *Shari'ah* Law as well - to overcome the disadvantages women experience as a result of these differences. Mandatory job security for pregnant women who leave work to bear children is one example. Formal equality adherents oppose such specific rules and special measures, on the grounds that differences between men and women are too easily exaggerated and rarely justify the consequences -harmful or corrective- that is attached to them. They urge the strategy of minimising women's differences, rather than calling attention to them. Thus they compare pregnancy with disabilities that men also experience, and insist it be treated no better no worse.

Unfortunately, observation of recruitment practices does not support this levelling, because no manager is willing to accept the disabled as part of his permanent staff. Furthermore, disabilities are considered as an unlucky accident, whilst a woman's need for maternity leave is well accepted and very much expected from any woman. It does not, therefore, seem a wise comparison.

Substantive Equality - While formal equality judges the form of a rule, requiring that it treat women and men on the same terms without special barriers or favour due to their sex, substantive equality looks to a rule's result or effect. Its critique of formal equality is that, as a result of current societal conditions and sex-based differences, equal treatment results in unequal outcomes. The advocates of substantive equality demand that the rules take account of these conditions and differences, so as to avoid unfair, gender-related outcomes. Just what differences should be recognised and how they should be taken into account, however, is a matter for considerable debate. The different possibilities have resulted in several overlapping versions of the theory, reflecting different forms of substantive equalities.

The fact is that to take the result, as a general measurement may never be practical. Furthermore, one can argue that decisions based solely on results cannot be practicable always and everywhere. There are many reasons behind it:

1. The decision must be taken before the result has been revealed in every single case.

2. Different individuals and changing circumstances may affect the results accordingly; therefore, it can never be a correct generalisation.

3. The individual circumstances may also change in a way that would lead to failure.

Equality Based on Balanced Dominance - The balanced dominance equality shifts the focus of attention from gender-based differences to the balanced dominance division of power between women and men to somehow rely on gender-based special rights or extra bonus. This is in order to create an objective division of power, while providing some classical stereotypes of measures for power. A theory in this framework takes into consideration the advantages of the second type of equality, and avoids the critique of the advocates of formal equality; while at the same time meeting the standard of practical life, and human needs.

The meaning of this equality is that every person should be given his rights and put in his proper place. For example, this equality between individuals and groups within a family implies that each shall get his due rights without any let or hindrance; no right shall be usurped or denied unjustly. The following words of Allah (swt) allude to this:

> ... And they have rights similar to those upon them in a just manner, and for the men is (the right) a degree above them...[14]

This verse ordains equality between the rights of both groups at the same time as it shows the differences between both.

3.4.2.3 Contradicting Interpretations

Unfortunately, some Muslims have been manipulated by inauthentic narrations, or have misunderstood a few of the canonical texts, in such a way, as to create the same sort of primitive mentality found in Medieval Europe. They support their claim with a few narrations or Qur'anic verses. Let us examine an example of the Qur'an, and a sample of a narrated speech of Imam Ali (as) in *Nahj ul-Balagha.*

The Qur'an states:

> Surely, it is a plot of you women! Certainly mighty is your plot.[15]

The crucial point, which attracts our attention, is that this phrase is not a statement of Allah (swt) but rather a quotation from the king, who is named *(Al-Aziz)*, in this chapter. Although one cannot refute the wisdom behind it, the context of the story must be taken into consideration as well as the fact that it was a quotation from a human being. As such, it can never be used as a proof that Allah (swt) has described women in this way.

The narration from As-Sharif Radi in the classical book *(Nahj ul-Balagha)* claims Imam Ali (as) has said:

> O ye peoples! Women are deficient in faith, deficient in shares and deficient in intelligence.[16]

---

[14] *Qur'an,* 2:228.
[15] *Ibid.,* 12:28.
[16] *Bihar ul-Anwar,* vol. 103, p. 228.

Criticising the authenticity of this specific narration is not possible in this paper. Although it is a narrated speech by the collector As-Sharif Radi, it is not a general judgment to criticise all women and place them under one category; because we cannot believe for a moment that Imam Ali (as) considered his wife Fatima Az-Zahra (as) to be one of those women. Presumably, he was referring to a certain woman who was the reason behind a fatal war, where the blood of thousands of Muslims was shed. The historical evidence surrounding this narration confirms this interpretation and the technical principle of hermeneutics supports it as well.

There are several points which contradict the principle we established, in our early discussion, that the two genders are equal. Therefore, the technical rule that is applied here is: whatever contradicts the Qur'an is invalid.

In addition, the Qur'an and Sunnah have supported a mentality of more respect and regard for women. For example, in the Sunnah, we read that Imam Musa ibn Ja'far (as) has narrated from his fathers that the Holy Prophet (saws) said:

> However much the faith of a man increases, his regard for women increases.[17]

It is also narrated that the Holy Prophet (saws) said:

> From the things of the world, I regard women and perfume highly, but prayer is the light of my eyes, (the love and worship of Allah).[18]

3.5   The Interrelation

In light of the above-mentioned analysis, one can draw the conclusion that both genders are entrusted to integrate and assist the other gender in achieving the highest level of perfection.

---

[17] *Bihar ul-Anwar*, vol. 76, p. 141, and *Al-Khissal* vol. 1, p. 183.

[18] As-Sahreef Radi, *Nahjul Balagha,* complied from Imam Ali's (as) words, S. Ali Reza (tran.), New York: Tahrike Tarsil Qur'an, 1985, p.204.

Therefore any claim of man's dominance can be met with the claim that the other way round might be the actual fact. It is supported by life, because woman is actually the dominant sex. Men have to engage in all sorts of activities designed to prove that they are worthy of a woman's attention and sincere love from which, if a man is deprived, he is unable to achieve perfection. Thus, it is a matter of how we look at things, or from which perspective they are observed. To arrive at a balanced and well-reflected claim, one must say that there is no dominance based solely on gender, but it is the reason and perfect decision-making, which dominate human society in general.

This elucidation reveals the meaning of the Prophet's (saws) sayings, which were narrated above. Woman is the crucial factor for a society to achieve perfection, taking into consideration her role as a mother or a good wife. The French novelist Honore De Balzac (1799-1850) said that a woman must be a genius to create a good husband. One may realise how a pious and intelligent woman is needed for an ambitious man to achieve the progressive performance in his life and to succeed. It is obvious that if the man were not able to be a good husband, it would be doubtful that he would achieve something special beyond family life.

3.6   Islam's Contribution to Humanity's Contemporary Problems

In light of what has been said concerning Islam's contribution in improving the condition of women throughout history, it is very apparent that Islam is able to produce a civilised alternative and can come with its own applied legal rules and practical ethics intact to resolve the modern socio-ethical crises. After decades, the Islamic movement has demonstrated its potential power and proved itself of being capable of ruling a country in our modern time.

Islam recognises the importance of women's life cycles, because they have been given different roles and responsibilities at different times of their lives and at each and every stage they are honoured and respected for that which they do. They argue that Islam at its inception has provided them with exemplary female role models and has delineated a path that can be honourably followed at each stage. Muhammad's daughter Fatima (as), for the Shi'ah in particular, provides an idealised role model as the daughter to the Prophet (saws) and wife to Imam 'Ali (as). For all Muslims, Khadija (as) represents a powerful representative of independence as well as being a supportive wife. Thus, revivalist contented Muslim women, and reformers have no need for Western examples, which are in any case alien and exploitative. They have their own path to happiness and liberation, which they wish to pursue.[19]

Conclusion

1- Woman is an equal partner in a balanced dominant division of power between the two genders. The fundamentals for this theory are all contained in the Qur'an, and the example of the Prophet (saws) and the female leaders surrounding him, and often even in early innovative *ijtihad*. The Muslim women's wish today is in developing a revival of Islamic values based on modern jurisprudence, which will drastically accelerate the process of improvement in the global society.

2- The relation of the two genders should be understood in the light of the above-mentioned unique principle. That is the complementarity and integration of the two genders. Therefore, any kind of schism is rejected as long as it contradicts both the Divine gifts and the natural role.

3- Islam, as a thorough and unique religion, can provide an extraordinary role in achieving the liberation of human beings from any kind of oppression. It has also the capability to provide the most sophisticated and civilised alternative for resolving contemporary humanity's problems.

---

[19] Haleh Afshar, "An Analysis of Political Strategies" in *Feminism and Islam*, Mai Yamani (ed.), London: Ithaca 1996, pp. 200-201.

Bibliography

Afshar, Haleh. 1996, "An Analysis of Political Strategies" in *Feminism and Islam*, Mai Yamani (ed.), London: Ithaca 1996, pp. 200-201.

Al-Hibri, Azizah. 1998, *A Companion to Feminist Philosophy*, Alison M. Jagger and Iris Marion Young (eds.), Blackwell, p. 545.

Gregory, R. L. 1987, *The Oxford Companion to The Mind*, Oxford University Press, p. 703.

Tabataba'i, Sayyid Muhammad Husayn. *Al-Mizan, An Exegesis of the Qur'an,* S. S. Akhtar Razawi (tran.), vol. 4, pp. 62-70.

Article 4

Exemplary Women in Islam and in the Holy Qur'an

Shahin Iravani

Abstract

In this paper, we will discuss the concept of feminine spiritual perfection as it is presented in the Qur'an. The Qur'an presents small spiritual biographies of numerous prophets, martyrs, and sages. Most of those examples given are of men; but there are, nonetheless, many detailed descriptions of perfect and exalted women.

We will first discuss the images presented of these women in great detail. Through a careful study of the Qur'anic text, we will attempt to elucidate precisely what virtues these women possessed, and what it was about them that made them so beloved by Allah (swt). We will then discuss those women who are praised in Islamic history, as the Qur'an only includes those women who preceded the Prophet (saws). We will focus on the exalted life of Fatima Zahra (as). There are numerous reports praising her as an embodiment of all virtue, so a careful study of her life will shed light on exactly how virtue is defined in Islam. After this discussion, we will also endeavour to demonstrate that, throughout history, women have achieved an elevated status in Islam.

Introduction

The developed world holds the belief that they are the sole discoverers of the concept of "women's rights". Armed with this presumption, they then attempt to offer such rights to the women of the undeveloped world. Islam has always had its own definition of women's rights and a clear definition of her position. However this is a position that has been covered in veils of ambiguity, and it is on this basis that we will attempt to elucidate the Islamic position on women.

The best method for such a study is to make recourse to the exemplary women presented inside the Qur'an and narrations. This will provide us with a panoramic view of the woman's position in Islam. It will also shed light on those virtues that have helped to make these women so exemplary, and those vices which must be eliminated from one's character. Finally, it will enable us to see whether there is any distinction between men and women in the Islamic image of human perfection.

4.1   The Qur'anic Modelling

First, it is necessary to understand the Qur'an's method of creating exemplary human beings. Every human being has an inherent drive to follow and emulate a person whom he considers to be special and exemplary. This drive, which is rooted in the human soul, makes one desirous of perfection. Every human being has some aptitudes that are to be discovered and developed in one's contact and conflict with their environment. But for the formation and development of these aptitudes it is necessary to have examples to which one can refer, as living embodiments, of his or her ideals. All human beings, consciously or unconsciously, follow the examples that they have in their environments. They look up to the ideal image until they manage to find their own way of life. However the choice of which example to follow is influenced by the person's basic beliefs, viewpoints, and values.

One of the best methods of education is the presentation of exemplary characters that are likely to be respected and emulated. Owing to its effectiveness, all social and cultural institutions use this method. We find extensive use of this in the mass media, including magazines, newspapers, television, radio and films. In reality this has been the main conduit for transmitting cultural beliefs from the Western nations to the developing nations.

The Holy Qur'an also makes use of this method, but with its own principles and criteria for selection. The phrase "example" is used frequently in the Qur'an. The original word, *osveh*, means some sort of embodiment or example. Qur'anically, this term refers to a person who should be emulated in their virtues and attitudes.

Since human beings are likely to make mistakes in their choice of example, the Holy Qur'an emphasises on the necessity of following *osveh hassaneh,* or the righteous example. Allah's Messengers are not the only examples given in the Qur'an. Their true followers are also explicitly put forward as *osveh* as well.[1]

The Qur'anic method is one of indirect introduction. Firstly, it reminds human beings of the messengers and their characteristics and then by repeated praise, not only shows its approval of their behaviour but also encourages all of humanity to follow them. It creates in the heart of the reader a desire to become a living example of human perfection. We read in this Qur'an the supplication:

Our lord, ...make us a model to the god fearing.[2]

In the renowned *Tafsir Al-Mizan*, the Qur'an Interpreter S. M. H. Tabatabaee states:

A prayer of all the believers is to be the model for the virtuous and the god fearing.[3]

This verse of the Qur'an is a plea, where one is asking one's Lord to provide one with an opportunity to surpass all others in the acquisition of good deeds. One is asking for a special grace to be brought down on oneself, so that others may love virtue through one's actions.

Examples, however, are often not sufficient and are subject to misunderstanding. The Holy Qur'an clearly explains its criteria for selecting examples. For instance, where it speaks of the prophets, it enumerates their specific virtues:

And Ishmael, Idris, Dhulkifl- each was of the patient.[4]

---

[1] Basic Reference of the Qur'an is "The Qur'an Interpreted, Arthur Arberry, New York, Collier book, 1955". *Qur'an,* 47:4.

[2] *Ibid.,* 25:74.

[3] Mohammad Hussein Tabatabaee, *The Standard Interpretation*, Tehran: The Knowledge & Thought Institute of Allameh Tabatabaee, 1988, vol. 16, p. 451.

[4] *Ibid.,* vol. 21, p. 85.

And about Zakaria, his wife, and John (as):

> Truly they vied with one another hastening to good works, and called
> upon Us out of yearning and awe; and they were humble to Us.[5]

We can see a similar process of exemplification in the annals of
Abraham (as) and his followers, where they are all collectively
described as *osveh*. The reader is immediately reminded that his
epithet is the result of their resistance to infidelity and polytheism.[6]

But sometimes even this sort of exemplification is not sufficient, as
human beings may take the wrong paths even with the best criteria.
They may err when it comes to the practical implementation of the
virtues. Here, the only road to the correct choice is the person's
power of discrimination. The Holy Qur'an demands that human
beings constantly reflect, and highly praises those endowed with
wisdom.[7] It also explicitly asserts that human beings should not
follow the things about which they do not have any knowledge.[8]

Lack of precise exemplary criteria or lack of discrimination can
lead to hero-worship and idolatry.

4.2   Gender and Introduction of Examples in the Qur'an

The Holy Qur'an employs two methods in presenting its desired
virtues: simple enumerations of virtues in general and introduction
of exemplary characters.

4.2.1   Enumeration of the Virtues in General

A study of Qur'anic verses demonstrates that in both methods, men
and women are equally important.

---

[5] *Ibid.*, 21:90.
[6] *Ibid.*, 60:4-6.
[7] *Ibid.*, 3:190-195.
[8] *Ibid.*, 17:36.

Men and women who have surrendered, Believing men and believing women, Obedient men and obedient women, Truthful men and truthful women, Enduring men and enduring women, Humble men and humble women, Men and women who give in charity, Men who fast and women who fast, Men and women who guard their private parts, Men and women who remember god often - for them God has prepared forgiveness and a mighty wage.[9]

The same attitude can be seen with the introduction of exemplary human beings:

Surely, there is virtue for you in following Abraham and his followers.[10]

You have had a good example in God's messenger for whosoever hopes for God and the Last Day, and remembers God often.[11]

God has struck a similitude for the believers the wife of pharaoh, when she said, 'my Lord, build for me a house in paradise, in thy presence, and deliver me from pharaoh and his work, and do thou deliver me from the people of the evildoers'. And Mary, Imran's daughter, who guarded her virginity; so We breathed into her of our spirit, and she confirmed the words of her Lord and his books. She was so prayerful.[12]

From these verses it is clear that gender is irrelevant. Man and woman can both develop the desired virtue and become exemplary beings. Furthermore, there is no border between the genders. Exemplary women are introduced as role models not only for women but also for all the faithful. The same is true of exemplary men; they are also examples for all who hope for God's grace on

---

[9] *Ibid.*, 33:35.
[10] *Ibid.*, 60:4.
[11] *Ibid.*, 33:21.
[12] *Ibid.*, 66:11-12.

the Day of Judgement.

The choice and introduction of exemplary characters in the Qur'an is thus done without any attention to gender. The last evidence is the clearest:

> And whosoever does a righteous deed, be they male or female, believing, we shall assuredly grant them to live a goodly life.[13]

4.2.2   A study of Exemplary Women

These women can be divided into two main groups, exemplary women in the Qur'an and exemplary women from the environment in which Islam gradually spread.

All the Qur'anic exemplary women, except one, belong to the nations of the past, whose history is common in Judaism, Christianity, and Islam. These women can themselves be subdivided into two groups: the virtuous, who are highly praised, and the evil ones, who are denounced. The virtuous include Mary (as), Mary's mother, John's mother, Moses' mother, Pharaoh's wife, Abraham's wife, Job's wife, and the Queen of Sheba. Examples of the evil are: Noah's wife, the Egyptian governor's wife and Abu Lahab's wife (whose husband was a leading figure of Mecca during the first years of Islam).

The examples who lived in the first years of Islam and later include the women from the House of the Holy Messenger (saws), some female followers, and the wives and daughters of some of the successors.

4.2.2.1 Exemplary Women in the Qur'an

It should first be noted that the reports presented in the Qur'an are completely different from those presented by man. Whatever is presented in the Qur'an is the specific representation of a universal

---

[13] *Ibid.*, 16: 99.

and timeless principle[14], not just a factual representation of a particular event that holds its truth only for that particular case. Thus, each one of the virtues mentioned for exemplary women in the Qur'an is an illumination of the potential and existential features of all women.

Mary (as)

The most prominent female figure in the Qur'an is Mary (as). She is the only woman whose name and pedigree is mentioned in the Qur'an. The other characters are mentioned by reference to their relations. Mary (as) is mentioned in the Qur'an with reverence and is exalted beyond imagination.

1. Mary (as) is the *Ayah* and the sign of God's presence, in the world. "Ayat" is a sign, the existence of which can lead the mind to an understanding of God and his grandeur. (Qur'an, 21:91 and 23:50)

2. Mary (as) is one of the elect. In the third chapter, God speaks of Imran's family as one of the elect families:

    God chose Adam and Noah and the house of Abraham and the house of Imran above all beings... (Qur'an, 3:32)

3. Mary (as) is the perfect example that God uses to reject the idea of gender as a criterion for human worthiness. During her pregnancy, Mary's mother vowed to give her baby in dedication to the Lord. But when she was born and she realised that she was a girl, she did not know what to do. The Holy Qur'an says:

    The boy she thought of could never be equal to the girl. (Qur'an, 3:36)

The verse emphasises the worthiness and the priority of the girl

---

[14] Abdullah Javadi Amoli, *Women in the Mirror of Elegance & Glory,* Tehran: Raja Cultural Publication Centre, 1996, pp. 280-281.

over any boy, rejecting gender as a criterion for worthiness.

4. According to Imam Sadiq's (as) report from the Holy
    Messenger (saws), Mary (as) has the spiritual status of a
    prophet. It is stated in religious texts that a prophet can see the
    heavenly angels in person and hear them present the words of
    God. According to the Qur'an, Mary (as) saw the heavenly
    angel as a man speaking to her and telling her of God's Will
    that "she will have a child" (Qur'an, Surah 3 & 19). This is the
    highest spiritual status a human being can achieve. Mary (as),
    however, was not responsible for delivering the message of
    God to her people. The reason for this will be clarified later.

5. Mary (as) is one of the truthful (Qur'an, 5:75 and 66:11). The
    truthful are those who alongside with the prophets, the
    righteous, and the martyrs form the leading group of the pious.

6. Mary (as) is the embodiment of humanity and a symbol of
    faith:

    God has struck a similitude for the believers. Mary, Imran's daughter,
    who guarded her virginity, so we breathed into her of our spirit, and
    she confirmed the words of her Lord and his books, and became one
    of the obedient. (Qur'an, 66:11,12)

7. God granted Mary (as) all His blessings in the various stages of
    life: when she lived in the temple (Qur'an, 3:37); when she
    was pregnant and during her delivery, He grew fresh dates and
    made a stream for her to brighten her eyes (Qur'an, 19:26);
    then when she was taking care of Jesus (as), he provided her
    with a peaceful place and refreshing water. (Qur'an, 23:50)

It can be seen that Mary (as) has a high status in the Qur'an. The
Qur'anic view of Mary (as) and her potentials reflect the potentials
and the existential possibilities for women, which as in the case of
Mary (as), are to be achieved with perseverance and devotion.

True, Mary (as) was a member of an elect family. Yet a simple comparison between her and Noah's son demonstrates that being a member of a pious family is not in itself sufficient for spiritual growth and salvation. The Qur'an's attitude towards Mary (as) and the term it uses to describe her character, prove that God appreciates the efforts of women in achieving perfection.

A Study of Required Criteria and Virtues

Verses 10-12 of the chapter 66 (The Forbidding) contain some important remarks about this matter:

> God has struck a similitude for the unbelievers the wife of Noah, and the wife of Lot; for they were under two of our righteous [worshipers], but they betrayed them, so they availed nothing whatsoever against God; so it was said, enter, you two, the fire with those who enter. God has struck a similitude for the believers the wife of Pharaoh, when she said, My Lord, build for me a house in Paradise, in thy presence, and deliver me from Pharaoh and his work, and do thou deliver me from the people of the evildoers. And Mary, Imran's daughter, who guarded her virginity, so we breathed into her of our spirit, and she confirmed the words of her Lord and his books, and became one of the obedient.

The following can be concluded from these verses:

1- Since men and women are introduced side by side as symbols of virtue and faith or impiety and sin, gender or being a man is not a pre-requisite for being exemplary.

2- A comparison between the two examples of impiety and those of virtue demonstrates that each example is contrary in a specific attitude to a counterpart of the opposite group. Noah's (as) impious wife who lived with God's Prophet and provided the ground for the education of Noah's (as) impious son is juxtaposed with Pharaoh's pious wife who lived with a man who claimed to be a god (Qur'an, 79:24) and provided the ground for the growth and education of a prophet; Moses (as). Both characters are mentioned first in their respective group. Lot's wife is then contrasted with Mary (as). Both are second in their respective groups. Mary (as) is the embodiment of chastity and piety while Lot's (as) wife provides the ground for the vilest kind of corruption and sin (Qur'an, 11:81). After pregnancy, Mary (as) managed to follow her virtuous path in spite of all the slanderous remarks which surrounded her. Lot's (as) wife, however, chose to be with the corrupt, although she belonged to the pious. Furthermore, Mary (as) was chaste although she was unmarried.

3- The Holy Qur'an demands two essential virtues in these verses: standing against oppression and leading a pious life. These two are the opposites of two essential vices: standing against the truth and moral corruption. Since standing against oppression demands involvement in socio-political activities, it is essential that all virtuous men and women be directly involved in these matters.

4- Another important point inferred from these verses is the emphasis on man's free will and independence in making decisions. The Holy Qur'an gives the examples of some women who managed to resist the temptations and pressures of their environment and make wise decisions. Considering the fact that women have always been under greater pressures than men, it has been common to imagine them as passive and submissive to the conventions and pressures. But the Qur'an demonstrates that women can choose freely and their fates are not determined by their milieu.

Another position assigned to women by the Qur'an is the governmental position. The Queen of Sheba was the monarch of a country, Sheba, and a contemporary of the great Prophet Solomon (as). The Prophet called her and her people to the worship of God and she ultimately converted to the true religion of the time. The Holy Qur'an speaks of her power and the vastness of her domain (Qur'an, 27:23). She had all that is needed for a great governor; that is resolution, providence, strong will, dignity, treasure and a powerful army. According to the Qur'an, her method of ruling was different from that of men. The terms she uses to refer to

Solomon's (as) letter are reverential: "A letter honourable has been cast unto me" (Qur'an, 27:2). Then, after perusing the letter, she consults her courtiers (all men). In spite of the courtiers' desire to wage a war against Solomon (as), she rejects war as causing only destruction and misery. Thus, she chooses a strategy of gradual encounter and makes peace with Solomon (as), especially because she realises his army is much stronger than hers. "But she also manages to keep her Queenly dignity in facing Solomon".[15] Then when she discovers the truth of Solomon's (as) call, she readily acknowledges his rightful position and does not conceal her belief behind the mask of arrogance and selfishness. Nevertheless, she never acts as an impotent and cowardly monarch.

She never says 'I' surrendered to Solomon (as) or believed in him, but speaks with self-esteem "I surrender with Solomon to God". God reminds us of the sublime and profound nature of her attitude.[16] (Qur'an, 27: 23-44)

The image of a woman's rule in the Qur'an differs greatly from those of men. She is the only monarch who surrenders to the words of Allah and does not wage war against His Prophet. She is the only ruler who prefers peace to war and has the courage to sacrifice her royal arrogance to truth.

Women and Moral Integrity in the Qur'an

Chastity, studied here in the case of Mary (as), is a virtue of great importance in the Qur'an. Some of the characters introduced in this regard are Mary (as), Joseph (as), the Egyptian governor's wife and her friends.

Mary and Joseph (as) are the embodiments of chastity because they were both put through intimidating tests and were able to come out

---

[15] Mohammad Hussein Tabatabaee, *The Standard Interpretation*, Tehran: The Knowledge & Thought Institute of Allameh Tabatabaee, 1988, vol. 15, p. 556, 559.

[16] Abdullah Javadi Amoli, *Women in the Mirror of Elegance & Glory,* Tehran: Raja Cultural Publication Centre, 1996, p. 286.

victorious and pure. But there is an essential difference between them. Joseph (as) managed to preserve his chastity; when women desired him, he did not even think to commit sin (Qur'an, 12:24). Mary's (as) case, however, was different. Mary (as) said to the angel:

I take refuge in the All-merciful from thee! If thou fearest God...

When the angel told her:

I am but a messenger come from thy Lord, to give thee a boy most pure.

Mary (as) responded:

When shall I have a boy and no mortal has yet touched me, nor have I been unchaste! (Qur'an, 19:18-20)

According to the Qur'an scholar Javadi Amoli, this is an act of calling to good deeds and forbidding evil deeds.[17] The words are of instructive value. Mary (as) not only takes refuge from the sin in the hands of God, but also warns the man against sinning by reminding him of God. Thus Mary's (as) spiritual influence goes beyond her own self and affects the other person.

To clarify the argument, it is now useful to refer to the chapter on Joseph, in which the attitudes of the Egyptian governor's wife and her friends are represented. Although married, this impious woman falls in love with the young servant, Joseph (as), whom her husband calls his son. She tries to trap and seduce him, but when her plot fails and her secret is revealed, she takes revenge by distorting the truth and pretending that he had tried to seduce her. Thus, Joseph (as) is sent to prison through her machination. The fact that the Holy Qur'an gives the example from among women but not men reflects the importance of women's attitudes in such

---

[17] *Ibid.,* p. 127.

conditions. Furthermore, the Holy Qur'an uses the phrase "great cunning" when it describes the attitudes of the woman and her friends who tried to seduce Joseph (as) and then later in revenge introduces him as the culprit.

In fact, a close study of Joseph's (as) story in the Qur'an reveals cunningness as one of the main themes. Joseph's (as) brothers deceive their father and try to get rid of Joseph (as). Joseph (as) later on conceals a valuable goblet in his brother's saddlebag and accuses him of theft. The Holy Qur'an states that Allah (sw) taught Joseph (as) the use of this cunningness. When the Egyptian governor's wife learns that her friends have criticized her for falling in love with Joseph (as), she invites them all and gives each of them a piece of fruit and a knife. She then displays the beauty of Joseph (as) to them; this dazzled group then cut their hands as they watch him, instead of the fruit.

However, among this cunningness and hidden plots, it is only the cunningness of the women, which creates a "great victory". The reason is because of the destructive effects of such deceptions in misleading others. It also reflects the power that women have in attracting men.

Considering the fact that Mary (as) is one step ahead of Joseph (as) in moral integrity and that women are given the power to attract men and thus are capable of "great cunningness", we can conclude that their role in preserving the moral integrity of society is more important than that of men.

This, however, does not mean that men have no responsibility in this regard. Joseph (as) is introduced in the Qur'an as the model of male chastity. Although single, attractive, and sought after by numerous women, he controls his desires and chooses imprisonment over moral corruption. It is narrated by Allah's Holy Messenger (saws), that Joseph (as) is the criterion of chastity for men and Mary (as) is the criterion for women, on the Day of

Judgement.[18]

In the section, which discussed the possibility of receiving revelation, it was emphasized that according to the Qur'an, Mary (as) was a prophet and received revelation. However, Mary (as) is not the only woman to have had communication with the supernatural; Moses' (as) mother is introduced in the Qur'an as having received revelation, (Qur'an, 20:38) and Abraham's (as) wife as speaking with the angels (Qur'an, 11:73). Thus the sublime status of receiving revelation does not belong solely to men. A question, however, is likely to be raised here: Why were all the prophets, who had the duty of delivering God's message to man, chosen from men?

The answer lies in the historical position of women in human society. Even now, it is very difficult for patriarchal societies to accept the leadership or management of women. Thus, how can it be expected that in the past millennia a woman be acknowledged as not only the religious and intellectual but also the political and military leader of people?

The features studied up to here are related to the essential identity of human beings as men and women. Now it is time to pay attention to the roles of women in life. The Holy Qur'an assigns numerous roles to women by discussing some exemplary characters, whose attitudes towards their lives and fulfilment of their duties are either praised or highly reproached. Among these roles, the most important ones are their roles as mothers and as wives. As wives, such women as Imran's wife, Zacharia's wife, Abraham's wife Sarah and his other wife Hajar, and Job's wife are referred to in the Qur'an. Two basic groups of virtues are praised in these women: first, they are praised as pious worshipers and performers of good deeds, and for some similar personal virtues; and then they are praised for being perfect companions for their

---

[18] Mohammad Hassan Horre Amoli, *The Means of Shiites*, Beirut: The Centre of Reviving Arabic Legacy, 1983, vol. 14, pp. 2-3.

husbands in the way of Allah (swt). It should be noted that mere accompaniment and obedience are not considered praiseworthy. These are valuable only when they are done for the sake of Allah (swt) and for His cause. Pharaoh's wife is praised for her disobedience of an oppressive husband; Noah's (as) wife and Lot's (as) wife are reproached for being disobedient towards their pious husbands and Abu Lahab's wife is reproached for being obedient towards and helping her evil husband. (Qur'an, 3:34-36; 21:89-90; 11:69-73, 14:37, 38:41-44)

As mothers, the Qur'an gives the examples of such women as Mary (Jesus' mother), Mary's (as) mother, Moses (as) mother, and also Pharaoh's wife who saved, protected, and educated Moses (as). Mary's (as) motherhood is from the beginning affected by suffering and pressure. But she manages to face her people bravely and bring up and educate Jesus (as) properly. (Qur'an, 19:22-33) Mary's (as) mother, on the other hand, vowed that the baby in her womb would be dedicated to God and after she had been born, asked God to protect her and her children. (Qur'an, 3:34-36)

Moses' (as) mother in great anxiety - but relieved by God's words- gave her son to the water of the Nile and followed him. Allah (swt) in His Mercy returned her son to her bosom to make her eyes 'bright with happiness'. (Qur'an, 20:36-40) Pharaoh's wife dissuaded her husband from killing Moses (as), performed all the motherly duties for him, and finally became his follower and sacrificed her life for her faith. (Qur'an, 28:7-9; and 66:11-12)

There is no direct reference to a bad mother in the Qur'an, but Noah (as) had an impious son who was brought up by an impious mother. Although the Holy Qur'an does not indicate a relationship, it can be inferred that there is a relationship between the irresponsibility of the mother and the wickedness of the son. This is not of any exemplary value because such a relationship is not seen in Lot's (as) family. The Holy Qur'an speaks of all the members of Lot's (as) family as being salvaged except his wife. (Qur'an, 11:81)

4.2.2.2 Exemplary Muslim Women

Those who grew up and lived under the Islamic system of education form the second group of exemplary models. The source of information about the first group, the women of ancient nations, is the Qur'an, the most important source of information in the Islamic world. But the source of information for exemplary Muslim personalities is the huge collection of historical records and the reported words of the first Islamic leaders. Some parts of this huge collection of information are not completely reliable. Thus, it is imperative that one refers to different historical documents to make sure the reported event or speech is authentic. However, they have the advantage of being fully detailed and, in comparison to the Qur'an, contain a wide variety of data on numerous exemplary characters. Thus one of the best ways of certifying an attitude as a virtue is to discover it in several pious people. Another important point is that women in the Qur'an are mostly depicted in their essential identity as female human beings and the study of their roles in life is given secondary importance. But in the available historical records, women are basically depicted in their roles in life and thus the descriptions are greatly affected by the assumptions of the parochial views of different historical periods. Thus, the Holy Qur'an is incomparable beyond all these texts for finding the true status of women in Islam. It is also imperative to use the Qur'an as the touchstone for these historical records, especially because most of the ambiguities and complications about the status of women in Islam are rooted in these historical reports.

Exemplary Muslim women belong to two basic groups: Women from the House of the Holy Messenger (saws), and his faithful female followers. Among the members of the first group, one can mention Khadijah (as), his wife; his daughter, Fatima (as); his grand-daughters, especially Zaynab (as); and some of the Imam's daughters and the daughters of some of the successors of the Holy Messenger (saws), such as Imam Hussein's (as) daughter, Fatima (as) and Sakinah (as); Imam Reza's (as) sister, Fatima (as); and Imam Naqi's (as) daughter, Hakimah (as). The wives of some of the Imam's also have their names in the list, such as the mother of the last Imam of the Shi'ahs, Narjes (as), who according to some historical reports was a descendant of one of Jesus' (as) disciples. There are also numerous female names mentioned as the faithful followers of the Holy Messenger (saws) and his successors, but it seems unnecessary to flood this paper with such names.

Fatima Zahra (as)

Fatima (as), our Messenger's (saws) daughter, holds the highest status among all these characters. Her characteristics are identical with whatever the Holy Qur'an holds valuable and praises in women. The following are some of the reports recorded about her spiritual status:

1- Fatima (as) is the elect of this world's women.[19]

2- Fatima (as) conversed with the angels[20] and even after the passing away of the Holy Messenger (saws), she had conversations with Gabriel and received some revelations from him.

3- Fatima (as) is held in high esteem by God and God has chosen her as one of His elect worshipers.[21]

4- Fatima (as) is the central pole of the House of the Holy Messenger (saws) and all the members are referred to in terms of their relationship with her. It is reported that God, speaking to Gabriel, refers to the members of this Holy family in the following terms: They are Fatemeh, her father, her husband,

---

[19] Mohammad Bagher Majlessi, *The Seas of Light*, Beirut: Al-Vafa Institute, 1983, vol. 11, p. 113.

[20] *Ibid.*, p. 99.

[21] Mohammad Hussein Tabatabaee, *The Standard Interpretation*, Tehran: The Knowledge & Thought Institute of Allameh Tabatabaee, 1988, vol. 4, pp. 233. See also Mohammad Bagher Majlessi, *The Seas of Light*, Beirut: Al-Vafa Institute, 1983, vol. 11, pp. 99, 113, 116.

and her sons.[22]

5- Fatima (as) is one of those who outrun all in the performance of good deeds.[23]

6- Fatima (as) is one of the all-patient human beings who endured all the sufferings and persecutions of cruel people, but never cursed any of them.[24]

7- Fatima (as) has the high status of a Holy being who can intercede with God on behalf of people.[25]

8- Fatima (as) is the criterion for people's deeds on the Day of Judgement.[26]

9- Fatima (as) managed to accomplish all these qualities and positions due to her unique attitude towards life and its vicissitudes and her relentless energy in her quest for spiritual growth and perfection.

Fatima's (as) Attitude towards Life

A close study of Fatima's (as) lifestyle demonstrates that her whole life is formed by one essential principle: Choosing hardship over ease.

One may be surprised to learn of such a principle; why should she choose such a principle and follow it throughout her life? In our modern world, in which all values are drastically metamorphosed and in which technology aims to reduce hardship and provide man with the utmost possibilities of ease and comfort, such a question is not so irrelevant. Islam, however, has its own point of view.

---

[22] Mohammad Hussein Tabatabaee, *The Standard Interpretation*, Tehran: The Knowledge & Thought Institute of Allameh Tabatabaee, 1988, vol. 4, p. 233.
[23] *Ibid.*, p. 248.
[24] *Ibid.*, p. 248.
[25] *Ibid.*, vol. 14, p.50.
[26] *Ibid.*, vol. 14, p. 50.

When dealing with self-discovery and spiritual growth, Islam approves of accepting and enduring hardship, to the extent that is proper for the individual. Building up character necessitates endurance of hardship;

> So truly with hardship comes ease. (Qur'an, 94:5)

This is the same principle that can be found in the life of all pious human beings, all great reformers, and all pursuers of worthy aims. Such examples are as follows:

1. Choosing poverty over wealth and welfare: Although she had a steady income from the Fadak estate, Fatima (as) lived in poverty and gave her income in charity to the poor.[27] She is reported as saying

   > I have nothing except a pair of worn out and patched up shoes and a dress and a cover, in the same condition.[28]

2. Preferring others to oneself: Her son, Imam Hassan (as) remembered,

   > Once my mother was at prayer from midnight until morning and she prayed for all except herself. I asked what about you? She said: 'My dear son! First the neighbour, then yourself'.[29]

3. Preferring simplicity over luxury: Fatima (as) gave out her ornaments necklace, earrings, her children's ornaments, and the beautiful curtain of her house in charity and in her wish to help the advancement of Islam. Her father (saws) was a source

---

[27] Mohammad Bagher Majlessi, *The Seas of Light*, Beirut: Al-Vafa Institute, 1983, vol. 12, p. 130.

[28] *Ibid.*

[29] Ali Gharani Golpayegani, *The Mysteries of Messenger's Ascension to Heaven*, Qom: Islamic Bookshop, 1979, p. 21.

of encouragement in this.[30]

4. Preferring work and hardship over ease and self-indulgence: Fatima (as) insisted on doing the household chores by herself and her hands showed the effects of hard work.[31]

5. Preferring midnight prayer to sleep and rest: Her son, Imam Hassan (as) once said,

> No one was more devout than Fatima. She stood on her feet for such a long time that her feet suffered inflammation.[32]

> Most nights, she prayed until mornings.[33]

6. Preferring opposition against oppression to silence: Fatima (as) was God's warrior against oppression,[34] especially after the passing away of the Holy Messenger (saws), when she objected to any injustice with great courage. Two of her important oppositions are the two speeches she made: one in the mosque before all the people and one at home in the presence of those who had come to visit her in her illness. She asked her husband Imam Ali (as), to bury her secretly so that the oppressors would not know the place of her grave and thus save her from the hypocritical show of reverence after her death. This was also a complex form of opposition of their oppression.[35]

---

[30] Mohammad Hassan Horre Amoli, *The Means of Shiites*, Beirut: The Centre of Reviving Arabic Legacy, 1983, vol. 3, Part 8.

[31] Mohammad Bagher Majlessi, *The Seas of Light*, Beirut: Al-Vafa Institute, 1983, vol. 12, p. 97.

[32] Mohammad Hussein Tabatabaee, *The Standard Interpretation*, Tehran: The Knowledge & Thought Institute of Allameh Tabatabaee, 1988, vol. 10, p. 505.

[33] *Ibid.*

[34] Zabihollah Mahallati, *The Flowers of Religious Law*, Tehran: The Centre of Islamic School, 1969, vol. 1, pp. 162, 213.

[35] Seyed Ahmad Alam Al-Hoda, *Zahra The Fruit of Revelation*, Tehran, Amir Kabir Publication, 1989, p. 52.

All the above were assiduously performed because Fatima (as) wished to achieve the high status of Allah's satisfaction and to be affiliated with His eternal being, the highest stage of perfection for humanity. Women who had lived with Fatima (as) spoke of her as having all the sublime characteristics of humanity,

I never saw a woman, more considerate than Zahra.[36]

The Holy Messenger gave me his daughter so that I educate her, but she was more courteous than I was.[37]

The Holy Messenger's wife, 'Aiesha said,

I never saw a woman more truthful than Fatima.[38]

I never saw anybody superior to Fatima except her father.[39]

It should be noted that the features mentioned in the different sources as evidence for Fatima's (as) spiritual status and her exemplary character are all common signs of perfection for the whole of humanity and gender plays no role in this regard.

Characteristics of Prominent Muslim Women

The aim here is to reveal all the characteristics, which are mentioned for women that hold a high status in Islam. These are virtues recommended for all women. There are altogether 134 virtues, which can be extracted from the texts of prayer and supplication and they can be divided into three groups: 47 of these virtues are related to personal behaviour, 48 to familial relations and the educational milieu, and the remaining 39 to spiritual and sublime virtues.

---

[36] Mohammad Hussein Tabatabaee, *The Standard Interpretation*, Tehran: The Knowledge & Thought Institute of Allameh Tabatabaee, 1988, vol. 10, p. 494.
[37] *Ibid.*
[38] *Ibid.*
[39] *Ibid.*, vol. 14, p. 23.

The first group deals with such subjects as perseverance, intellectual potentials, faith and attitudes resulting from faith, and motherly behaviour. Some of them are as follows:

- Kindness towards the child entrusted to her by God

- Care and protection of that child

- Education and discipline of that child

- Ever conscious of the call of God's Messenger

- To gain knowledge

- To work hard in the path of God

- To prefer God's satisfaction over one's own

- To endure hardship because of faith in God

- To be pious

- To fight for Divine causes

- To be liberal and noble

- Consistency

- Perseverance

- Relentless in the way of faith

- To regularly perform night prayer

- To be iron-willed

- To be a protector of the weak

- Courageous

- To obey God, when both alone and in company

- Denunciatory towards the hypocrites and conspirators

- Thankful for God's blessings

- To uprise against oppression

- To seek marriage with the pious

The second group concerns the environment in which these exemplary women grew up in and their familial relations. There are also references to the sufferings they had to endure. Some of these are related to the women from the House of God's Holy Messenger (saws), and the focus is on the presence of those women in the environment in which the revelations were received. Some of these are:

- Being educated in the house of the Holy revelations

- Being born at the centre of piety and infallibility

- Being the heiress to nobility and virtuousness

- Being educated by the rhythmical recital of the Qur'an

- Growing up in the Holy places of Mecca, Mina, Zamzam and Safa

- Growing up with the profound and strong signs of faith (God's Holy Messenger and the Imams)

There are attributes referring to the relationship of these women with the Infallible Imams (as) such as: the carriers of the pious in their wombs; the child of God's dear follower and friend; the sister of God's dear follower and friend; the aunt of God's dear follower

and friend; the miracle of Muhammed; the dearly beloved of the
Holy Messenger (saws).

There are also attributes related to the hardship that these women
endured, such as: the persecuted; captive; oppressed; bereaved; a
noble soul humiliated by vulgarity; the lonely and homeless. These
attributes, which refer to their suffering, depict them as passive
sufferers, but there are others reflecting their perseverance and
power. It should be noted that these attributes reflect the pressures
of a suppressing milieu, in which they built up their exemplary
characters.

The third group reflects the levels of their spiritual growth and is
the result of their tireless attempts in their quest for perfection.
Some of these are: the matured and perfect: the illuminated; the
magnanimous; the pure and pious; the knowledgeable; the highly
reputable with God.

The third group is in fact, the result of self-education and is totally
regardless of gender. These attributes are the virtues that any
human being, in quest for perfection, must acquire. Thus, Islam
demands that women, like men, improve their spirituality, stability,
perseverance, courage, knowledge and wisdom.

Islam does not view women as passive and frail; on the contrary, it
considers them as capable of changing their milieu in spite of all
pressures. Consequently, in many cases it introduces its exemplary
women to all the people of the world as perfect models.

4.3   The Activities of Muslim Women in the Past

At the end, it seems necessary to cite some statistics concerning
Muslim women who have played their roles in important social and
cultural activities and who have had their names recorded in the
Islamic historical texts. These statistics are the results of a
quantitative analysis of the activities of Muslim women, and they
reflect the fact that in spite of all the limitations imposed on them
in their patriarchal societies, they have been able to be socially
active and influential:

The total number of women surveyed is 2600.

Women educated in Islamic studies	1400
Literary women and poetesses	520
Mystics and hermits	200
Women who look after the poor	290
Revolutionary women	200
Physicians, artists, and craftswomen	30
Musicians	Less than 30

Some of these women were active in several fields and were especially interested in composing poetry.[40] It should be noted that the recorded names are just the names of a small fraction of Muslim women who participated in social activities. However there are many women who wish to remain unknown and thus the number of women who were active and influential are much more than this.

> O mankind! Lo: We have created you male and female, and have made you nations and tribes that ye may know one another. Lo! The noblest of you, in the sight of Allah, is the best in conduct. Lo! Allah is knower, Aware. (Qur'an, 49:13)

Conclusion

It is human nature to emulate one's ideal, in Islam such an ideal is embodied in certain personalities, who uphold the loftiest spiritual values.

---

[40] Omar Reza Kahalleh, *The Names of Famous Women in the Arab & Islamic World*, Beirut: Al-Resaleh Institute, 5th Edition, Five volumes.

Through a study of characters in the Qur'an and Islamic texts, it becomes clear that spiritual perfection is accessible to both men and women alike. We are provided with various examples of women who have attained such proximity to God, and they are paradigms for men and women the world over. In the personalities of the above mentioned, 'four perfect women', timeless virtues are expounded such as patience, chastity and courage. As women they also provide the Muslim woman with the ideal role models in their duties as wives and mothers. In Mary (as) we witness the direct influence of her purity in the upbringing and education of her son the Prophet Jesus (as). In Khadija, we see the importance of companionship a wife has to her husband in supporting him in a God-orientated life, and in the character of Asiya (as) we observe the personification of courage and devotion to God in her stand against the tyranny and oppression of her husband. All goodness and virtue culminates in the enduring spirit of Fatima Zahra (as). She is indeed the most sublime woman in creation and her light shines forth as a beacon for all of mankind.

The Muslim woman is eternally blessed with such exemplars who provide her with the guidance and inspiration necessary to reach perfection and stand exalted amongst her contemporaries.

Article 5

Personalities of Women in the Qur'an and their Reflection on Women in Islamic History

Halimah Krausen

Abstract

The paper will begin by analysing certain women mentioned in the Qur'an in order to illustrate the ontological position, religious and social responsibilities, and ethical framework of women, that was implemented amongst the Prophet's contemporaries. The paper then proceeds to show how women in Islamic history received and reflected these impulses, being active and even famous in various fields.

We will ask what other role models can be found for present-day Muslim girls and women that can encourage them to unfold their potential and to use their abilities in a meaningful way. In a final step, it will be questioned why and how Muslim women in recent centuries suffered the setback that has created their present situation in many Muslim countries, and what strategies can be developed to overcome this situation.

Introduction

"The Position of Women in Islam" is currently one of the most popular topics discussed by Muslims and in inter-cultural dialogue. The discussion is often triggered by burning questions based on the encounter with a non-Islamic value system and a re-evaluation of past experiences within the Muslim community. In any case, the background is the need for orientation concerning the implementation of Islamic values in the modern world. In this context, we are often presented with descriptions of "The Ideal Muslim Woman" in an attempt to oppose the stereotypes we are confronted with from outside, ranging from critical sociological studies of the actual situation of our sisters between Indonesia and Morocco to romantic images from 'Arabian Nights'. Sadly, what is often missing is an idea of how women actually endeavoured to realise their ideals, to overcome obstacles, and to contribute to the development of the community side by side with the men. Such an idea can motivate our present and future generations and help them to develop visions of their own.

5.1   The Exemplary Women in Islam

I must admit that, if I am an expert in this field at all, then I am an involuntary one. As a Muslim woman, I can not avoid being challenged into making statements on this topic. Besides, at some point in my life, when looking for role models for the young people I was teaching, I collected materials on women in Islamic history that were then integrated into various educational projects. You will probably be familiar with some of the facts, which I am going to mention. What matters to me is a perspective slightly different from the traditional one, that can help us to use them both to encourage women and girls to take initiatives along these lines and to remind them and the men that:

> The faithful men and the faithful women are protecting friends of each other. They enjoin what is good and prohibit what is evil and establish prayer and give the Zakat and obey God and His messenger. They are those on whom God has mercy. God is Mighty, Wise.[1]

There is no doubt that this verse, like many others, especially 4:1 and 33:35, points out the fact that men and women have the same ontological status, the same ethical values apply to them, and that they have the same religious obligations, whichever way they otherwise share their socio-economical responsibilities. These abstract principles are illustrated by examples that are outlined for the reader to think about more carefully. Thus, in 66:11-12, Pharaoh's wife and Mary (as) are pointed out as being "examples for those who have faith" (both men and women, as the grammar indicates). Both show remarkable confidence and courage - the former by persuading her tyrannical husband to let her bring up Moses (as) (the trouble she must have gone through is best illustrated by her prayer to be liberated "from Pharaoh and his machinations and from the oppressive people")[2], the latter by confronting her suspicious clan with baby Jesus (as) for whose

---

[1] *Qur'an*, 9: 71.
[2] *Ibid.*, 66: 11.

education she then bears the responsibility. A third example is the Queen of Sheba who is described as a wise ruler who, instead of following her ambitious advisors, pursues her own peaceful diplomacy that eventually opens the way for insight and guidance: she surrenders "with Solomon" to the Lord of the worlds.

All three of them are exactly the opposite of the socially convenient woman who uncritically conforms to the role that is expected of her. Qur'anic "family stories" are often stories of conflicts about right and wrong, e.g. between the generations like in the case of Abraham (as) and his father about the latter's idolatry, or between husband and wife like in the aforementioned case of Pharaoh's wife, all of them illustrating the Qur'anic main topic of individual responsibility that applies to every male and female human being. Remarkably, the story that could traditionally be considered a "harmonious family story" - the one of Zakaria (as), his wife and his son John (as) - concludes with the comment,

> They (plural, not dual!) used to compete with each other in good actions and to call upon Us in hope and fear and to be humble before Us.[3]

As a condition for being able to fulfil this human responsibility, the Prophet Muhammad (saws) declared:

> The search for knowledge a religious duty for every Muslim, man and woman.[4]

How was this new concept reflected in Muslim women? A few examples are mentioned here:

5.1.1   Khadîja bint Khuwailid (as)

She was a Meccan businesswoman who, after the death of her two

---

[3] *Ibid.*, 21:89.

[4] Allamah Al-Majlesi, *Bihar Al-Anwar*, Beirut/ Lebanon, 1984, vol. 57, p. 68.

former husbands, succeeded in continuing their businesses for the benefit of her children. She remained respected in a role most unusual for a woman in pre-Islamic society. Impressed by the sincerity and reliability of young Muhammad (saws), whom she had employed in her business, as well as by his thoughts and attitudes - both of them being actively committed to the cause of the poor and underprivileged - Khadija married him. Thus, her personality was most suited to receive those new impulses. As a spiritually mature woman she was the first one to recognise the Prophet's (saws) message and to support him in every possible way. Through her, many relatives and friends found their way to Islam. She stood by her husband through the time of moral and economic pressure and persecution, and being a true "Mother of the Faithful", who was worthy to be personally greeted by Gabriel (a), finally died from exhaustion.

5.1.2   Umm Salama (as)

She emigrated to Abyssinia with her first husband. Having decided to emigrate to Medina after their return, she had to overcome immense hardship from the side of her clan who forcibly tried to keep her back and separate her from her baby. Her husband later died from his wounds after a campaign, and the Prophet (saws) received her and her four children into his family. With her presence of mind and her wise counsel she played a decisive role when the peace treaty of Hudaibiya was made. She accompanied the Prophet (saws) on several expeditions and was one of the teachers of the community. Later on, her daughter Zaynab became one of the best scholars of her time.

5.1.3   Our Lady Fatima (as)

Of the innumerable noteworthy traits of Fatima (as), I would like, in this context, to mention of only three:

- Her simple everyday life - she contributed to the family income by spinning, and even when the economic situation in Medina improved she never tried to gain personal advantages but spent her income on the poor.

- Her commitment to the cause of social justice, being, like her father, especially sensitive to this.

- Her distinct sense for community matters that made her perceptive to the forces that promoted discord and a relapse into tribalism and greed for power. She admonished the leaders of the community reminding them to remember their responsibilities and to fulfil their duties.

It is no wonder that the Prophet (saws) said about her:

Fatima belongs to me. Whoever hurts her, hurts me.[5]

5.1.4 Zaynab (as)

Fatima's (as) daughter, Lady Zaynab (as), is as it were, an embodiment of the Prophet's (saws) statement:

The greatest jihad is a just word in front of an unjust ruler.[6]

Being the sister of Hassan (as) and Hussein (as) and a scholar in her own right, she was a well-known teacher and a recognised authority on legal issues. In this context, she was called the "Proxy of the Imam". Being especially close to her brother Hussein (as), she left her family in Medina with her husband's consent to accompany him on the journey that was to end in the tragedy of Karbala. In a well-known speech she reproached Yazid for his behaviour against the Prophet's family members, saving Imam Zainul-Abidîn's (as) life with her courageous intervention, exposing the tyrant's injustice and cruelty so that the fear of public opinion compelled him to set his prisoners free.

---

[5] Al-Majlesi, *Bihar Al-Anwar*, vol. 27, p. 62, narrated from Misbah As-Shari'ah which is wrongly related to Imam Ja'far As-Sadiq (as).
[6] See Ibn Abi Jumhour Al-Ihsa'i, *Awali Al-la'ali'*, vol. 1, no. 131, p. 432 and *Ibn Warram Collection of Narrations*, vol. 2, p. 1.

5.2   Exemplary Women of Later Generations

Active women from later generations are probably less well known:

5.2.1   Sayydah Nafisa

She was a great-granddaughter of the Prophet (saws)'s grandson Hassan (as). She was born in 762 A.D. Growing up in Medina, she profited both from the education within her own family and from the numerous centres of scholarship that had meanwhile been established there. Besides being familiar with the Qur'an and its explanations and commentaries, she had a profound knowledge of Islamic law, the principles of which were at that time arranged systematically. After her marriage with Ja'far as-Sâdiq (as)'s son Ishâq, Nafisa moved to Cairo where they had a son and a daughter. Nafisa taught her knowledge in public lectures and classes and was soon well known as a scholar. Even ash-Shâfi'i to whom one of the Sunni schools of law is traced back to, was among her regular audience attendees, discussing various theological and legal issues with her and sharing part of her spiritual life. Because of her friendly, open and generous manner, she was respected and loved far beyond the circles of scholars and students, and when she died at the age of 63 years, a huge crowd assembled from everywhere and persuaded her husband to have her buried right there among them in Cairo.

5.2.2   Râbi'ah al-Adawîya

No account on Islamic mysticism can be imagined without mentioning Râbi'ah al-Adawîya whose name has become proverbial for the exclusive love of God (swt). She was born around 717 AD in a poor family and lost her parents at an early age. Captured in a hold-up, she was enslaved. Her master who had ambitious plans for her was, however, so impressed with her conscientiousness and religious devotion that he set her free. After a pilgrimage to Mecca, Râbi'ah settled in Basra, studying and teaching and leading an ascetic life that was based on her love for God. Among her companions, there were numerous well-known scholars and mystics like Sufyan ath-Thawri who used to challenge her with complicated questions, and she had several male and female students. Some of her prayers and poems are still available today. Râbi'ah was one of the first to teach the pure love for God for His sake rather than for the sake of His gifts.

5.2.3 Shuhda

Let us stop for a while to consider how teaching and research was done in those days. Mosques were then not only places of prayer, but also important centres of intellectual and spiritual life. Teachers used to offer lectures and classes there - unless they offered them in their homes. The most important mosques later on developed into academies and universities. From contemporary accounts, we get a rather clear idea of the activities. Among other things, we learn about women who studied there. Compared with modern expectations, their percentage was certainly not high, but on the other hand, it was not so low that a female student would have been considered something questionable. There were women not only among the students but also among the teachers and they were highly respected. Among the more famous examples there was Shuhda, nicknamed Fakhr an-Nisâ' (Glory of Women). Another nickname al-Kâtiba (the Writer), points to her brilliance in calligraphy, an art that was carefully cultivated and only taught by real experts. Shuhda taught a large number of male and female students at Baghdad University in various branches of theology and was one of the most significant scholars of her time until she died in 1178 A.D. She was far from being the only one.

During the early centuries, quite a number of women were also experts in Islamic law (*Shari'ah Law*)- even though they were denied the practice of law as judges (while significant scholars like e.g. Abu Hanîfa demanded "women judges in every city so that women are guaranteed their rights"), it was quite usual that female muftis were asked for their opinions.

A critical reader of the biographies of scholars will soon be surprised to find that very often male scholars were motivated and encouraged by their mothers, grandmothers, aunts etc. while female scholars were motivated and supported by their fathers, grandfathers and other male relatives. Moreover, those authors who took biographical notes on their contemporaries (e.g. Ibn Arabi, Ibn Khallikan etc.) never hesitated to mention their female teachers and other well-known women with great respect alongside the men.

Mathematics, physics and astronomy (in order to calculate the times of prayers, religious holidays, shares of inheritance, Zakat etc.) were a self-evident part of theological studies, so it would be absurd to assume that women were exempted, although it is a challenge for the historian to find famous names. As we can see from contemporary reports, in families with a tradition of scholarship, daughters enjoyed the same careful education as their brothers and also had possibilities to pass it on, e.g. as private teachers in similar families or in schools. The same applies to medicine. During the classical period it was considered normal to have women physicians treat female patients both at home and in hospital. Since in those days professions were usually handed down in a family and young people often married into a family with a similar tradition, it was not uncommon that a married couple of physicians co-operated in looking after their respective male and female patients.

5.2.4   Ijlîya

Women were admittedly less involved in the sciences that were linked with military aims. Nevertheless, there was Ijlîya, the daughter of an "astrolabe"[7] builder in Aleppo who learnt this trade from her father and continued it after his death. She was obviously successful, for she was then employed as an astrolabe builder at the court of Saif ad-Dawla, who ruled Northern Syria from 944 to 967

---

[7] An instrument used by early astronomers to measure the altitude of stars and planets and also as a navigational aid. It consists of a graduated circular disc with a movable sighting device. *Collins English Dictionary*, Australia: Harper Collins Publishers, 2000, p.93.

AD, safeguarding the borders of Syria from the Byzantine Empire.

Concerning women in politics, we find a problem quite different from the one with women's contribution to science. For while there is no lack of names and facts, there is - like with politically significant men - the question of their moral integrity, not to mention the legitimacy of the political system. In the Qur'an, women in two extreme political situations are highlighted: women under oppression like the wife of Pharaoh as well as Moses' mother and sister, and the Queen of Sheba - a female ruler. With all their differences, they share an exclusive trust in God, emphasised by the prayer quoted from Pharaoh's wife in Qur'an (66:11) and by the extraordinary courage of Moses' mother.

5.2.5   Asma and Arwa

Everywhere in world history, women rulers are an exception. Among the most well known examples in Islamic history are two queens called Asma and Arwa. Asma was the wife of Ali as-Suhaili, the founder of a Fatimid dynasty in Yemen, who was murdered in 1080 AD on his way to Mecca. After having spent two years as a prisoner, she became queen. She obviously succeeded in promoting the economic and social wellbeing of her people, by constructing roads and gardens, and avoiding military conflicts by skilful diplomacy. She was famous for conscientiously keeping her contracts. After her death in 1137 AD, her daughter-in-law Arwa succeeded her and continued her style of government but had to defend herself against all kinds of intrigues. The Yeminite poets highly praise both these women.

5.2.6   Radiya Sultana and Khadîja

Other examples are Radiya Sultana who succeeded her father Iltutmish to the throne in Delhi in 1236 A.D. She made great efforts to promote social justice. There was also a queen called Khadîja in the Maldive islands, who employed the world traveller Ibn Battuta as a judge. As late as the 17th century, we hear about Muslim women rulers in the Malay Archipelago. No-one ever complained that the Muslim society in parts of Africa, South India and Indonesia were matriarchal societies; only the Europeans tried, in the colonial ages, to change their structures.

5.3   Women in Social and Political Life

The contribution of Muslim women in situations of defence during the first generations is probably the most at variance with the traditional stereotype. Women certainly did have priorities other than that of the armed struggle. They used to look after their children's education and absent husbands' businesses, or they accompanied the troops in order to treat the wounded and to take the responsibility for the supplies. However, this did not mean that they were unable to interfere wherever it proved to be necessary, and there are quite a few reports of a woman's presence of mind that saved the situation or decided the outcome of a battle, e.g. in the Battle of Maysan, the women made flags out of clothes and marched towards the battle field, giving the Persians the impression that the Muslim troops were reinforced so that they withdrew, or in the Battle of Damascus where Umm Aban shot a golden cross, held by a priest - as a symbol for the Byzantine victory - out of his hands.

However, political activities are by no means identical with being a ruler, or with armed struggle. The literal meaning of politics is community building, and men and women must not forget that this responsibility already starts in our immediate vicinity, in family life, among neighbours and colleagues. We must not underrate the efforts of all those men and women who, by guiding their children and students to an ethical life, kept alive Islamic values and ideals.

In fact, stagnation in social development and moral degeneration were the characteristics of the age immediately preceding the colonial age. Social reality was then too far away from the ideals of the Qur'an and Sunnah. Women are hardly mentioned at all; they disappeared into a doubtful private sphere and shared their brothers' fate of ignorance, cultural alienation and exploitation. It is therefore no surprise that, in the beginning of this century, Muslim women started to struggle for their rights, demanding equal chances in education, the abolishment of prostitution and protection against legal discrimination with the same voice as their European sisters and, tragically enough, sometimes without being conscious that, according to the Islamic sources, these are their legitimate rights anyway. Women like Halide Edib-Adivar and Sultan Jahan Begum, pioneered work in the field of girls' education. Women's organisations publicised the problems and demanded solutions.

Together with the rediscovery of Islamic values, examples of women from the early days of Islam were revived. There were serious programmes for the liberation from colonial influences, to which women made a significant contribution. Thus, for example, Fatima Jinnah who co-operated with her brother Muhammad Ali Jinnah for the establishment of Pakistan initiated programmes for women's education and social projects and was a candidate in the presidential elections long after her brother's death. Women played a significant role in the liberation of Algeria, in the Palestinian resistance, in Afghanistan, in the Islamic revolution of Iran as well as the Islamic movement all over the world.

5.4   Qur'anic Guidance for a Successful Society

The meaning of learning from the past cannot consist of 'resting on our laurels' or complaining of present grievances, but to obtain 'food for thought' that enables us to deal with the demands of our own time. In many countries, Muslims are in a process of revival after some centuries of stagnation and colonialism, struggling with materialist standards that do not recognise any ethical, spiritual, cultural, or human development. This is coupled with a widespread ignorance concerning the essence and intention of Islam. There is a work situation due to industrialisation and migration that tends to destroy family structures without offering alternatives. This causes loneliness for the elderly, disadvantages for children who have no chance to grow into a society with a healthy relationship between the generations, and a difficult situation for women.

> God does not change the situation of a people before they change what
> is within themselves.[8]

with these words, the Qur'an expresses a law operative in human society, the intellectual and spiritual and the social and political component being closely linked with each other. What are then the characteristics of the strong Muslim women in history that can encourage us when shaping our future?

- *Education-* One central point is certainly education. People who acquire and teach knowledge were compared by the Prophet (saws) to those who are in *jihad* on God's path, the struggle to refine one's character used to be termed the "Greater *Jihad*". For women, acquiring and transmitting knowledge serves their own benefit as a safeguard from oppression and exploitation and as a building ground for the life to come. It is beneficial for the community and its future generations. Those of our brothers, who are not yet used to this idea for traditional reasons, should at least realise that their own children would be at a great disadvantage if their mothers were kept uneducated and ignorant of the world. If there are no other opportunities, knowledge can be shared and pooled the way it was done in the early generations, if necessary in our homes, or by making use of modern means of communication wherever possible. The example of Rabi'ah the mystic illustrates how a woman who literally started off from a point where there was nothing but obstacles took the initiative to learn, achieve spiritual maturity, and teach and become one of the great personalities of Islam.

- *Solidarity-* Another important point is solidarity. It is no coincidence that the word *insan* - human being, indicates a social aspect that is also contained in all Islamic rituals and includes qualities like compassion, patience, courage, perseverance and the readiness for co-operation. Justice

---

[8] *Qur'an,* 13:11.

demands that we not only stand up for our own legitimate interests, but also become aware of our sister's needs and possible ways of fulfilment. This might be a matter of material and practical help or sympathetic listening and counselling. It might be a matter of developing good ideas and projects or a matter of praying for each other and expressing moral support. It certainly does not exclude solidarity with men (cf. the Qur'anic verse quoted in the beginning), for together, as human beings, men and women; we share the responsibility for our society and for this earth. The example of the interaction of Moses' mother and sister as well as Pharaoh's wife in bringing up the messenger who was to save the people from oppression illustrates solidarity across the limits of nationality and social class.

- *Confidence-* Last but not least, there is confidence. A faithful person should never give up hope. "Faith in the unseen" not only implies faith in God and His angels etc. but also the perspective that values of justice and peace will some day be realised in our society. This will help us to fulfil our responsibility to speak out for what is right, enjoining what is good and prohibiting what is evil, in our personal lives, in our families, in our community and in any kind of political decision making, with the insight that our responsibility before our Creator bears more weight than any considerations of "social control". The best example for this confidence and courage is Mary (as) who, after extreme loneliness during labour and birth, trusted in God enough to go and confront her community with Jesus (as).

Based on these principles and experiences, Muslim women can build up their strategies. Individual efforts and self-help as well as informal sharing and networking can be first steps, especially in an environment, which may bear hostilities against Muslims and women. In the long run, systematic social and political considerations and steps are necessary e.g. to give children and young people future-oriented impulses beyond the mere preservation of Muslim tradition, to encourage women to stand up for Islamic values rather than to blindly conform to social control, to create an infra-structure that supports women in emergencies, to find ways of integrating the elderly in a dignified manner and to respect and learn from their experiences, to value volunteer work (that, in a materialist society, is often marginalised) on the same basis as a paid job, to contrast the prevalent images with visible examples of our own efforts to realise our visions, to organise and structure individual efforts in order to increase their efficiency and weight to the point where they gain respect and are taken seriously in political decision making. Thus we will gradually revive the richness of our religious and cultural heritage for ourselves and for the greater benefit of humankind as a whole.

Conclusion

It can be observed in the outstanding personalities of women highlighted in the Qur'an, their strength of will in holding fast to their faith and unwavering principles. This consequently led them to break with acceptable stereotypes and oppose any socially convenient expectations of the time at which they lived. We recognise such traits reflecting in the lives of prominent women throughout Islamic history.

In order to reclaim her status, the Muslim woman of today needs to firstly delineate her principles and reach a firm conviction and certainty of faith. Armed with thorough knowledge of her Islamic rights and duties, she must confront the mire of ignorance and stagnation she is sadly surrounded by today. As Muslim women, we must endeavour to exemplify our heritage, which has been bequeathed to us by our foremothers. Thus we will be able to have a direct impact and influence on the future of the Islamic society.

Bibliography

The Holy Qur'an

Al-Ihsa'i, Ibn Abi Jumhour, *Awali Al-la'ali'*, Edited by S. M. Najjaf, Qum/ Iran.

Al-Majlesi, 1984, *Bihar Al-Anwar*, Beirut/ Lebanon.

Misbah As-shari'ah which is wrongly related to Imam Ja'far As-Sadiq (as) [Editor's remark].

Article 6

Women and Intellectualism

Saedah Siraj

Abstract

In this paper, we will attempt to discuss the unique spiritual status of women in Islam. We will begin with an analysis of the "four perfect" women: Asiya, Maryam, Khadija and Fatima Zahra. These women, being infallible, serve as a perfect guide for emulation.

Spiritual wayfaring is ultimately an intellectual endeavour, and a struggle for knowledge. But it is a special kind of knowledge, one that can only be achieved through hard spiritual struggle. As such, we can refer to spiritual wayfaring as an attempt to achieve "high intellectualism". We will attempt to discover what is required in terms of belief and actions in order to reach this stage of "high intellectualism". This will shed light on the spiritual path of women.

Introduction

Women are endowed with their own distinctive qualities, and God has created both men and women equally with the purpose of devoting themselves solely to Him. (Qur'an, 51:56)[1] It is for this very reason that women were created with the potential to possess unshakeable faith in order to gain piety *(al-muttaqi)*.[2] Having

---

[1] The belief in God of some Christians is similar to the belief in God of Muslims as stated in Lonsdale and Laura Ragg, (ed. & tr. from Italian: MS. In the Imperial Library at Vienna), *The Gospel of Barnabas* (1st published Oxford: The Clarendon Press, 1907, 8th edition, Karachi: Begum Aisha Bawani Waqf, 1980, pp.17-8: "Jesus answered: 'Philip, God is good without which there is naught good; He hath no beginning, nor will he ever have an end, ... He hath no father nor mother; he hath no sons'" is the only One God, Allah 'Azza Wajalla', as Muslims believe in. Accordingly, the working paper presenter use the word "God" which refers to the only One God, Allah 'Azza Wajalla, as the belief of some Christians; On Barnabas, see, "Kashkul" in *Al-Tawhid,* 1990, vol. 7, no. 3, pp. 145-6.

[2] *Taqwa* does not imply a negative attitude rather it is 'a spiritual faculty which appears as a result of continued exercise and practice' see Murtada Mutahari, "Glimpses of the Nahju ul-Balaghah" in *Al-Tawhid,* 'Ali Quli Qara'i (tran.), 1986, vol. 3, no. 3, pp. 119-27; On the pious *(al-muttaqi)*

obtained piety, the woman would then live her life in accordance with the commands and dictates of God, creating a foundation based on truth and justice (Qur'an, 16:92, 57:25). The result would be perfect human beings (*insan-ul-kamil*) who have the capability of balancing their 'animal elements' such as jealousy, anger and envy. Thus they could not become classified as being of those people with 'animal personalities' (Qur'an, 59:19), or of those with an, 'intermingled personality', which consists of both human and animalistic traits.[3] Likewise their souls would become purified from all the diseases of the heart (Qur'an, 2:10), and they would acquire, practice and teach others about the knowledge of God. They would possess a high and distinct level of intellectualism and

---

characteristics see lbn Abi 'al-Hadid, *Sharh Nahjul ul-Balagha,* Dar ul-Rashad wa'l-Hadithah, vol. 2, p.551.

[3] Muhammad 'Abduh, *Nahju'l-Balagha,* Beirut: Daru 'ul-Balagha, 1985, pp. 74-5, states 'human elements' are in every soul as stated by Amiru'l-Mu'minin 'Ali (as) namely: a) The brain; b) Intellectualism (intellectual capacity, the faculty of knowing, mental power, intelligence, superior reasoning power, understanding); c) Wisdom *(al-hikmah),* (which one can use to differentiate between right and wrong); and d) Knowledge.

Derived from: 'Abduh, *Nahju'l-Balagha,* pp. 74-5; Muhammad Hosayni Beheshti & Javad Bahonar, *Philosophy of Islam*, Salt Lake City, UT: Islamic Publications, n.d., pp. 186-97, 201-5; Murtada Mutahari, "History and Human Evolution" in *Al-Tawhid,* 'Ala'uddin Pasargadi (tran.), 1984, vol. 1, no. 2, p. 104; Murtaza Mutahari, *Fundamentals of Islamic Thought,* R. Campbell (tran.), Berkeley: Mizan Press, 1985, pp. 25-31; Murtada Mutahari, "Sociology of the Qur'an: A critique of historical materialism" in *Al-Tawhid,* Ali Quli Qara'i (tran.), 1984, vol. 1, no. 4, p. 90; Ali Shari'ati, *Marxism and other Western Fallacies.* R. Campbell (tran.), Berkeley: Mizan Press, 1980, pp. 24-6. The two main natural elements made in man are:

A) Human elements namely: a) Brain; b) Intellect, intelligence, the faculty of knowing; c) Self-consciousness; d) Faith; e) Wishes for perfection; f) Knowledge.

B) Animal elements namely: a) Desire - such as sexual desire, eating and drinking; b) Like to settle at birthplace; c) Building relationship by means of blood connection; d) Enmity; e) Materialistic etc.

wisdom (*al-hikmah*),[4] which can be used for discerning between right and wrong, leading them to be of those on 'the right side' (*as-shabu 'l-yamin*) (Qur'an, 56:27), and not of those on 'the left side'. (*as-shabus-shimal*) (Qur'an, 56:41)[5]

Women will only achieve the above qualities when they take for role models the four perfect women of Paradise (*sayyidatun-nisa ahli'l jannah*). As such, this paper will focus on:

- The four perfect women – Role models

- Intellectualism

- The achievement of intellectualism

6.1   The Four Perfect Women – Role Models

According to an authentic tradition, within Islam there are four perfect women:

---

[4] Mutahari, '*Glimpses,*' p. 115 states the word *al-hikmah* in the Qur'an, 16:125 is referring to: a) Instruction and conveying knowledge; b) Struggle against ignorance; c) Deals with intellect (The faculty of knowing, mental power, intelligence, superior reasoning power); d) Educates (edifies, enlightens); e) A lamp (which beams darkness or the ignorance); f) Ratification (justification, rationalisation); and g) Language (expressions) of the intellect. Thus, *al-hikmah* could change an individual, alter one's course of life, transform one's personality, and bring about one's spiritual change.

[5] a) 'The left side' (*as-habus-shimal*) (Qur'an, 56:41) such as Nimrod, Pharaoh (nation leaders who are classed in 'the left side') and Korah (Qarun in the Qur'an, 28:79) (influential and rich person who is classed in 'the left side').

b) In hereafter, God will blind 'the left side' due to their evil words, ideas and actions (The Qur'an, 2:16-18; 41:1-5). They will also be humiliated in front of 'all the noble slaves of God' (*al-akhyar*) (Qur'an, 17:72).

c) The hypocrites (Qur'an, 2:8-13; 63:1-11) are classed in 'the left side.' According to Imam Khumayni, *Risalah nawin,* 'Abdu'l-Karim Bi Azar Shirazi (collec.), Qum: Daftar Nashr Farhang Islami, 1373 AH, vol.4, 7th edition, p.105, as referred to the Qur'an, 4:145, in hereafter, the hypocrites are placed at the lowest depths of hell fire; On the hypocrite characteristics, see, 'Abduh, *Nahj,* p. 444-6.

- Asiyah (as), daughter of Mazahum and wife of the Pharaoh

- Mary (as), daughter of Imran and mother of Jesus (as)

- Khadija (as), daughter of Khwailid and wife of the Prophet (saws)

- Fatima Zahra (as), daughter of the Prophet (saws) [6]

These great women reached the utmost degree of intellectualism, and are the wisest of all women from the beginning to the end of time.

The following delineates the status and ranks of man according to his obedience (ta'abud ilallah) and closeness (taqarrub) to God.

Levels of Intellect

Members of the 'Right side:

- Friend's of God (Awliya'Allah):

  - The Prophet (An-nabi)

  - The Truthful (As-sadiq)[7]

  - The Martyr-witness (As-shahid)[8]

  - The Pious (As-salih)[9]

---

[6] Ahmad bin Muhammad bin Hanbal (Ahmad Ibn Hanbal), *Al-Musnad,* Ahmad Muhammad Shakir, (commentary and index), al-Husaini 'Abdu'l-Majid Hashim (completion and arrangement), Egypt: Daru'l Ma'arif, 1975, vols. 3&4, pp. 232, 323, narrations no: 2668 & 2903 - *Isnad* (chain of transmission) of the two narrations are authentic.

[7] *Qur'an,* 2: 23, 31; 11: 32; 12: 27, 51.

[8] *Ibid.,* 2:154; 3:169.

[9] *Ibid.,* 3:45,113; 21:105; 12:101.

- Followers of the leaders of God:

  - The one who is close to God (*Al-muqarrab*)[10]

  - The Devotee (*Al-muttaqi*)[11]

  - The True believer (*Al-mu'min*)[12]

  - The one who surrenders to God (*Al-muslim*)[13]

If we look at the above scale[14], we can see that the highest degree is that held by the prophets (as), and the lowest status is that of the Muslims. For women, the status of Prophethood is the only one which they cannot hold. However the four perfect women have achieved the level of the Truthful. Prior to this station they also reached the positions of the Devotees and the True believer.

Some of the characteristics of the True Believer (*al-mu'min*) [15] will

---

[10] *Ibid.*, 19:57; 20:75; 83:18,21.

[11] *Ibid.,* 3:44.

[12] *Qur'an,* 3:75,114,132,137; 11:49; 13:30-1; 19:86; 21:48.

[13] *Ibid.*, 2:133,136; 3:51,83,10l; 21:10.

[14] *Ibid.*, 2:97,223,248,238; 3:67,138,170; 14:11; 15:77; 16:64,79.

[15] a) On 'the true believer' *(al-mu'min)* characteristics, see, Abduh, *Nahj,* pp.204-207.

b) Amiru'l-Mu'minin 'Ali (as) 'the Leader of the true believers' is referring to the narrations: "God, the Most High, has not revealed the verses (O you the believers) except 'Ali is their Head and Leader" See 'Abdur Rahman Jalaluddin as-Suyuti, *Ad-durru'l-manthur fi tafsir bil-ma'thur,* Beirut: Daru'l-Fikr, 1983, p.254; 'Ala'iddin 'Ali al-Muttaqi al-Hindi, *Kanzu'l-'ummal fl sunan al-'aqwal wa'l-af'al,* Beirut: Mu'assasah Ar-Risalah, 1989, p.249.

c) Amiru'l-Mu'minin 'Ali (as) 'the Leader of the true believers' is similar to that of the Prophet's, referring to an authentic narrations: "Aren't you pleased, you and me are as similar to the status of Aaron and Moses ... you are the Guardian of every believer after me." See Ahmad bin Hanbal, *Al-Musnad,* vols. 5&6, p. 1l, narrations no. 3062; Abi 'Abdallah Muhammad b. 'Abdallah al-Haakim an-Nisaburi, *Al-Mustadrak 'alas-sahihayn,* Beirut: Daru'l-Fiqr, 1978, vol. 3, p. 133; Abi 'Abdillah Muhammad b. Isma'il b. Ibrahim b. al-Mughirah b. Barzirbah al-Bukhari, *Sahih al-Bukhari,* Beirut: Daru'l- Jiil, n.d., vols. 4&6, p. 3; Abi'l-Husayn Muslim ibni'l- Hajjaji'l- Qushayri an-Naysaburi (Muslim), *Sahih Muslim,* Beirut:

be mentioned below:

- The destroyer of ignorance

- The problem solver

- The guide

- The one who conveys the truth and acts in accordance to it.[16]

Characteristics of the Devotee (al-muttaqi) are as follows:

- The one who is patient and struggles to achieve piety and knowledge

- The one who is satisfied with true guidance and thus follows it

- The one who avoids worldly luxury, wealth and fame. Knowledge becomes patience and words become actions.[17]

It is for this reason that the four perfect women have joined their souls with a Holy world in the heavens,[18] which cannot be perceived by normal sight. This is the 'angelic world' (al-Malakut) and the 'great world' (al-Jabarut), which are mentioned in two narrations: 'Most Glorious of the Great world and the Angelic world'. Such individuals receive teaching from God, which includes 'merciful inspirations' (ilham rahmani) from the angelic world.

So fear Allah; for it is Allah that teaches you. (Qur'an, 2:282)

Daru'l-Fiqr, 1983, vol. 4, p. 1870; 'al-Muttaqi, Kanzu'umall, vol. 13, p. 106; Abi Ja'far Muhammad b. Jarir at-Tabari, Tarikh at-Tabari Tarikhu'l-oumam wal-muluk, Beirut: Daru'l-Kutub Alamiyyah 1988, vol. 2, p. 73; Ibn Sa'ad, At-Tabaqat al-Kubra, Ihsan 'Abbas (ed.); Beirut: Daru'l-Fiqr, 1985, vol. 3, pp. 24-5.

[16] 'Abduh, Nahj 'ul-Balaghah, pp. 204-7.

[17] Ibn Abi'l Hadid, Sharh, vol. 2, p. 551.

[18] See Imam Khumayni, Nawin, p. 97.

Subsequently, every Muslim woman must understand, experience and reflect upon the lives of these perfect women, in order that they may attain a high status in the Eyes of Allah (swt) and thus reach a high degree of intellectualism.

6.1.1   Asiya (as)

Asiya (as) is amongst the Holy women. She is from the lineage of Isra'il, which God chose as His blessed slaves (Qur'an, 19:58). She raised the Prophet Moses (as) with love, inside of Pharaoh's home. Asiya (as) is a paradigm of courage as she was willing to denounce her position as Queen and abandon all her worldly luxuries and wealth for the sake of Allah (swt). She did not obey her husband's command to believe in him as god and was subsequently tortured and crucified until she died as a martyr.

6.1.2   Mary (as)

Mary (as) the daughter of Imran and mother of Jesus (as) is also from the lineage of Isra'il. She is one of those 'close to God' (*al-muqarrabin)*, which the Qur'an refers to in 83:21:

> To which bear witness those Nearest to Allah.

Accordingly Mary (as) was able to see things by Allah's will.[19] such as the angelic world, which is unperceivable to ordinary sight.

> He (Zakaria) said: O Mary! Whence comes this food to you? She said: From God; For God provides sustenance to whom He pleases, without measure. (Qur'an, 3:37)

The Prophet (saws) said that both Mary (as) and Fatima (as) were (*al-Batul*) purified, since both were free from menstruation and

---

[19] See Imam Khumayni, *Nawin,* p. 97.

post-natal bleeding.[20] Being free from menstruation and post-natal bleeding, Mary (as) was able to constantly devote herself to Allah (swt), as compared to the other women of her time. For this reason she is a role model, because during her teenage years she completely devoted herself to Allah (swt), and never met with a man except those permitted by the religious laws (Qur'an, 3:37)

6.1.3   Khadija (as)

Khadija (as) was the daughter of Khuwailid, and first wife to the Prophet Muhammad (saws). She was the first woman to believe in the message of Islam, whilst other women of that time rejected the belief in the Oneness of Allah (swt). She was of the wealthiest businesswomen of the era and gave all her wealth to assist the religion of Islam. Khadija was deeply loved by the Prophet (saws) and was known to be from amongst the best of people (*khaira ummatin*), as stated in the Qur'an:

> Ye are the best of peoples, evolved for mankind. (Qur'an, 3:110)

According to an exegesis by As-Suyuti,[21] this verse refers to the family of the Prophet (saws) and includes Khadija (as).

6.1.4   Fatima Zahra (as)

Fatima Zahra (as)[22] was the most loved child by the Prophet (saws), and one of the holiest women in the Eyes of Allah (swt), as

---

[20] Narrations in as-Shaykh Sulaiman al-Qunduzi al-hanafi, *Yanabi' ul-Mawaddah*, p. 260, in al-Allama 'ul-Hujjah al-Haj as-Sayyid Ghulamarda al-Kasa'i al-Kawakini, *Monaqib Az-Zahra'*, Qum: Matba'ah Mahr, 1397 AH, p. 55.

[21] As suyuti, *Ad-Durrar*, vol. 2, p. 293.

[22] Fatimatuz-Zahra' daughter of Abu'l-Qasim Muhammad (saws) son of 'Abdulla son of 'Abd 'ul-Muttalib son of Hashim son of 'Abd 'ul-Manaf son of Qusayy; On Fatimat Uz-Zahra' (as), see Ali Shari'ati, *Fatima is Fatima*, Laleh Bakhtiari (tran.), Tehran: The Shari'ati Foundation, 1980; Sayyid Saeed Arjmand Hashemi (tran.) *A Summary of Fatima's Biography*, Islamic Republic of Iran: Islamic Research Foundation of *Astan Quds Razavi*, 1992; H. M. H. Al-Hamid al-Husaini, *Riwayat Hidup Sitti Fatima Azzahra r.a.* (tran. as: *The story of Sitti Fatima Azzahra' (as)*), Kuala Lumpur: Victory Agencie, 1989.

expressed by the Prophet (saws) in two authentic narrations:

> Narrated by 'Aisha: When the Prophet was dying he said: 'O Fatima, aren't you pleased to become the Leader of all women, the Leader of the women of this community and of all faithful women'.[23]

Fatima is the Leader of the women in Heaven.[24]

In respect to the above narrations, Fatima (as) has been bestowed with the following titles:

- Leader of all women – *as*- (سيدة نساء العالمين)

- Leader of women of this community Muslim women) – *as*-

  (سيدة نساء هذه الأمة)

- Leader of all faithful women from the time of Adam (as) until the end of time – *as*- (سيدة نساء المؤمنين)

- Leader of the women in Paradise – *as*- (سيدة نساء أهل الجنة)

Besides having these four famous titles, Fatima (as) is also known as:

- The most intelligent – *Az-Zakkiyah*

- The Resplendent – *Az-Zahrah*

---

[23] Al-Hakim, *Al-Mustadrak,* vol. 3, p. 156; Al-Hakim had confirmed this is an authentic narrations but al-Bukhari and Muslim did not record it in their two authentic books. See also, Ibn Sa'ad, *At-Tabaqat,* vol. 2, p. 248.

[24] Al-Bukhari, *Sahih,* vol. 4 & 6, p. 36; Al-Hakim, *Al-Mustadrak,* vol. 3, p. 151. Al-Hakim confirmed it was an authentic *(sahih)* narration.

- The Purified – *At-Tahirah*

- The one free from menstruation and post-natal bleeding – *Al-Batul*

Like Mary, Fatima Zahra (as) being free from the above-mentioned bleeding could worship continuously, unlike other women of her time.

Hassan al-Basri (b. 21H) said that the most pious amongst the community was Fatima (as), and it is reported that her feet became swollen due to continual prayer.[25]

Like Khadija, Fatima (as) is one of the best people mentioned in the Qur'an, which was explained to mean the family of the Prophet (saws).[26]

These four perfect women possess the highest level of intellectualism by constantly purifying their souls[27], being obedient to the commands of God, devotion to God, willingness to abandon worldly positions such as popularity, fame, luxuries and wealth for the sake of God, and offering all their wealth to assist the religion of God.

6.2   Different Kinds of Intellectualism

In order to reach a high level of intellectualism, the Muslim woman has to study and reflect the attributes of these great women in their everyday lives. It seems that there are two kinds of Intellectualism: High and low.

---

[25] As-Sayyid 'Abdur-Razzaq Kamunah al-Husaini, *Al-Mishkhatu 'ul-Qudsiyyah fi-'anwaril Fatimiyyah,* ch. xxiii, p. 45, in Siratuz-Zahra', Kuwait: Zayna'l-'Abidin Library Mosque, in H.M.H. Al-Hamid, p. 16.

[26] As-Suyuti, *Ad-durr ul-Manthur,* vol.2, p.293.

[27] Referring to the Qur'an, 33:33, God Himself purified 'the Prophet's family', including Khadija and Fatima (as), from all sins and wrongdoings.

6.2.1   Low Intellectualism

For centuries the main aim of education systems, all over the world, has been the intellectual development of man. However the definition of 'intellectualism' has been limited to 'low' intellectualism or 'wisdom at a visual state' or a 'system's implantation of animal elements', leaving the spiritual aspects behind and upholding materialism. This includes the opinion of Western thinkers such as Immanuel Kant (1724-1804), who focused only on rationalism synthesis while discussing the intellect[28]; Georges Politzer (1903-1942), who stressed intellect according only to communistic views[29]; Binet and Simon (1905), who argued that the intellect could be measured by conducting an IQ test in order to assess one's intellectual level[30]; Guilford (1967), who introduced the intellectual structure and developed a basic dimensional model of the individual[31]; Buros (1972), who introduced 'the seventh mental measurement'[32]; Lazear (1991), Khatena (1992) and Renzulli (1992), who introduced 'multiple intelligence', which consisted of creativity, problem solving, academicals potential, leadership potential, visual and art ability.[33]

The concept of intellectualism spread in the 19th century, changing from time to time. Choice of information and knowledge was made on the definition of intellectualism put forward by the Western scholars and philosophers, which focused on the 'animal elements',

---

[28] Allama Muhammad Baqir as-Sadr, *Our Philosophy,* Shams C. Inati, (tran.), London: The Muhammadi Trust, 1987, p. 41.

[29] *Ibid*, p. 44.

[30] A. Binet & T. Simon, "Methodes nouvelles pour le diagnostic du niveau intellectuel des anormaux," in *Annee Psychologique,* 1905, vol. 11, pp. 191-244.

[31] J. P. Guilford, *The Nature of Human Intelligence,* New York: McGraw-Hill, 1967.

[32] O. K. Buros, (ed.), *The Seventh Mental Measurement,* Highland Park, NJ: Gryphon Press, 1972.

[33] D. Lazear, *Seven Ways of Teachings - The Artery of Teaching Eight Multiple Intelligence,* Illinois: Skylight Publishing Palatine, 1991; Joe Khatena, *Gifted,* Itasca, Illinois: F.E. Peacock Publishers, Inc., 1992; J. S. Renzulli, "The Multiple Menus Model for Developing Differentiated Curriculum for the Gifted and Talented" in *Gifted Child Quarterly,*1988, vol. 32, no. 3, pp. 298-309.

thus upholding materialism and hence abandoning all spiritual aspects. The curricula and education system (the modern Western education system all over the world) was made to adopt low intellectualism.

6.2.1.1 Development of Materialism in the Modern Western Educational System

The origins of the modern Western educational system can be found in five major educational philosophies: perennialism, idealism, realism, experimentalism and existentialism. In the early 20th century, perennialism and idealism were more influential in the educational system. During this period, religious education (of all religions) was still secure. However, after the 30's, realism, experimentalism and existentialism whose emphasis was more on materialism (based entirely on 'worldly achievements') became dominant, and the measurement of goodness was based on the laws of nature and public tests, instead of religion.[34]

At present, realism, experimentalism and existentialism influence the modern Western educational systems in schools all over the world. In schools, physical reality and social sciences have developed into new ideologies and are causing the educational system to place emphasis on providing jobs for man in order that they may offer the services to society. This resulted in the spiritual aspects being abandoned and de-emphasised. Hence, the system develops a generation, which does not hold religion as a way of life and causes a severe catastrophe of morality. In other words, the modern educational system has failed to develop a generation of high intellectualism in the sight of God, due to the system's implantation of 'animal elements', upholding materialism and forsaking spiritualism.

The ideologies of realism, experimentalism and existentialism are parallel to the Platonic theory of recollection, the rational theory of

---

[34] Jon Wiles & Joseph Bondi, *Curriculum Development,* Upper Saddle River, N.J., Columbus, Ohio: Merrill, 1998, pp. 41-4.

Rene Descartes (1596-1650) and Immanuel Kant, the empirical theory of Alfred Ayer (b. 1910) and the Marxist theory of Lenin (1870-1924), which uphold materialism and leave the spiritual aspects behind.[35] These theories do not consider morality and religion as a means to provide answers, and they fail to provide an even balance for man's intellect, inner voice and desires (including materialism). This demonstrates that the above philosophers fail to possess high intellectualism in the sight of God.

6.2.2   High Intellectualism

'High intellectualism' is a term referring to the clarification of one's reasoning capacities. The Western view of this differs to the Muslim view.

Some psychologists hold the opinion that the term 'intellectualism' is a 'mental strength, which can produce one's ability to live in a community'. But to what extent does this intellectualism comply with high intellectualism in the sight of Allah (swt).

The achievement of high intellectualism in the sight of God, is when one learns to use his intellect (the faculty of knowing, intelligence) and the five other 'human elements' (brain, self-consciousness, faith, desire for perfection, and knowledge), and successfully overcome all his 'animal elements'[36], which is in compliance with the commands of Allah (swt), as follows:

> And be not like those who forgot God; so they forgot their own souls; these are the transgressors. (Qur'an, 59:19)

> By the soul, and the proportion and order given to it; and its enlightenment as to its wrong and its right; truly he succeeds that purifies it; and he fails that corrupts it.' (Qur'an, 91:7-10)

---

[35] Baqir as-Sadr, *Our Philosophy,* chap. 1; Qara'i, *Martyr,* pp. 156-61.

[36] Derived from: 'Abduh, *Nahj,* pp. 74-5; Behishti & Bahonar, *Philosophy,* pp. 186-97, 201-5; Mutahhari, *History,* pp. 104, 114-9; Mutahhari, *Fundamental,* pp. 25-31; Mutahhari, *Sociology,* p. 90; Shari'ati, *Marxism,* pp. 24-6.

He who lets his carnal desires dominate him is abasing himself. (Imam Ali (as))[37]

Among the main objectives of high intellectualism and inquiry are:

a) Piety (*taqwa*) so that one is constantly obedient (*ta'abud ilallah*)[38] and close to God (*taqarrub ilallah*).

b) To cure the soul so as one would not possess the disease of the heart like the hypocrites (Qur'an, 2:8-13).

c) To found one's life in accordance with justice and equality so that one is constantly in line with the teachings of the Qur'an. (Qur'an, 16:92 and 57:25)

The individuals who receive Allah's (swt) blessings and are close to Him are those who successfully prevent their desires from dominating their intellect. This is because when one follows one's desires, the intellect becomes weak.[39] Martyr Mutahari states in his exegesis on the Qur'an, 16:125, that wisdom becomes weak when it is not in conformity with its nature, which is a) Instruction and conveyance of knowledge b) Struggle against ignorance c) Intellect d) Education e) Enlightenment f) Ratiocination or justification, rationalisation g) Language or expressions of the intellect.[40]

Thus when one follows one's desires, one has separated oneself from the True Believers and the Devotees; one has failed to cure the heart and instead possesses the heart of the hypocrite (Qur'an, 2:8-13); and one has failed to found one's life according to justice

---

[37] Murteza Mutahhari, *Spiritual Sayings,* Aluddin Pazargadi (tran.), M. Salman Tawhidi (ed.), Tehran, Islamic Republic of Iran: Islamic Propagation Organization, 1983/1403, p. 572.

[38] *Qur'an,* 5:56.

[39] Referring to the Qur'an 59: 19; 91: 7-10 and the sayings of Amiru'l-Mu'minin 'Ali (as): "...he who lets his carnal desires dominate him is abasing himself" (Cf. Mutahhari, *Spiritual,* p.52).

[40] Mutahhari, *Glimpses,* p. 115.

and equality (Qur'an, 16:92, 57:25).

Those who possess high intellectualism are those who are able to dominate their 'animalistic' tendencies.

6.3   Intellectualism and its Relation to the 'Inner Voice' (Which Desires Righteousness)

Certainly, I (God) know (the human elements) what you (angels) do not know (the angels only know man's animal elements). (Qur'an, 2:30)

Both Rumi's (b. 1207) poetry[41] and Mutahari's exegesis[42] on the above Qur'anic verse reveal that the most amazing phenomenon in man is his 'inner voice' or consciousness, which guides him towards righteousness. Since the creation of man, every soul has desired this righteousness, and it is this element, which is the most important factor for balancing the desires of the self. For this reason, the 'animal elements' within humans such as jealousy, anger and envy will be evenly balanced by this 'inner voice'. When a person achieves this they will benefit their own soul as opposed to putting themselves in loss.

Thus in the creation of man, every external action (including words) is affected by this 'inner voice', which if the person is successful, will balance the desires of the self resulting in righteous words and deeds.

No-one can deny that factual research and results, which have a moral base, are to be held in a higher position than such research and results that do not have such a base.

---

[41] Mutahhari, *History,* p. 117; On Rumi, see also, William C. Chittick, *The Sufi Path of Love,* Albany: State University of New York Press, 1983; Annemarie Schimmel, *Mystical Dimensions of Islam,* Chapel Hill: The University of North Carolina Press, 1975, pp. 309-43.
[42] Mutahhari, *History,* p. 115.

The following reasons show how such research and results are unnecessary in upholding morality. The mind has a constant awareness concerning knowledge of 'objects outside the brain', which can be seen by normal sight, such as research results. It constantly receives such knowledge, termed as 'reality' by modern education, which can be interpreted by the intellect. This shows that the reality of the 'knowledge of objects outside the mind which can be interpreted by the intellect' is separated and situated outside the brain. Accordingly the 'inner voice' has a higher position than observations and research analysis even though scientific findings are accepted as the reality.

In contrast, Freud (1856-1940) denied that the 'inner voice' existed naturally in man. For him the 'inner voice' resulted from socialisation and has no concern with the human psyche. Freud's denials lowered the human status, which has been created far more excellent than other creations. He also denied all natural morality so that all moral values such as justice and trust become meaningless and absurd; and all internal conflicts such as anger; frustration and depression within the human become external factors – i.e. socialisation.[43]

It is very rare for this inner voice to commit error in decision-making. In fact, improper reasoning causes one's intellect to make mistakes and the 'inner voice' to be balanced by desires.[44] Mulla Sadra (1050-1640 AD) clarifies this as 'Improper reasoning equal in everything' as 'there are many kinds of individuals as there are individuals'.[45] When this situation occurs, one's faith will balance out the desires.

---

[43] Baqir as-Sadr, *Our Philosophy,* pp. 110-3; Mutahhari, *Fundamentals,* p.191; See, Ali Quli Qara'i, "Martyr Muhammad Baqir al-Sadr's critique of Marxist philosophy: A critical summary of his book Our Philosophy (Part I)" in *Al-Tawhid,*1998, vol. 1, p. 171.

[44] Behishti & Bahonar, *Philosophy,* p.56; See, the Qur'an, 39:17-8.

[45] Cf. Mutahhari, *Spiritual,* p.17; On Mulla Sadra, see also, Roberts Avens, "Theosophy of Mulla Sadra" in *Hamdrad Islamicus* IX, 3 (Autumn 1986): 3-30; Mahdi Dehbashi, "Mulla Sadra Conception of Motion" *in Al-Tawhid,* 1984, vol. 2, no. 1, pp. 68-78.

Each one can freely use his intellect and can freely choose to follow the 'inner voice' or not. However, this freedom is possessed when one tries to balance his desires (i.e. when the intellect and inner voice evenly balance the desires).[46]

Intellect and the 'inner voice' will always hold an exalted position as long as there is no conflict between the two and there is no psychological interference (because one follows his desires). Intellectual strength is in fact higher than external power.

6.4   Achievement of High Intellectualism

High intellectualism may be achieved by:

a)   Dominating one's 'animal elements' and developing 'human elements'

b)   Developing intellectualism by means of Allah's knowledge

c)   Dominating one's 'animal elements' and developing 'human elements'

According to Imam 'Ali (as), when Allah (swt) created man, He breathed His (created) soul into his human form Adam (as). This human form was endowed with the brain (fikarin), which makes him noble, the intellect, wisdom, physical body, and knowledge so he can differentiate between right and wrong.[47]

If we look at the following Qur'anic verse: 'Certainly, I (God) know what you know not.' (Qur'an, 2:30), Imam Ali's (as) above statement and Martyr Mutahari's exegesis on the above verse[48], we see that the two main elements in man are:

---

[46] Behishti & Bahonar, *Philosophy,* pp. 57-8.

[47] Abduh, *Nahj,* pp.74-5.

[48] Mutahhari, *History,* pp. 114-19.

A. The human elements

- Brain

- Intellect

- Self-consciousness

- Faith

- Desire for perfection

- Knowledge[49]

B. The Animal Elements

- Desire

- Building of relationships by means of blood ties

- Enmity

- Love of worldly goods[50]

The Messengers (as) and the Prophets (saws) were endowed with the highest levels of intellectualism and the highest degrees of wisdom. Their roles are to:

a) Enlighten man to faith in Allah (swt)

b) Teach man to dominate his animal self and develop his human qualities[51]

---

[49] 'Abduh, *Nabj,* pp. 74-5.

[50] See 'Abduh, *Nahj,* pp. 74-5; Mutahhari, *History,* pp. 104, 114-19; Behishti & Bahonar, *Philosophy,* pp. 186-97, 201-5; Mutahhari, *Fundamental,* pp. 25-31; Mutahhari, *Sociology,* p.90; Shari'ati, *Marxism,* pp. 24-6.

[51] Mutahhari, *History,* p. 104; See, Behishti & Bahonar, *Philosophy,* pp. 223-31.

Every Muslim should take these exemplars as role models in their lives in order to try to reach the highest degrees of intellectualism and wisdom.

When his animal self dominates a person, he will become influenced and deceived by Satan. Such people are known as humans with animal personalities. Imam Ali (as) said:

The shape is human, but the mind may be a beast.[52]

such as individuals like Yazid son of Mu'awiya and Shimr. The Qur'an in (4:47) describes how the inhabitants of an Israelite fishing village were turned into apes because they persisted in breaking the Sabbath. When a person is partially dominated by his animal self, he will be known as a human with an 'intermingled personality', consisting of both animal and human elements. For this reason humans have the responsibility to follow the divine teachers so as they will not be raised up with these beastly personalities on Judgement Day.

By correctly utilising the human elements, man can possess a strong faith in God and strive towards becoming the perfect man dominating the animal elements, thus becoming true Muslims.

Those who follow their animal self, in fact deny the unique characteristics[53] bestowed on them by their Creator. They are also not capable of fulfilling their own needs. For instance, a murderer (who follows the animal self) who is captured, cannot be trusted to be set free again. As he is following his animalistic desires, he becomes influenced and deceived by Satan, therefore a murderer is not free to choose the correct way, i.e. by not committing murder.

---

[52] See Mutahari, *Spiritual,* p. 17.
52. Shari'ati, *Marxism,* p. 25.
[53] Imam Khumayni, *40 Narrations,* Ilyas Hasan, (tran. from English) & Faruq bin Shina, (tran. from Persian), book.3, Bandung: Penerbit Mizan, 1994, p. 55.

6.5   Intellectualism Development by means of Allah's (swt) Knowledge

The developmental process of 'high intellectualism' will be achieved as long as one acquires and teaches others the 'three knowledge's of God.' This is based on a narration, which states that there are three types of knowledge:

a) (العلم بآية محكمة), which refers to 'the knowledge of spiritual obligation and mind perfection'.

b) (العلم بفريضة عادلة), which refers to 'the knowledge of actions and soul obligations'. (Moral knowledge)

c) (العلم بسنة قائمة), which refers to 'the knowledge of actions and obligations in life'.[54]

6.6   The Knowledge of Spiritual Obligation and Mind Perfection

This knowledge teaches and improves one's intellectualism in the 'spiritual and intellectual spheres'; in this case, intellectualism discusses 'the unseen' such as the Actions and Essence of God, types of angels, Holy Books, messengers (as), prophets (as), 'friends of God' *(awliya' Allah),* and the Hereafter.[55]

By acquiring, conducting research and practicing all the above forms of knowledge, the Greatness of Allah (swt) and His Power and also the situation in the Hereafter will become known. All these forms of knowledge are included in *('ilm bi-ayatin muhkama)* (literally: 'the knowledge with strong or clear signs'), which refers to the "...knowledge of spiritual obligation and mind perfection".[56]

---

[54] *Ibid.,* p. 57.
[55] *Ibid.,* p. 62.
[56] *Ibid.,* p. 57.

The main characteristics of the 'knowledge of spiritual obligation and mind perfection' are:

1) It can be accepted by the intellect (rational)

2) The contents of the knowledge are genuine in the Eyes of God, its truth cannot be denied and its qualities are *(jabr)* fixed by God

3) The contents of the knowledge are the teachings of Allah (swt) as stated in the Qur'an and authentic narrations.[57]

The 'knowledge of spiritual obligation and mind perfection' consists of six kinds of knowledge:

1) Knowledge of the Essence of God;

2) Knowledge of the Actions of God;

3) Knowledge of the 'Unseen world', which discusses all the kinds of Angels of a high status such as:

   a) Angels of a high status who reside at the highest *Jabarut* ('Great world' - in the skies)

   b) Angels of a high status who reside at the highest *Malakut* ('Angel world' - in the skies) to all types of angels of low status who reside on earth (the low level angel world)

   c) Angels who are in the world

   d) Angels who become God's army

4) Knowledge of the prophets and 'the friends of God' *(awliya 'Allah)* and their status

---

[57] *Ibid.*

5) Knowledge of the Qur'an and the Holy Books such as the Torah and the Bible

6) Knowledge of the Hereafter, which also discusses the realities of each soul when it returns to the 'Unseen World' (*'alamu ul-ghayb*); the situation in the 'grave' and in the Hereafter.[58]

The above knowledge can be obtained by utilising 'high intellectualism,' which is referring to the Qur'an and authentic narrations.[59]

6.7   Moral Knowledge

Moral knowledge is knowledge based on the education, discipline and acts of the heart. Such knowledge has to be equally balanced between two extremes.[60] Its main characteristic is that it guides one between the two extremes of exaggeration (*ifrat*) and insufficiency (*tafrit*). God detests both extremes. By knowing and understanding these two extremes, one is able to discern the correct balance. For instance:

One should possess courage because courage can be found between:

- The one who has no fear regardless of the situation (*tahawwur*), he has no fear even when he should, i.e. he should fear disobedience to God.

- The coward who is afraid when he should not be (*jubn*), i.e. one should fear God alone, not people etc.

One should possess courage because courage can be found between:

---

[58] *Ibid.*, p. 62.
[59] *Ibid.*
[60] *Ibid.*, p. 57.

- Misusage of intellect *(ifrat)* i.e. one who uses his intellect to ruin a person's reputation

- Not using the intellect when one is required to do so *(tafrit)*, i.e. when an intellectual uses his intelligence to cheat on people instead of using it to help people.

Moral knowledge comprises of four branches:

1) Procedures to hinder moral decay *(munjiyat)*. This branch of knowledge discusses patience *(saber)*, thankfulness *(shukr)*, shyness *(haya')*, humility *(tawadu')*, courage *(shuja'ah)*, mercy *(sakhawah)*, piety *(taqwa)* and self-perfection *(tahleeah)*.

2) The process of achieving patience, thankfulness, shyness, humilty, courage, mercy, piety and self-perfection.

3) The ways to recognise bad morality such as boasting *('ujub)*, egotism *(kibr)*, showing off *(riya')*, enmity *(hiqd)*, lying *(ghishsh)*, self-love and love of the world *(Ananeeah wa hub Ad-dunia)*.

4) The knowledge to discuss the factors and reasons why one has displeasing morals and ways whereby one can free oneself from them.[61]

The prophets (as), their legatees and ethical and mystical experts such as Suhrawardi, Rumi and Mulla Sadra[62] preserved such moral knowledge.

Some Muslims hold the opinion that obtaining and practising moral knowledge and mysticism is innovation *(bid'ah)*. This was due to the fact that those who hold such an opinion fail to understand the link between the three different worlds that man

---

[61] *Ibid.*, p. 57
[62] *Ibid.*, pp. 56, 59.

will inhabit, namely the earth, world of the grave and the Hereafter.[63]

6.8   The Knowledge of Actions and Obligations in Life

This knowledge discusses the acts of loyalty to God and the obligatory duties incumbent on every Muslim according to *Shari'ah Law*[64], in order to gain proximity to God. Its main characteristics are:

1) To remain loyal to the commands of Allah (swt), gaining His proximity.

2) Obligatory duties such as prayer, fasting …etc.

3) Those things, which are incomprehensible by intellect alone.[65]

This knowledge consists of six branches:

- Science of Islamic jurisprudence *(Al- fiqh)*

- Islamic law *(Shari'ah Law)*

- Ethics *(Adab)*

- Social interactions *(Mu'asharah)*

- Home administration *(tadbir al-manzil)*

- Politics *(siyasatu'l-mudun)* [66]

---

[63] *Ibid.,* pp. 57, 63.
[64] *Ibid.,* p. 63.
[65] *Ibid.,* p. 57.
[66] *Ibid.,* pp. 57-8.

6.9   The Status of Knowledge other than the Three Main Fields of Knowledge

When one studies other forms of knowledge such as engineering, western education, medicine, astronomy, mathematics, architecture, accounting, history, geography, computing or agriculture with the purpose of:

- Knowing the signs of the greatness of Allah (swt) – such knowledge will hold the same status as that of the knowledge of spiritual obligation and mind perfection;

- Gaining lessons – such knowledge will hold the same status as that of Moral knowledge;

- Upholding the *Sunnah* – such knowledge will hold the same status as the knowledge of actions and obligations in life.[67]

If one studies the above knowledge without the intention to strengthen one's faith in God and the Hereafter, or for the sole reason of self-interest, he is in loss.[68]

Conclusion

The theories of Western philosophers unevenly balance materialism and spiritualism and are not considered to be 'high' intellectualism in the Eyes of God. A woman can reach a degree of high intellectualism by understanding and practising the three-mentioned knowledge's of God. If she learns with the intention of drawing closer to Allah (swt), she can form a link to the Holy and Unseen Worlds. Consequently she will be rewarded by merciful inspirations (*ilham rahmani*) from the angels (Qur'an, 91:8). The knowledge she acquires will make her in line with truth, justice and equality.

---

[67] *Ibid.,* p. 68.
[68] *Ibid.*

A woman's main goal of self-purification is to achieve the same status as the friends of God, not worldly status and recognition. When a woman can reach such an exalted status, she will become one of Allah's (swt) noble slaves and possess a high intellect. She will be rewarded with a supreme status and recognition from God, which will save her from the burning fire of Hell.

Bibliography

'Abduh, as-Shaykh Muhammad. 1985, *Nahjul-Balagha,* Beirut: Daru'l-Balagha.

Abi 'al-Hadid, Ibn. n.d., *Sharh Nahju'l-Balagha,* 4 vols., Dar 'ul-Rashad 'al Hadithah.

Avens, Roberts. 1986, "Theosophy of Mulla Sadra" in *Hamdrad Islamicus,* vol. IX, no. 3, pp. 3-30.

As-Sadr, Allama Muhammad Baqir. 1987, *Our Philosophy,* Shams C. Inati (tran.), London: The Muhammadi Trust, 1st ed.

As-Sadr, Allama Muhammad Baqir. 1986, *Iqtisaduna,* Beirut: Darut-Ta' lil-Matbu'at.

Barker, B. 1958, *The Politic of Aristotle,* London, Oxford, New York: Oxford University Press, 1st ed.

Behishti, Muhammad Hosayn and Bahonar, Javad. n.d., *Philosophy of Islam,* Salt Lake City, UT: Islamic Publications.

Binet and Simon, T. 1905, "Methodes nouvelles pour le diagnostic du niveau intellectuel des anormaux", in *Annee Psychologique,* vol. II.

Al-Bukhari, Abi 'Abdillah Muhammad b. Isma'il b. Ibrahim b. al-Mughirah b. Barzirbah. n.d., *Sahih al-Bukhari (*6 vols.), Beirut: Daru'l-Jil.

Buros, O. K. 1972, *The Seventh Mental Measurement,* Highland Park, N.J.: Gryphon Press.

Chittick, W. C. 1983, *The Sufi Path of Love, the Spiritual Teachings of Rumi,* Albany, N.Y.: State University of New York Press.

Dehbashi, Mahdi. 1984, "Mulla Sadra Conception of Motion" in *Al-Tawhid*, vol. 2, no. 1, pp. 68-78.

Guilford, J. P. 1967, *The Nature of Human Intelligence*, New York: McGraw-Hill.

Al-Haakim (Abi 'Abdallah Muhammad b. 'Abdallah al-Haakim an-Nisaburi) 1978, *Al-Mustadrak 'alassahihayn.*, 4 vols., Beirut: Daru'l-Fiqr.

Hanbal, Ahmad bin Muhammad bin. 1975, *Al-Musnad*, Ahmad Muhammad Shakir (commentary & index), Al-Husaini 'Abdu'l-Majid Hashim (completion & arrangement), 20 vols., Eygpt: Daru'l-Ma'arif.

Hashemi, Sayyid Saeed Arjmand. (tran.) 1992, *A Summary of Fatima's Biography*, 1st ed., Islamic Republic of Iran: Islamic Research Foundation of *Astan Quds Razavi.*

Hodgson, Marshall G. S. 1974, *The Venture of Islam*, 3 vols., Chicago and London: The University of Chicago Press.

Al-Husaini, H. M. H. al-Hamid. 1989, *Riwayat hidup Sitti Fatima Azzahra r.a.* (tran. as: *Life Story of Sitti Fatima Azzahra' -as-*). 1st. ed., Kuala Lumpur: Victory Agency.

Ibn Manzur, (Abi al-Fadl Jamaluddin Muhammad ibn Marqam ibn Manzur al-Ifriqi al-Misri), n.d., *Lisanu'l-'Arab*, 13 vols., 1st ed., Beirut: Dar Sadr.

Al-Kawakini (al-'Allamatu'l-Hujjah al-Haj as-Sayyid Ghulamarda al-Kasa'i) 1397 AH, *Manaqib az-Zahra'*, Qum: Matba'ah Mahr.

Khatena, J. 1992, *Gifted*, Itasca, Illinois: F.E. Peacock Publishers, Inc.

Khumaini, Imam. 1373 AH, *Risalah Nawin*, 'Abdu'l-Karim Bi Azar. Shirazi (collector), vol. 4, 7th ed., Qum: Daftar Nashr Farhang Islami.

Khumaini, Imam. 1994, *40 Hadith* (tran. as: *40 Narrations)*, Hasan, Ilyas. (tran. from English) & Shina, Faruq bin. (tran. from the Persian), 4 books. 1st ed., Bandung: Penerbit Mizan.

Larson, R. (tran. & ed.) 1979, *The Republic Plato,* Arlington Height, Illinois: Harlan Davidson, Inc.

Lazear, D. 1991, *Seven Ways of Teachings - The Artery of Teaching Eight Multiple Intelligences,* Illinois: Skylight Publishing Palatine.

Lonsdale and Ragg, Laura. (ed. & tran.) 1980, *The Gospel of Barnabas,* Karachi: Begum Aisha Bawani Waqf.

Al-Mufid, Shaykh. 1981, *Kitab al-Irshad (*The Book of Guidance), I. K. A. Howard (tran.), 1ˢᵗ ed., Elmhurst, New York: Tharike Tarsile Qur'an.

Muslim (Abi 'al-Husayn Muslim ibn Hajjaji'l-Qushayri an-Naysaburi) 1983, *Sahih Muslim,* 5 vols., Beirut: Daru'l-Fiqr.

Mutahhari, Murtada. 1985, *Fundamentals of Islamic Thought,* R. Campbell (tran.), Berkeley: Mizan Press.

Mutahhari, Murtada. 1983/1403, *Spiritual Sayings,* Aluddin Pazargadi (tran.), M. Salman Tawhidi (ed.), Tehran: Islamic Propagation Organization.

Al-Muttaqi, Ali. ('Ala'iddin 'Ali al-Muttaqi b. Hisamuddin al-Hindi), 1989, *Kanzu'l-'ummal fi Sunan Aqwal Wa'l'afal,* 16 vols. Beirut: Mu'assasah Ar-Risalah.

Qara'i, Ali Quli. 1988, "Martyr Muhammad Baqir al-Sadr's Critique of Marxist Philosophy: A Critical Summary of his Book Our Philosophy (Part 1)" in *Al-Tawhid,* vol. 6, no. 1, pp. 153-177.

Qara'i, Mahliqa. 1984, "Sociology of the Qur'an: A Critique of Historical Materialism" in *Al-Tawhid,* vol.1, no. 4, pp. 77-135.

Renzulli, J. S. 1988, "The Multiple Menus Model for Developing Differentiated Curriculum for the Gifted and Talented" in *Gifted Child Quarterly,* vol. 32, no. 3, pp. 298-309.

Reza, Sayed Ali. (tran.) 1985, *Nahjul Balagha,* 4 vols., rev. ed., New York: Tahrike Tarsile Qur'an, Inc.

Sa'd, Ibn. 1985, *At-Tabaqat al-Kubra,* Ihsan Abbas (ed.), 9 vols., Beirut:

Daru'l-Fiqr.

Schimmel, Annemarie. 1975, *Mystical Dimensions of Islam,* Chapel Hill: The University of North Carolina Press.

Shari'ati, Ali. 1980, *Fatima is Fatima,* Laleh Bakhtiari (tran.), Tehran: The Shari'ati Foundation.

Shari'ati, Ali. 1980, *Marxism and other Western Fallacies,* R. Campbell (tran.), Berkeley: Mizan Press.

As-Sijjistani, 1994, *Sunan Abi Da'ud,* Abi Da'ud Sulayman ibn al-Ash'ath (ed.), 2 vols., Beirut: Daru'l-Fiqr.

As-Suyuti, 'Abdur-Rahman Jalaluddin. 1983, *Ad-Durru'l-Manthur fi Tafsir al-Ma'thur,* 8 vols., 1st ed., Beirut: Daru'l-Fiqr.

At-Tabari, Abi Ja'far Muhammad b. Jarir. 1988, *Tarikh at-Tabari, Tarikhu'l-imam wa'l-muluk,* 6 vols., 2nd ed.. Beirut: Daru'l-Kutub Al-'Alamiyyah.

Tabataba'i, 'Allamah Sayyid Muhammad Husayn. 1983, *Al-mizan,* Sayyid Saeed Akhtar Rizvi (tran.), 3 vols. 1st ed., Tehran: WOFIS.

Wiles, J. and Bondi, J. 1998, *Curriculum Development,* 5th ed., Upper Saddle River, N.J., Columbus, Ohio: Merrill.

Part Two

Islam and Feminism: Applications

Article 7

A Glance at Women's Socio-Political Roles in Islamic Government

Ashraf Borujerdi

Abstract

Disagreement arises amongst the scholars of Islamic jurisprudence regarding the competency of women for political activity. Much of this revolves around the potential held by women for political leadership.

In this paper, we will attempt to discover the boundaries and limitations of women's rights and duties when we extend this discussion into the political realm.

It will then be argued that women are quite capable of contributing to the needs of their society through political participation, especially when they are able to assess the achievements and approaches of the government and its political leaders. The late Imam Khomeini argued that women should play a key role in the guidance of society, and based on this, we will seek to vindicate the position of women within Islamic government.

Introduction

Fatima Zahra (as) has been and always will be the greatest exemplar of human perfection. In the current era, there is a definite need for the definition of the woman's role inside the social and political arena. The great daughter of Prophet Muhammad (saws) can help shed light on this role and provide for us a comprehensive framework of study. The main goal of human life is to achieve perfection, the kind of perfection achieved by Our Lady Fatima Zahra (as). In addition, the thoughts of the late Imam Khomaini have also opened a door for illuminating the role of women in society. Without detecting the ties between the modern approaches of *Ijtihad* and the classical understanding of practical Law one cannot conclude a perfect solution and thus cannot achieve a perfect society. Imam Khomeini states that:

Obeying the Shari'ah Practical Law and following theological teaching is the best path for achieving perfection.[1]

The disagreement of opinion amongst the jurisprudents concerning the role of women for leadership has prompted me to begin this investigation. Some jurisprudents have argued for a total prohibition on women's activities in this area, whilst others have allowed room for change in this classical ruling, a change based on time and place. In this discussion, it is very important that we clearly separate actual Divine rulings from injunctions that are merely social and traditional in nature. Frequently, we may find a conflict between such traditional practices and the actual injunctions of *Shari'ah* Law.

However, the fact is that many jurisprudents have consistently rejected the idea of women being competent for leadership, and that a consensus supports this claim. They are arguing uniformly that women are not competent for such a task.[2]

The Islamic Revolution has paved the way for the intertwining of politics and religion. New issues were brought up by the revolution, and much revision of traditional thought accompanied it. The late Imam Khomeini spearheaded this. Much of this was based on the necessity of maintaining Islamic rule, to which secondary legislative principles were subordinated:

Regarding the role of time and place in Islamic legislation or ijtihad, we see that it is one of the most important issues...Gaining an ability to govern, an ability that is based upon a scientific philosophy, that allows us to counter paganism and solve internal problems, could not be achieved in the form of the ongoing discourse amongst the clergy,

---

[1] Mateen Quarterly, 1999, vol.1, no. 2, p. 4.

[2] M. Mahdi Shamsuddin, Preface to *The Scale of Women's Political Participation in Political Arena*, Mohsin Abedi (tran.), Tehran: Be'sat Publication, 1997.

a discourse that takes us into deadlock and that violates the Constitution.[3]

This is also in line with the opinion of a wise scholar:

Ancient narrations cannot grant holiness to what has been said by those who have come before, or give legitimacy to the route that they paved, unless those narrations can be proved to have a timeless reality or truth...A text that proves to be a changeable unfounded truth is open to dispute. In spite of the text making recourse to a vocabulary of transcendence, this nonetheless does not grant it any eternal validity.[4]

Taking this into consideration, we are able to open a door for contemporary legislators to find the truth. Some may be of the opinion that there is already too much to deal with in terms of women's issues, to then throw the problem of political participation into the fray. But it should be clear from the other presenters at this conference that the study of the other issues regarding women's rights will lead directly to a study of the problems of women's political participation.

7.1   Enlightenment on Women's Social and Political Participation

Within a real social environment, the woman's share of socio-political participation could be put in such a way that collective activities are based on a free, voluntary, conscious, and active will. This is a situation where the individuals of society organise and manage social affairs (directly or indirectly), and help shape the life of civil society.[5]

We can define the concept of political participation as the will of

---

[3] Imam Khomeini, *Sahifah Noor*, Tehran/Iran, vol. 20, p. 6.
[4] M. Hussain Fadhlullah, *Payameh Hajar*, 1997, vol. 8, no. 8, p. 45.
[5] Dawood Mirmohammedi, *Islamic Consultative Bodies*, Iranian Interior Affairs Ministry, Political Affairs publication, 1998, pp. 9-10.

individuals to act in such a way as to gain, individually or collectively, the power of rule. This can be done through legislative or administrative means. Those who engage in political participation are able to give their assent or criticisms to government policy.

Insofar as the *Shari'ah* Law has not neglected the role of women in society and assigned to them a neutral position, and insofar as the Qur'an and *Sunnah* advocate gender equality in the social sphere, women have a right to political participation. Women are free to express their views, and give their assent or criticism to government policies. This is in line with their acceptance of the Qur'anic injunction:

> And as for the believing men and the believing women, they are guardians of each other; they enjoin good and forbid evil and keep up prayer and pay the poor-rate, and obey Allah and His Apostle. For these, Allah will have Mercy. Surely Allah is Mighty, Wise.[6]

7.2   Dimensions of Women's Socio-Political Participation

7.2.1   Charting the Country's Destiny

When the late Imam Khomeini was residing in Paris, a reporter asked him about the role of women in shaping the Islamic government, in terms of *Shari'ah Law*? In response, he said:

> Thanks to Islam, women have a great and sensitive role in organizing the society. This is because this religion has promoted women to a place where they may gain their rightful position as human beings, and are no longer treated as mere material objects.[7]

The possibility for becoming involved in the society's destiny and having a say in its administrative trends, demonstrates that the

---

[6] *Holy Qur'an*, surah Al-Tawbeh, verse 71.
[7] Imam Khomeini, *Sahifah Noor*, Tehran/Iran, vol. 2, p. 101.

government is not a form of absolute sovereignty emerging from Divine principles. Rather, it is a kind of leadership that is shaped with the framework of established institutions and organisations, which grants a ruler the power to serve. This power is not to be used in accordance with a person's own wishes, but rather according to some sort of institution of consultation. An example would be the Queen of Sheba as presented in the Qur'an. She adhered to a policy of consultation in the management of her kingdom, rather than adopting a top-down authoritarianism. Lacking royal pride, she accepted the invitation to Islam offered to her by Solomon (as). She possessed an internal consciousness towards the truth, a consciousness that impelled her to accept the right and resolve the political crisis precipitated by Solomon's (as) overtures of war.[8]

This story demonstrates that it is human beings, as such, who have the right of leadership. It is painful to see the segregation of the sexes that occurs in the modern world. Human beings are, in fact, a single essence that is manifested in two forms, and there is no difference between the works of these two manifestations. The Holy Qur'an says:

O people! Be careful of your duty to your Lord, who created you from a single being.[9]

On this basis, it must be asked: Why, then, have women been excluded from their natural rights? It is beyond the scope of this paper to prove the woman's right to rule entirely, but I rather intend to highlight the issues laid out by the *Shari'ah* Law. In spite of the refusal by the cultures of Islamic countries in granting women a right to rule, there is no evidence that the *Shari'ah* Law grants any sort of legislative base for such a prohibition. An examination of Islamic history would bear this out.

---

[8] Monireh Gorji, "Woman and Leadership", *Farzaneh* Magazine, 1983, no. 1, p. 9.
[9] *Holy Qur'an*, surah Al-Nissa'a, verse 1.

During all the political struggles associated with Prophet Muhammad's (saws) mission and struggle, during all the wars and campaigns that he was forced to fight, women were never neglected and were assigned a full role. They were not limited to mere acceptance of Islamic ideology; rather they were given a full role in helping to spread the religion. They bore all the sufferings needed to protect the new faith, and took part in the emigration that was necessary for its protection. They helped the fighters and, when necessary, became combatants as well.[10]

As such, women have a full role in all political activities. Nonetheless, we still find a position, held by many jurisprudents, that prohibits women from engaging in this sort of righteous activity, and binds women into a family and child-rearing role. There are others amongst the jurisprudents that argue for the banning of women from the national electoral process, allowing them to serve on municipal councils, but not in national positions of leadership as ministers or cabinet members. There are also jurisprudents that believe that women can achieve any sort of degree of managerial authority, except the position of supreme executive authority.[11]

The evidence for this position is based on the following verse of Qur'an:

> Men are maintainers of women, because Allah made of some of them
> to excel over others, and because they spend some of their property.[12]

The interpretation of this verse revolves around the phrase maintainers, or *quawam* in Arabic. Some argue that this comes from the root word meaning "superiority". But if this were the case

---

[10] Abdulhalim Abushegheh, *The Emancipation of Women during the Early Period of Islam*, Kuwait: Darul-'ilm, 1990, vol. 2, p. 54.

[11] M. Mahdi Shamsuddin, Preface to *The Scale of Women's Political Participation in Political Arena*, Mohsin Abedi (tran.), Tehran: Be'sat Publication, 1997, p. 41.

[12] *Holy Qur'an*, surah Al-Nissa'a, verse 34.

it would collide with the Qur'anic verse 13 of chapter (49) Chambers *(Al-Hujjarat)*, which states:

> O people! Surely we have created you of a male and a female and made you into tribes and families that you may know each other, surely the most honourable of you with Allah is the one amongst you who is careful [of his duty]. Surely Allah is Knowing, Aware.

Other meanings of this word exist, however. This would include protector, guide, support, and so forth. Furthermore, we must also be clear about the scope of this verse. It clearly only refers to the issues of family life, and not those of government. We would argue that the "superiority" of men in terms of their family role is based upon capacity, but this capacity does not grant them a superior role in all fields of life.[13] Another verse, used for proof of female inferiority, is this:

> And they have rights similar to those against them in a just manner, and the men are a degree above them, and Allah is Mighty, Wise. (Qur'an, 20:228)

This verse, again, does not refer to the field of government. It is not a correct conclusion to infer from the Arabic word *(darajah)* degree used in this context, a general ruling upon all fields. And as far as the discussion refers to the relations between men and women, most jurisprudents are agreed that these verses deal only with family affairs. A third verse is:

> And stay in your houses and do not display your finery like the displays of the days of ignorance. (Qur'an, 33:33)

This verse is only applicable to the wives of the Prophet

---

[13] M. Mahdi Shamsuddin, Preface to *The Scale of Women's Political Participation in Political Arena*, Mohsin Abedi (tran.), Tehran: Be'sat Publication, 1997, p. 68.

Muhammad (saws), that they should avoid displays in line with the behaviour during the pre-Islamic period. This has no relevance on government and ruling.

Finally, there is a very famous narration from Prophet Muhammad (saws). He was informed about the female ruler of the Sassanid Empire, to which he replied:

> A nation that puts its destiny into the hands of a woman will never experience salvation.[14]

This narration does not come in a form that indicates obligation. It has already been discussed that the legitimacy of a woman's rule may be formulated with the structure of law. Absolute sovereignty is desirable neither for men or women. If we speak in terms of consultative government, the ruler gains power through a consultative assembly and allows people to make their own observations.

We would concur with the argument of the late Imam Khomeini, who has stated that the political participation of women is a duty, and one that will demonstrate their responsibilities.[15] In another discussion he argued that women must participate in social activities along with men, within the framework of Islamic law.[16] There is no difference between the two sexes in drawing the destiny and fate of the nation. The destiny of the country is the destiny of all.[17]

7.2.2   Participation in Administration

The victory of the Islamic Revolution in Iran, in spite of the absence of a recognised public assembly in place at the time of the

---

[14] *Sahih Albokahari*, vol. 3, p. 90; *Sunan Nessa'i*, vol. 8, p. 227; *Sahih Tarmazi*, vol. 3, p. 360; *Musnad Ahmad*, vol. 5, p. 38; *Alnehaye*, vol. 4, p. 135.

[15] Imam Khomeini, *Sahifah Noor*, Tehran/Iran, 1980, vol. 9, p.136.

[16] *Ibid.*, vol. 18, p. 263.

[17] *Ibid.*, vol. 4, p. 259.

victory, created self-motivated acts of political participation. The most prominent of these were those established within the consultative bodies and local non-governmental organisations. Feminist NGOs were shaped after the revolution's victory, and included more than one hundred registered organizations. Insofar as the consultant bodies are public ones in an Islamic community, such entities have a religious origin.

7.2.3   Involvement in Social Guidance

In Imam Khomeini's view, the virtue of a society is dependent upon the virtue or corruptness of its women.[18] The pillar of social development is based upon the status of woman, and social development, as such, remains in their hands. Women can be considered as rightful leaders of society and every community. The creators of human happiness are women, and the corruption or salvation of a society is in their hands.[19]

The late Imam Khomeini drew a beautiful picture of Our Lady Fatima (as) and her role in guiding society by these words:

> The woman that guided the universe from her tiny home and trained human beings, that their shining lights and lustres went from the earthen soil to browse beyond the spheres and from land to the heaven.[20]

According to the Imam's point of view, the responsibility of society's training is hidden within the hands of women either in the field of culture or in social change.

Conclusion

In conclusion, we may discuss the causes and structures for the lack of women's socio-political participation, on a macro and

---

[18] *Ibid.*, vol. 16, p. 125.
[19] *Ibid.*, p. 162.
[20] *Ibid.*, p. 125.

microcosmic scale. On the macrocosmic scale, we may speak of socio-political scenes, which discourage the motivation for participation. As Samuel Huntington says, the view of the political elites towards public participation is shaped in such a way that it blocks people from effective political participation. On the microcosmic scale, we find the main problem is the women's own lack of confidence in their abilities, and the reason behind this lies behind their education within their family environment.

Bibliography

Abushegheh, Abdulhalim. 1990, *The Emancipation of Women during the early Period of Islam*, Kuwait: Darul-'ilm.

Alnehaye, vol. 4.

Fadhlullah, M. Hussain. 1997, *Payameh Hajar* Magazine, vol. 8, no. 8.

Khomeini, Imam. *Sahifah Noor*.

Mateen Quarterly, 1999, vol. 1, no. 2, pp. 4.

Mirmohammedi, Dawood. 1998, *Islamic Consultative Bodies*, Iranian Interior Affairs Ministry, Political Affairs Publication.

Musnad Ahmad, vol. 5.

Sahih Albokahari, vol. 3.

Sahih Tarmazi, vol. 3.

Sunan Nessa'i, vol. 8.

Article 8

The Shari'ah Law and Education for Women

Saedah Siraj

Abstract

This paper seeks to highlight the role women have had in the history of *Shari'ah,* along with discussing the position of women before the law itself. Issues concerning apparent restrictions on the position of women prior to the implementation of *Shari'ah* Law will be discussed. It will be shown that, contrary to many unfounded opinions; Islam gives women important spiritual and leadership roles. Islamic laws may sometimes be different for men and women, but this paper will seek to prove that there is no injustice in such an arrangement.

Finally, the practical requirements for proper Islamic legal education for women will be addressed and a broad plan for Islamic education, with emphasis on the traditional study of the *Shari'ah*, will be presented.

Introduction

Only a small number of studies and discussions have been made on the *Shari'ah* Law[1] and women's education. At the same time, not many Muslim women have been exposed to the *Shari'ah Law.* This is due to the fact that schools in the Muslim countries have, since the colonial ages up until the present day, given more emphasis to Western education as opposed to Islamic education. It is for these reasons mentioned, that this paper will focus on the following main subjects:

- The *Shari'ah* Law

- The importance of educating women in the *Shari'ah* Law

- How to educate Muslim women in the *Shari'ah* Law

---

[1] In Law of Islam, the term *as-shari`a* (pl. *as-shara`i*) means 'the revealed, canonical, law of Islam' as stated in *A Learner's Arabic-English Dictionary,* 1978, p. 573; *A Dictionary of Modern Written Arabic*, 1980, p. 466; see also, the Qur'an, 5:48; 42:13,21; 45:18; "Shari`a" in *Shorter Encyclopaedia of Islam*, 1953, p. 524.

8.1   The Shari'ah Law

Muslims believe that the Qur'an contains a system of Divine laws and instructions for man to follow, and also emphasises a direct and universal human responsibility before Allah (swt). In light of the Qur'an, everyone, with no exception, has to obey the commands of Allah (swt); these commands are what constitute the *Shari'ah* Law, and they are from a Divine source.

The Qur'an teaches justice and equality. It does not discriminate against man by looking towards superficialities such as wealth or power. Everyone is of equal status. The only legitimate distinction among the Muslims is the degree of *(taqwa)* piety.[2] Parallel to the teachings of the Qur'an, every Muslim, regardless of nationality, political boundary and sexual difference, has to refer his/her activities to the *Shari'ah* Law. By referring to the *Shari'ah* Law, Muslims are also fulfilling Allah's (swt) Will, incumbent upon them as stated in the Qur'an:

There is no judgement but Allah's. (Qur'an, 12:40)

And whoever judgeth not by what Allah hath sent down; these then are the transgressors. (Qur'an, 5:47)

The above verses of the Qur'an explain that authority belongs to Allah (swt) (the Most Truthful, the Most Righteous), while individual interests are subordinate to it.

The main feature of the Shari'a law is fixed and unchangeable. This is in contradiction to the ordinary social laws (penal codes and customary laws), which are legislated according to the wishes of the majority.

Schools of law (*madhhab*; pl. *madhahib*) did not exist during the

---

[2] *Taqwa* (piety, abstinence) does not imply a negative attitude, see, Martyr Murtada Mutahhari, "Glimpses of the Nahj al-Balaghah" in *Al-Tawhid*, `Ali Quli Qara'i (tran.), 1986, vol. 3, no. 3, pp. 119-27.

Prophet's (saws) lifetime (Medinian period, 1-10/622-32). Muslims only practiced the *Shari'ah* Law, revealed to the Prophet (saws) and problems that arose would be referred straight to him. As a Prophet, he gave judgements on cases related to penal laws (*hudud*) and social rules (*munakahat*) etc. In later periods these judgements became part of the narrations.[3]

During the period of rule of the first four caliphs (10-40 AH/632-61 AD), the Muslim empire had spread over a vast area, and the caliphs had appointed provincial governors. The judge and magistrate of the Shari'ah court, the revealed law court of Islam used to be under the authority of the governor.

During the rule of *Amiru'l-Mu'minin* 'Ali b. Abi Talib (as) (r. 35-40/656-61), (the fourth caliph for the Sunnis and the First Imam[4] of the ummah according to the Shi'ah), certain rules for the appointment of governors were put into place. Ali (as) directed his governor of Egypt and surrounding areas Malik al-Ashtar an-Nakha'i as follows:

> For the settlement of disputes among people select him who is the most distinguished of your subjects in your view. The cases (coming before him) should vex him, disputation should not enrage him, he should not insist on any wrong point, and should not begrudge accepting the truth when he perceives it; he should not lean towards greed and should not content himself with a cursory understanding (of

---

[3] In the Sunni School, 'narrations' means 'words, actions and approval of the Prophet Muhammad (p.b.u.h.)' whereas in the Imamite School, 'narrations' means 'words, actions and approval of the Prophet Muhammad (p.b.u.h.) and all the infallibles of his family'.

[4] 'Imam' means 'Leader' of the community (ummah). The Imamites believe that the Twelve Imams, from 'the Family of the Prophet' (*Ahlu'l-Bayt Rasulallah*), are the successors of the Prophet (p.b.u.h.). The first Imam is Amiru'l-Mu'minin 'Ali b. Abi Talib (k.w.) and ends with the twelfth Imam, Imam Muhammad al-Mahdi b. Hasan al-`Askari (a.s.). Their names appeared in authentic narrations in the Sunni's source, *Fara'idus-simtayn* of al-Hamawi, in as-Shaykh Sulayman al-Qunduzi al-Hanafi, *Yanabi` al-mawadda*, chap. 76.

matter) without going thoroughly into it. He should be most ready to stop (to ponder) on doubtful points, most regardful of arguments, least disgusted at the quarrel of litigants, most patient at probing into matters and most fearless at the time of passing judgement. Praise should not make him vain and elation should not make him lean (to any side). Such people are very few.

Then, very often check his decisions and allow him so much money (as remuneration) that he has no excuse worth hearing (for not being honest) and there remains no occasion for him to go to others for his needs. Give him that rank in your audience for which no one else among your chiefs aspires, so that he remains safe from the harm of those around you. You should have a piercing eye in this matter because this region has formerly been a prisoner in the hands of vicious persons when action was taken according to passion, and worldly wealth was sought.[5]

In Islam, the role of the ruler is to ensure that the *Shari'ah* Law is preserved and implemented. This role, according to the Shi'ahs, is undertaken by the Twelve Imams (as) from the family of the Prophet (saws), who are the religious scholars (*al-'ulama'*) and the rulers of the *ummah*. This is based on the argument that the religion of Islam and each *ummah* are to be both preserved and administered by the Imams appointed by God, as clearly stated in the Qur'an, 17:71; 2:30,124,247; 21:73,105; 32:24; 38:26. Moreover, according to authentic narrations as stated in the authorised sources of narrations in the Sunni school, the Prophet (saws) will be succeeded by twelve Imams (as), who will be in authority until the end of time[6], and who are similar to the twelve

---

[5] Cf. Sayed Ali Reza (tran.), *Nahjul Balagha*, New York: Tahrike Tarsile Qur'an Inc., 1985, pp. 539-40.

[6] Ahmad bin Muhammad bin Hanbal (Ahmad Hanbal), *Al-Musnad*, vols. 5&6, Egypt: Daru'l-Ma'arif, 1975, p.294. Narrations no.3781, the *isnad* (chain of transmission), of this narrations is authentic (*sahih*); Abi'l-Husayn Muslim ibni'l-Hajjaji'l-Qushayri an-Naysaburi (Muslim), *Sahih Muslim*, Beirut: Daru'l-Fiqr,

Chieftains from among the children of Israel. (The Qur'an, 5:12)[7]

However, during the Umayyad (r. 41-127/661-744) and the 'Abbasid (r. 132/750) periods the religious scholars, namely, the Twelve Imams (as) from the family of the Prophet (saws), were denied their rightful positions in the Muslim Empire. Thus, a deviation of the *Shari'ah* Law from the right and pure teaching of Islam occurred.

Nevertheless, in agreement with the Sunnis' belief that: "the religious scholars among the masses are the rulers of the ummah after the Prophet (saws)", local Sunni religious scholars adopted the role of leadership during these periods.[8] Some of them obeyed the government and warned against disobedience to the caliph, such as Abu Yusuf (d. 182/798), disciple of Abu Hanifah, who was appointed as 'Chief Judge of the Supreme Court' (*qadi al-qudat*) by Harun ar-Rashid (r. 170-93/789-809).[9]

It was during the 'Abbasid period that the four Sunni schools were founded, namely, the Malikite, Hanafite, Shafi'ite and Hanbalite schools. Religious scholars, (who were 'specialists in the *Shari'ah* Law' or *al-fuqaha*[10] of the Sunni school), such as Abu Hanifah (80-150H), 'Abdul-Rahman al-Awza'i (d. 157/774), Malik b. Anas (93-179H), as-Shafi'i (150-240H) and Ahmad Hanbal (164-241H)

1983, vol. 3, pp. 1452-4; Abi Da'ud Sulayman ibn al-Ash`ath as-Sij-jistani, *Sunan Abi Da'ud*, Beirut Daru'l-Fiqr, 1994, vol. 2, p. 314, narrations no. 4279, 4280.

[7] "... and We (God) raised up from among them (the children of Israel) Twelve Chieftains; ... (*waba`athna minhum ithna `ashara naqiban*)". (The Qur'an, 5:12)

[8] Since the beginning of the twentieth century until the present, modernists or reformers, (namely, the Sunni activists all over the world), believe the religious scholars (*al-`ulama'*) among masses are the rulers of the ummah after the Prophet Muhammad (p.b.u.h.) and *al-khulafa' ar-rashidun*.

[9] J. Schacht, "Abu Yusuf" in *Encyclopaedia of Islam* (new edition), 1960, p. 164; Danial Latifi, "Rationalism and Muslim Law" in *Islam and the Modern Age*, 1973, vol. 4, no. 4, p. 43.

[10] Such as Abu Hanifa who resided in Kufa, Iraq; 'Abdul-Rahman al-Awza'i who resided in Damascus; Malik b. Anas who resided in Medina; as-Shafi`i, who was born in Yemen, then migrated to Medina, Kufa and Baghdad and finally resided in Egypt; and Ahmad Hanbal who resided in Baghdad.

started to teach the Shari`a law to the locals, partly based on local narrations and with their (i.e. *al-fuqaha'*) 'religious verdicts' (*al-fatawa*); and also based on the Qur'an and the Sunna. Medina, Kufa, Damascus and Baghdad became places where the Sunni schools were developed.

The Sunni *fuqaha* developed the Shari`a law on the basis of the following sources:

- The Qur'an

- *As-Sunnah* (the words, actions and approval of the Prophet Muhammad (saws))

- *Al-Ijma'* ('consensus' of the Sunni jurists' religious verdicts)

- *Al-Qiyas* (analogical reasoning)

In contrast, the Shi'ah Muslims, who were in opposition to the rulers (the Umayyad and the 'Abbasid), upheld their Imams (as) and referred straight to them for solutions to their problems. Beginning from the middle of the first century of Hijra to the middle of the second century of Hijrah, categorisation and organisation of the *Shari'ah* law were arranged by the fifth and the sixth Shi'ah Imams, Imam Muhammad al-Baqir (as) (57-114H) and Imam Ja'far as-Sadiq (as). (83-148H)

In the Shi'ah School, the *Shari'ah* law is to be formulated according to the following sources:

- The Qur'an;

- *As-Sunnah* [the words, actions and approval of the Prophet (saws) and his family (as)]

- *Al-Ijtihad* ('effort' of a religious scholar's independent reasoning in light of the Qur'an, the *Sunnah* and earlier religious verdicts).[11]

In the Sunni school, the process of finding a rule of the *Shari'ah* law (*hukm*) should be obtained from the four main sources, the Qur'an, *Sunnah, ijma'* and *qiyas* accordingly. As for the Imamites, a rule of the *Shari'ah* law is found by referring to the Qur'an, *Sunna* and *ijtihad* of the *mujtahid* (a religious scholar who is able to perform independent reasoning), namely, a living *al-marja`-al-fatwa* (the one who is referred for religious verdict), which will be further discussed.

The above sources for the two Shari'ah laws (the Shi'ah and the Sunni schools) will produce one of the following *hukms* (a rule of the *Shari'ah* law), which are *wajib* (compulsory), *haram* (forbidden), *sunnat* (advisable), *halal* (permissible) and *makruh* (unadvisable). Accordingly, based on the Qur'an, (2:43,277), when a sane Muslim has reached puberty, he is obligated (*wajib*, compulsory) to perform the five daily prayers. It is also forbidden (*haram*) for him to eat dead (*not-halal*) meat and all kinds of blood (The Qur'an, 5:4). Besides performing the obligatory five daily prayers, he is 'advised' (*sunnah*) to perform extra prayers at night. For the case of *hukm* that is 'unadvisable' (*makruh*), it is unadvisable to sleep after having sex before taking a bath during the night.

---

[11] On *Ijtihad*, see, Muhammad Ibrahim Jannati, "The Meaning of Ijtihad" in *Al-Tawhid*, Martyr Mahliqa Qara'i (tran.), 1988, vol. 5, no. 3&4, pp. 179-200; Muhammad Ibrahim Jannati, "The Beginning of Shi'i Ijtihad" in *Al-Tawhid*, A. Q. Qara'i (tran.), 1988, vol. 6, no. 1, pp. 45-64; Martyr Murtada Mutahhari, "Ijtihad in the Imamiyyah Tradition" in *Al-Tawhid*, Mahliqa Qara'i (tran.), 1986, vol. 4, no. 1, pp. 26-48; Martyr Murtada Mutahhari, "The Role of Ijtihad in Legislation" in *Al-Tawhid*, `Ali Quli Qara'i (tran.), 1986-87, vol. 4, no. 2, pp. 21-52; Abdulaziz Abdulhussein Sachedina, *The Just Ruler (Al-Sultan al-`Adil) in Shi`ite Islam*, New York: Oxford University Press, 1988, chaps. 4-5; Asaf A. A. Fyzee, *Outlines of Muhammadan Law*, London: Oxford University Press, 1955, pp. 21-27; Reuben Levy, *The Social Structure of Islam*, Cambridge: Cambridge University Press, 1962, pp. 150-91; H. Lammens, *Islam: Beliefs and Institution*, London: Methuen & Co. Ltd., 1929, pp. 97-110; J. Schacht, "Idjtihad" in *Encyclopaedia of Islam* (new edition), 1965, vol. 3, pp. 1206-27.

In a matter needing new *ijtihad*, according to the Sunni school, 'the followers' (*al-muqallidun*) 'hold' and follow the *ijtihads* of Abu Hanifa, Malik b. Anas, as-Shafi`i and Ahmad Hanbal which can be found in their jurisprudence books - written around the beginning of the second century of Hijrah until the first quarter of the fourth century of Hijra such as *Al-Muwatta'* of Malik b. Anas, *Al-Kharaj* of Abu Yusuf and *Al-Umm* of as-Shafi'i.[12]

Around the beginning of the 4th century of Hijrah (10th century AD), *ijtihads* were no longer carried out (in the Sunni school) - this was known as 'Closing the Door of *ijtihad*' (*insidad babu'l-ijtihad*) - because they believe the *ijtihad* had been completed.[13]

A thousand years after 'Closing the Door of *ijtihad*' occurred, the Sunni religious scholars such as-Sayyid Jamaluddin al-Afghani (1839-1897)[14], and as-Shaykh Muhammad 'Abduh (1849-1905), modernists and founders of the modern age movements of Islam, were of the opinion that *ijtihad* had never been closed to the Muslims. These opinions gave a vital impact to the understanding of Islam among the Sunnis. Millions of Sunnis all over the world

---

[12] Muhammad b. al-Hasan as-Shaybani (narrator), *Muwatta' al-Imam Malik*, `Abdu'l-Wahhab `Abdu'l-Latif (ed.), n.p.: Al-Maktaba Al-`Alamiyya, n.d.; As-Shafi`i, *Al-Umm*, 8 vols., Beirut: Daru'l-Fiqr, 1983.

[13] Abu al-Qasim Gorji, "A Brief Survey of the Development of `Ilm usul al-fiqh" in *Al-Tawhid*, `Ali Quli Qara'i (tran.), 1986, vol. 3, no. 3, p. 95; J. Schacht, *An Introduction to Islamic Law*, Oxford: The Clarendon Press, 1964, pp. 70-71; N. J. Coulson, *A History of Islamic Law*, Edinburgh: Edinburgh University Press, 1971, pp. 80f; W. W. Montgomery Watt, "The Closing of the Door of Ijtihad" in *Orientalia Hispanica*, 1974, vol. 1, p. 675; see also, Mutahhari, "The Role of Ijtihad in Legislation" in *Al-Tawhid*, `Ali Quli Qara'i (tran.), 1986-87, vol. 4, no. 2, pp. 26-27; Wael B. Hallaq, "Was the Gate of Ijtihad Closed?" in *IJMES*, 1984, vol. 16, no. 1, pp. 3-41; Wael B. Hallaq, "On the Origins of the Controversy about the Existence of Mujtahids and the Gate of Ijtihad" in *Studia Islamica* lxviii, 1986, pp. 9-141.

[14] Murtada al-Mutahhari, *Al-Harakat al-Islamiyyah fi'l-Qarni ar-Rabi` `Ashara'l-Hijri*, Albany, California: Muslim Student Association (Persian Speaking Group), n.d., pp. 22,43,62-63 states that as-Sayyid Jamaluddin al-Afghani i.e. as-Sayyid Jamaluddin al-Asad-abadi, (As-Shaykh Muhammad `Abduh's teacher) was an Iranian Shi`ite scholar.

started to follow suit of the modernists' ideologies. They became more and more progressive, coping with the advancing and developing technologies. With their new spirit injected by the modernists, they were now very hopeful for the possibility of building an Islamic state. This situation became a threat to the secular rulers.[15]

At present, the rulers of Sunni countries are referring to 'the Verdict Committee'[16] led by a *mufti*, concerning a matter requiring new *ijtihad*. These committees are under the administration of a secular ruling authority, which results in some verdicts being made to correspond with policies of the secular ruling powers.[17]

As for the Shi'ahs, they hold on to a living *al-marja`-a'l-fatwa* (the one who is referred for religious verdict) for reference on matters needing new *ijtihads*.[18]

In this respect, Islam has divided human laws and regulations into two classes:

---

[15] On modernist thought, see Hamid Enayat, *Modern Islamic Political Thought*, Austin: University of Texas Press, 1988, pp. 69-83; Albert Hourani, *Arabic Thought in the Liberal Age 1798-1939*, New York: Cambridge University Press, 1984, pp. 103-244; On modernist thought, which includes a threat to the secular ruling authority, see Chandra Muzaffar, *Islamic Resurgence in Malaysia*, Petaling Jaya: Penerbit Fajar Bakti Sdn. Bhd., 1987, pp. 33f.

[16] In Malaysia, 'The National Verdict Committee' (*Jawatankuasa Fatwa Kebangsaan*).

[17] "Keputusan Mesyuarat Jawatankuasa Fatwa Kebangsaan (*Results of the National Verdict Committee Meeting*)", Islamic Centre of Malaysia, Prime Minister Department, Kuala Lumpur, (Unpublished, n.d.).

[18] On *al-Marja`-a'l-Fatwa*, see Ayatullah `Ali Mishkini, "Wilayat al-Faqih: Its Meaning and Scope" in *Al-Tawhid*, Shahyar Sa`adat (tran.), 1985, vol. 3, no. 1, pp. 29-65; Hamid Enayat, "Iran: Khumayni's Concept of the Guardianship of the Juriconsult" in *Islam in the Political Process*, James Piscatori (ed.), Cambridge, London, New York, New Rochelle, Melbourne, Sydney: Cambridge University Press, 1983, pp. 160-80; A. K. S. Lambton, "A Reconsideration of the Position of the Marja` al-Taqlid and the Religious Institution" in *Studia Islamica* xx, pp. 114-35.

- The fixed laws - the Shari`a law - for instance, criminal law or penal code

- The alterable laws - the laws, which are open to alteration and can be formulated according to the changing conditions of place and time. For instance, during the Prophet's (saws) lifetime there was no need for road regulations and procedures because vehicles did not exist. As time passed, technology improved and it gave birth to various kinds of transportation such as the car. Consequently, road regulations and procedures were made – which are open to alteration and can be modified according to the changing conditions of place and time.

The following institutions have the authority to formulate the alterable laws:

- *Ahlu'l-halli wa'l-`aqdi* (those who are given authority by the community to rule a nation or a government)

- 'The *fatwa* (verdict) committee' according to the Sunni school.[19]

- *Al-Khilafah* (Leader of the community chosen by man), according to the Sunni school, or *Wilayat ul-`ammah* (General Guardianship) according to the Shi'ah school.[20]

In the Shi'ah school, the alterable laws are subject to the judgement of the Prophet (saws), his successors (as) and those appointed by him. These laws and regulations are formulated by *al-Wilayah* (Guardianship) or *al-Imamah* (Leadership) in light of the Shari`a law in accordance with the situation, time and place.

After the fall of the 'Uthman Empire in 1924, the *Shari'ah law* was

---

[19] *Ahlu'l-Halli wa'l-`aqdi* is one of the modern thinker's principles.

[20] On *al-Wilayah al-`Ammah*, see also Abdulaziz Abdulhussein Sachedina, *The Just Ruler (Al-Sultan al-`Adil) in Shi`ite Islam*, New York: Oxford University Press, 1988.

no longer practised in Muslim countries because of the colonisation of the Western powers.[21] As a result of colonization, the Muslims did not receive the proper education concerning the *Shari'ah* Law – including the women - this will be discussed in the following topic.

8.2   The Importance of the Education of Women in the Shari'ah Law

Women and men complement one another. A woman is not complete without a man and a man is not complete without a woman. As a family educator, women hold the responsibility of educating their children. If a woman is deficient in the correct education, she will produce uneducated children - this will be further discussed. Hence, women have significant roles in developing the *ummah* and hold the keys to its success.

Islam has provided a great service of which no previous example exists in history. Islam saves women from oppression and elevates them to a special place. Islam never sought to degrade women but instead encouraged women to progress, and sought to preserve the respect and honour of their gender. This includes the proper education of women in the areas of the Qur'an, narrations and *Shari'ah* law.

The following facts will show how Islam wants women to perform certain responsibilities just as men do:

8.2.1   Women Possessing Documented Reading Materials at the Time of the Prophet (saws)

An-Najashi's (d. 450/1058) *Kitabu'l-rijal* says:

> One day, when Sayyidatun-Nisa' il-'Alamin Fatima (as) couldn't find
> a recorded narrations manuscript, she asked her housemaid to search

---

[21] Marshall G. S. Hodgson, *The Venture of Islam*, Chicago and London: The University of Chicago Press, 1974, vol. 3, pp. 149-58.

for it, saying: "Look for it. It is as precious to me as my sons Hassan and Hussayn".[22]

This example shows how Islam encourages women in education. During the Medinian period, those who knew the narrations (the words, actions and approval of the Prophet (saws) and the exegesis of the Qur'an) were considered to be highly intellectual. Consequently, 'the chosen slaves of God' (al-akhyar) who possessed such knowledge, would also possess Divine knowledge from the Unseen world, namely the knowledge of the 'angel world' (al-malakut) and the 'great world' (al-jabarut).[23]

No one would disagree that by possessing narration manuscripts, Sayyidatun-Nisa'il-'Alamin Fatima (as), was considered a person of high intellect and for this reason, she was known as (az-zakiyya) the intelligent one. For this cause, Islam offers women the opportunity of higher education – such as those who are in universities at the present can specialise in the study of Narrations.

8.2.2   Women as Narrators of Narrations

Sayyidatun-Nisa'il-'Alamin Fatima (as) is among the earliest narrators (ruwat, sing. rawi) as are Amiru'l-Mu'minin 'Ali (as), Abu Rafi` and Salman al-Farsi.[24] This fact indicates that Fatima (as) was given the appropriate educational background by her father, the Prophet (saws), in all aspects of life, which includes the Shari'ah law. Furthermore, her husband, Amiru'l-Mu'minin 'Ali (as), was the most knowledgeable person after the Prophet (saws). This fact is stated in all of the authorised sources of narrations in the Shi'ah and Sunni schools.

---

[22] Cf. Mustafa Awliya'i, "Outlines of the Development of the Science of Narrations", Al-Tawhid, A. Q. Qara'i (tran.), 1404 AH, vol. 1, no. 1, p. 28.

[23] Based on the narrations in Lisanu'l-`Arab 4:113, "Most Glorious of the Great (world) and the angels (world) (in the skies) (Subahana zi'l-jabarut wa'l-malakut and Thumma yakunu mulkun wa-jabarut ayyu `utuwun wa-qahrun)".

[24] Mustafa Awliya'i, "Outlines of the Development of the Science of Narrations", Al-Tawhid, A. Q. Qara'i (tran.), 1404 AH, vol. 1, no. 1, p. 29.

Umm Salama (as), wife of the Prophet (saws), was also one of the earliest narrators, and it was she who reported the famous (narration of *al-kisa'*) the blanket tradition.[25]

This shows how Islam treats men and women equally concerning education, and how the Prophet (saws) himself directly conveyed the teachings of Islam to women. Accordingly, in 'the Study of Narration', we will find women who became trustworthy narrators – such as Fatima (as) and Umm Salama (as).

8.2.3   Women could be Appointed as Judges according to the Sunni School

In the Sunni schools, namely, the Hanafite and the Shafi'ite schools, from around the beginning of the second century of Hijrah until the first quarter of the 4th century of Hijrah, formulated a law which allowed women to become judges (*qadi*) in all cases except criminal cases. This was in compliance with the rule that the testimony of a woman was permissible in every case, except in criminal cases.[26]

In contrast, the Shi'ahs believe women cannot be appointed as judges. This is because, in Islam, there are 124,000 prophets and none of them are female. One of the numerous duties of a Prophet is to pass judgement in cases related to penal laws and social rules. Hence, the appointment of the male *(qadi)* judge is in accordance with Islam.

Women from the prophets' families were created 'without menstruation and postnatal bleeding.[27] Without menstruation and

---

[25] Sayyid Muhammad Husayn Tabataba'i, *Al-Mizan fi Tafsir al-Qur'an*, Beirut: Mu'assasah Al-'Alami li'l-Matbu'at, 1983, vol. 4, p. 411.

[26] Anwar Ahmad Qadri, *Islamic Jurisprudence in the Modern World*, Lahore: Sh. Muhammad Ashraf, 1973, pp. 482-83.

[27] An authentic narration, in as-Shaykh Sulayman al-Qunduzi al-Hanafi, *Yanabi' al-Mawadda*, p.260 cited in al-'Allamatu'l-Hujjah al-Haj as-Sayyid Ghulamarda al-Kasa'i al-Kawakini, *Manaqib az-Zahra'*, Qum: Matba'ah Mahr, 1397 AH, p.55.

postnatal bleeding, the great 'heavenly women' from the prophets' families, namely, Mary (as) and Fatima (as) could constantly devote themselves to God in comparison to other women of their times. They were of 'those closest to God' (*al-muqarrabin*) (Quran, 83:21), but neither of them were elected to become judge. Thus, there is no such false accusation that there is injustice, oppression and inequality between the two sides according to the *Shari'ah* law.

In addition, not a single source of Islam mentions that the Prophet (saws) and the first four caliphs had ever appointed a woman as a judge. It is worth noting that in trials of a sexual nature, it is considered inappropriate for women to examine and question the accused concerning matters of a sexual nature.

8.2.4   A Male Witness is Equivalent to Two Female Witnesses during a Trial

One of the most crucial issues at present is regarding witnesses during a trial. Islam says that a male witness is equivalent to two female witnesses, but this does not imply discrimination towards women.

In bearing witness, two women are required in place of one man, the Qur'an states:

> Call to witness two witnesses from among your men, and if there not be two men, then (take) a man and two (women), so that should one of the two (women) forget, the (second) one of the two may remind the other; … (Qur'an, 2:282)

This verse does not belittle women, but rather helps women defend themselves during a trial. Moreover, Islam wants to preserve the women's reputation; if there is only one female witness, she may be subjected to insult by the other party. On this point, Weiss (1986) argues that a single female witness was accepted in early Islam, but Weiss' argument that *Sayyidatuna* Khadija (as) (d. 3 before Hijrah/619), the first wife of the Prophet (saws), was the only witness to the prophethood of Muhammad (saws) cannot be applied to the case of the trial witness. This is because it was not only Sayyidatuna Khadija (as) who witnessed the prophethood of Prophet Muhammad (saws), but many other Muslim women and men as well.[28]

Weiss' argument cannot be applied to the case of female witnesses in court. This is because every narration is subject to the narration of different narrators. For instance, a narration which was narrated by 'Aisha may also be narrated by another narrator. However, Islam teaches that there is no difference in human rights between men and women because both are human beings, and women, just like men, have the right to issues about there own lives. The Qur'an (4:1), clearly indicates that men and women are branches from the same root - the Prophet Adam (as). Simultaneously, the decision of the Pakistani Council on Islamic Ideology in 1984, fixing the testimony of two women to that of one man, is in accordance with the Qur'an.[29]

8.2.5   Women and Social Issues

Women in Islam are not forbidden to participate in social issues on the basis of two principles:

First, a woman cannot, for the sake of possession and wealth, sacrifice the important responsibility and duty of managing the family, and training the children who will become the future worthwhile members of society. One of the crucial responsibilities of a woman in Islam is being a mother and training righteous children. Activities outside the home are secondary to this until the children have grown up. Women are responsible for raising the young of our society. If it were ever to be that these women, who rear human beings, were to be taken from society, the condition of Islam would be threatened. Women, by using the correct methods

---

[28] Anita M. Weiss, *Islamic Reassertion in Pakistan,* New York: Syracuse University Press, 1986, p. 102.
[29] *Ibid.*

of training, build individuals and improve the state of Islam. The training takes place in the environment of the home, on the mother's lap. Consequently, it is reasonable to believe that the role of women in society is as important if not more so than that of men.

The second principle is that, a woman cannot, by means of cosmetics and ornamentations, turn herself into a doll-like creature to advertise products, attract customers, meet the lustful desires of men and flirt with them. This is because the role of women contains special characteristics. The goodness or corruption of a society stems from the goodness or corruption of the women in that society. A woman is a unique creature who has the awesome responsibility of rearing children and instilling values into them, and thus actively determines the future of her society. The Qur'an states:

> Whosoever does good, whether male or female and is a believer, We (God) will certainly make him (or her) live a happy life and We will most certainly give them the reward of the best of what they did. (Qur'an, 49:13) And they must remember their pledge to God, and guard themselves against evil. (Qur'an, 16:97)

8.2.5.1 A Woman as a Model of Virtue, Chastity and Obedience

The Qur'an states:

> So her Lords accepted her (Mary) with a good acceptance and made her grow up a good growing and gave her into the charge of Zakaria. (Qur'an, 3:37)

It is then Mary (as) whose existence is directly linked to the prophethood, and God says in the Qur'an:

> And Mary, Imran's daughter, who guarded her virginity, so We breathed into her of our spirit (created by God) and she confirmed the

Words of her Lord and His books and became one of the obedient. (Qur'an, 66:12)

Mary (as) a woman, as stated in the Qur'an, is a model of virtue and chastity, a model of obedience, to whom Allah (swt) gave a great role to play in society.

8.2.5.2 Women as Important Agents for Changing Society

Women are also important agents in changing society. Women have their own responsibilities and so do men. They help each other to determine the success and the failure of a society. In Islam, there is no case of oppression or injustice to either sex. The calmness and affection of women are appropriate attributes for educating and raising children at home. On the other hand, men - with their strength- are suited to outdoor work, thus earning a living for the family.

We cannot claim that women (by residing at home to educate and bring up the children) are oppressing men and taking advantage of them, by asking them to work hard outside and earn a living and vice versa. Therefore there can be no suggestion that there is injustice, oppression and inequality between the two sides according to the *Shari'ah* law.

8.2.6 Both Adam and Eve were Responsible for the Temptations of Satan

Sunni accept theological narrations concerning the creation of women (Eve) from the rib of Adam (as). This is also stated in the *New Testament* and *The Gospel of Barnabas* (39) as follows:

Seeing the man alone, God said: 'It is not well that he (Adam) should remain alone. Wherefore he (God) made him (Adam) to sleep, and took a rib from near his (Adam) heart, feeling the place with flesh. Of that rib made he (God) Eve and gave her (Eve) to Adam for his wife...'[30]

The above statement and the Sunnis' theological narrations concerning the creation of women from the rib of Adam demean women. In contrast, the Shi'ahs believe that Allah (swt) created Eve

...from the clay left over from the creation of Adam which lay near his lowest rib.[31]

and this does not differentiate women from men.

The Qur'an clearly tells us both Adam (as) and Eve (as) were responsible for following the temptations of Satan:

And We (God) said: 'Oh Adam, dwell you and your wife in the garden and eat thereof easefully where you desire; but draw not nigh this tree, least you be of evildoers.' (Qur'an, 2:35) And Adam disobeyed his Lord, and so his life became evil (to him). (Qur'an, 20:121)

Consequently, in Islam, there are no original sins to be blamed on women. According to the Qur'an, God forgave both Adam and Eve and sent them out from the Garden of Paradise.

8.2.7   Women's Political Roles

The history of Islam records many stories of brave women, for instance, Asiyah (as) the Pharaoh's wife, who braved the cruelty and injustice of her husband. As a result, God gave her a

---

[30] Lonsdale and Laura Ragg (ed.), *The Gospel of Barnabas*, Karachi: Begum Aisha Bawani Waqf, 1980, p. 50.
[31] Sayyid Muhammad Husayn Tabataba'i, *Al-mizan*, Sayyid Saeed Akhtar Rizvi, (tran.), Tehran: WOFIS, 1983, vol. 1, pp. 209-10; for additional meaning on 'rib', see Ali Shariati, *Man and Islam*, Fatollah Marjani, (tran.), Houston: FILINC, 1981, pp. 4-5.

permanent place in heaven, as stated in the Qur'an:

> She (`Asiyah) said: 'O my Lord, build for me a house in the Garden
> and deliver me from the Pharaoh and his doing, and deliver me from
> the unjust people'. (Qur'an, 66:11)

Other examples *Sayyidatun-Nisa'il-'Alamin* Fatima (as) the
daughter of the Prophet Muhammad (saws), who bravely opposed
Caliph Abu Bakr (r.11-3/632-4) in defending her inheritance,[32] and
Sayyidah Zaynab (as), the granddaughter of the Prophet
Muhammad (saws) and sister of Imam Hussain b. `Ali (as), who
bravely opposed the cruelty of *Caliph* Yazid b. Mu'awiyya (r. 59-
61/680-3).

In Islam, there are some special rules which apply only to women.
A woman cannot be a leader over men and women, but can be a
leader over women. In respect to this, Weiss argues:

> There have been rulers in Muslim history, such as Balqis or the Queen
> of Sheba ... in Yemen (during the time of Prophet Solomon (as)....[33]

Balqis, however, had become a ruler when she was still an
unbeliever. Later, she converted to the religion of God, before her
marriage to the Prophet Solomon (as), as stated in the Qur'an:

> ...My Lord! Verily I have been unjust to myself, and I submit (along)
> with Solomon unto God, the Lord of the worlds. (Qur'an, 27:44)

---

[32] Guillaume, (tran.), *The Life of Muhammad: A Translation of Ishaq's Sirat Rasul Allah*, New York: Oxford University Press, 1978, pp. 650-2, states that 'Fadak' is an area in the North-East of Khaybar in Arabia. Fadak was the Prophet's private property because horse or camel had not attacked it. Accordingly, as-Sayyidatun-Nisa' `il-`Alamin Fatima (`a.ha.s.), the daughter of the Prophet, has the right of inheriting her father's property. This is in accordance to the Qur'an, 27:16 but Abu Bakr, the First Caliph, denied this claim. However, finally as-Sayyidatun-Nisa' `il-`Alamin Fatima (as) won the case.

[33] Weiss, *Islamic*, p. 103.

So when she converted to Islam she was no longer ruling her country. Consequently, Islam disqualifies women from being the head of state, and this is in accordance with the Qur'an.

8.2.8   Hijab (Veil)

The use of *hijab* by women was not unknown in pre-Islamic 'Arabia. The Prophet (saws) never abolished the wearing of *hijab* and up to the time of the first four caliphs, the women kept the face and hands unveiled.

The action of some Muslim women abandoning their *hijabs* in order to engage in everyday activities has nothing to do with Islam. This is because Islam never prevents any woman from being involved in any normal everyday activity. During the lifetime of the Prophet (saws), women were serving food and drink to the army and treated the injured in war without abandoning their *hijabs*. Wearing and abandoning the *hijab* has nothing to do with the participation of women in activities of life because the command to wear the *hijab* is a Divine injunction, and its purpose is to save women from immoral men. Moreover, it is also an Islamic political symbol, because the wearing of *hijab* means Muslims are successful in protecting their women, as stated in Qur'an (3:59). This verse stresses that men must first "wear the *hijab*" by lowering their gaze in the presence of women. Then, it advises the women to wear *hijab*. Accordingly, this verse gives equal rights to both sexes.

The philosophy behind wearing the *hijab* is to save and to protect women from the roaming eyes of men. Eyes are understood to be the most important means of creating the feeling of sexual desire. By wearing the *hijab*, both men and women are safe from bad acts, including rape and fornication.

8.2.9   Producing Highly Intellectual Women

Education of the *Shari'ah* law is also essential for the production of highly intellectual women. These women place their 'human elements' above their 'animal elements'.[34] Consequently, they become true human beings. Here, according to Imam Khumayni (ra), women as well as men may initiate the process of improving their devoutness to God - in which they have to ascend from one stage of devoutness to God to the other as follows:[35]

- *Al-Muslim* (the one who surrenders to God) [36]

- *Al-Mu'min* (the true believer)[37]

- *Al-Muttaqi* (the devotee)[38]

---

[34] Anita M. Weiss, *Islamic Reassertion in Pakistan,* New York: Syracuse University Press, 1986, p.103.

[35] Muhammad `Abduh, *Nahju'l-Balagha,* Beirut: Daru'l-Balagha, 1985, pp. 74-75, states that 'human elements' are in every soul as stated by Amiru'l-Mu'minin `Ali (k.w.), namely: a) The brain (*fikarin*); b) Intellectualism (intellectual capacity, the faculty of knowing, mental power, intelligence, superior reasoning power, understanding); c) Wisdom (*al-hikmah*); and d) Knowledge, which one can use to differentiate between right and wrong.

Derived from the Qur'an, 2:30: "... Certainly, I (God) know (the human elements) what you (angels) do not know (angels only have knowledge of 'animal elements' such as enmity, wickedness and mischief)"; Amiru'l-Mu'minin `Ali's above statement; Murtada Mutahhari, "History and human evolution", `Ala'uddin Pasargadi, (tran.), in *Al-Tawhid,* 1404 AH, vol. 1, no. 2, pp. 104, 114-19; Muhammad Hosayni Behishti & Javad Bahonar, *Philosophy of Islam,* Salt Lake City, UT: Islamic Publications, n.d., pp. 186-97, 201-5; Murtaza Mutahhari, *Fundamentals of Islamic Thought,* R. Campbell, (tran.), Berkeley: Mizan Press, 1985, pp.25-31; Murtada Mutahhari, "Sociology of the Qur'an: A Critique of Historical Materialism", Mahliqa Qara'i (tran.) in *Al-Tawhid,* 1404 AH, vol. 1, no. 4, p. 90; Ali Shari`ati, *Marxism and other Western Fallacies,* R. Campbell (tran.), Berkeley: Mizan Press, 1980, pp. 24-6, the two main natural elements made in man are: 1)Human elements namely: a) Brain; b) Intellect, intelligence, the faculty of knowing; c) Self- consciousness; d) Faith; e) Wishes for perfection; f) Knowledge; and 2) Animal elements namely: a) Desire - such as sexual desire, eating and drinking; b) Like to settle at birth place; c) Building relationship by means of blood connection; d) Enmity; e) Materialistic etc.

[36] Imam Khumayni, *Risalah Nawin,* `Abdu'l-Karim Bi Azar Shirazi (collector), Qum: Daftar Nashr Farhang Islami, 1373 AH, vol. 4, p. 81.

[37] *Qur'an,* 2:133; 21:108.

- *Al-Muqarrabi* (the one who is close to God)[39]

According to Imam Khumayni (ra), the above-mentioned group of people are known in a position of as *a'la `illiyyin* (those who are high in the eyes of God).[40] After completing the above stages, one must further ascend from one stage of devoutness to God to the other as follows:

- *As-Salih* (the pious one)[41]

- *As-Shahid* (the martyr)[42]

- *As-Sadiq* (the one who is most truthful and obedient to the Divine commands)[43]

- *An-Nabi* (the prophet)[44]

The above four groups of people are known as *awliya' Allah* (God friends). God friends in an *a'la `illiyyin*, both are known as *as-habu'l-yamin* (those who are on the right side)[45]

8.3   How to Educate Women

The following are a few suggestions on how to educate Muslim women in the Muslim countries:

The *Shari'ah* law should be made one of the core subjects in schools in Muslim countries. Here, the details of the *Shari'ah* law

---

[38] *Ibid.*, 2:97,223,238,248; 16:11.

[39] *Ibid.*, 2:177,241; 3:75,114,132,137.

[40] *Ibid.*, 3:44.

[41] *Ibid.*, 3:57; Imam Khumayni, *Risalah Nawin*, `Abdu'l-Karim Bi Azar Shirazi (collector), Qum: Daftar Nashr Farhang Islami, 1373 AH, vol. 4, p. 81.

[42] *Qur'an*, 3:45,113; 21:105.

[43] *Ibid.*, 19:58.

[44] *Ibid.*, 2:23,31; 11:27,51.

[45] Imam Khumayni, *Risalah Nawin*, `Abdu'l-Karim Bi Azar Shirazi (collector), Qum: Daftar Nashr Farhang Islami, 1373 AH, vol. 4, p. 81.

should be emphasised.

As a whole, the world is lacking educated women writers, who are able to discuss the Shari`a law. Alongside this, there should be more grants and scholarships offered to women, so that they may further their studies on the *Shari'ah* law at a higher level. After completing their studies, they should be encouraged and funded to write in relation to this subject.

At the moment, discussions are focused on explaining the rights of women. But there is hardly any focus on how to educate Muslim women in *Shari'ah* law. In families, the *Shari'ah* law should also be emphasised. Accordingly, their children will develop a better understanding of the *Shari'ah* law and consequently, this will reduce moral decay among Muslim teenagers.

The Muslim NGO's all over the world should group together and discuss the arrangement of programs regarding the education of *Shari'ah* law for women in Muslim countries. Muslim governments and NGOs should carry out researches into the effectiveness of the education of *Shari'ah* law. Research findings will then help in formulating strategies depending on the specific nation. Religious scholars from all over the world should discuss and decide on the most important aspects of the *Shari'ah* law, which should be endowed for every Muslim woman.

When all the above suggestions are fulfilled, women will have the opportunity to educate their children according to the *Shari'ah* law. Yet, at the present, the lack of emphasis that is placed on the education of the *Shari'ah* law among the Muslim women lays the ground for moral decomposition amongst the Muslim generations.

Conclusion

Derived from the Qur'an and the Sunnah, the *Shari'ah* law covers all aspects of life, ideal and perfect in every way. It is a complete system of law and procedures for man. However, nowadays, Muslim women still lack the proper education in this field. This is due to the impact of Western colonisation on Muslim countries.

This phenomenon brings about moral devastation among the present Muslim generation – resulting from the fact that women are the educators of families.

Every single party concerned towards the education of Muslim women should make collaborative efforts. Alongside, a joint effort should also be made for professionalism in the education of the *Shari'ah* law, which aims to produce more women thinkers and scholars.

All Muslim nations should accept the reality that Muslim women are intelligent beings who may achieve the same high level of intellectualism as men.

Muslim women need intellectuals from amongst themselves so as to solve their own problems which arise due to the changing of time, place and situation. In consequence, their status will rise above that of women of other religions. Armed with willpower and spirit, they will be more determined in achieving their life goals and will also be capable of competing with others, and hence will become courageous in facing the challenges in life.

Bibliography

A Dictionary of Modern Written Arabic, 1980.

A Learner's Arabic-English Dictionary, 1978.

Abduh, As-Shaykh Muhammad. 1985, *Nahju'l-Balagha*, Beirut: Daru'l-Balagha.

Abi Da'ud, Abi Da'ud Sulayman ibn al-Ash`ath as-Sij-jistani. 1994, *Sunan Abi Da'ud*, 2 vols., Beirut: Daru'l-Fiqr.

Ahmad Hanbal, Ahmad bin Muhammad bin Hanbal. 1975, *Al-Musnad*, 20 vols., Egypt: Daru'l-Ma`arif.

Ahsan, Abd Allah. 1987-88, "The Identity Crisis within the Modern Muslim Nation-States" in *Al-Tawhid*, vol. 2, pp. 97-130.

Al-Kawakini, al-`Allamatu'l-Hujjah al-Haj as-Sayyid Ghulamarda al-Kasa'i. 1397 AH, *Manaqib az-Zahra'*, Qum: Matba`ah Mahr.

As-Shafi`i, Abi `Abdillah Muhammad Idris. 1983, *Al-Umm*, 8 vols., Beirut: Daru'l-Fiqr.

As-Shaybani, Muhammad b. al-Hasan. (narrator) n.d., *Muwatta' al-Imam Malik*, `Abdu'l-Latif, `Abdu'l-Wahhab. (ed.), Al-Maktabah Al-`Alamiyyah.

Awliya'i, Mustafa. 1440 AH, "Outlines of the development of the science of narrations" in *Al-Tawhid,* Qara'i, A. Q. (tran.), vol. 1, no. 1, pp. 26-37.

Campbell, R. (tran.) 1980, *Marxism and other Western Fallacies*, Berkeley: Mizan Press.

Campbell, R. (tran.). 1985, *Fundamentals of Islamic Thought*, Berkeley: Mizan Press.

Coulson, N. J. 1971, *A History of Islamic Law*, Edinburgh: Edinburgh University Press.

Enayat, Hamid. 1983, "Iran: Khumayni's concept of the guardianship of the juriconsult", in *Islam in the Political Process*, Piscatori, James. (ed.), Cambridge, London, New York, New Rochelle, Melbourne, Sydney: Cambridge University Press, pp.160-80.

Fyzee, Asaf A. A. 1955, *Outlines of Muhammadan Law*, London: Oxford University Press.

Guillaume. (tran.) 1978, *The life of Muhammad: A Translation of Ishaq's Sirat Rasul Allah*, New York: Oxford University Press.

Hallaq, Wael B. 1986, "On the Origins of the Controversy about the Existence of Mujtahids and the Gate of Ijtihad" in *Stvdia Islamica* lxviii, pp. 9-141.

Hodgson, Marshall G. S. 1974, *The Venture of Islam*, Chicago and London: The University of Chicago Press.

Hourani, Albert. 1984, *Arabic Thought in the Liberal Age 1798-1939*, New York: Cambridge University Press.

Ibn Manzur, Abi al-Fadl Jamaluddin Muhammad ibn Marqam ibn Manzur al-Ifriqi al-Misri. n.d., *Lisanu'l-`Arab*, Beirut: Dar Sadr.

Jannati, Muhammad Ibrahim. 1988, "The Meaning of Ijtihad" in *Al-Tawhid,* Qara'i, Martyr Mahliqa. (tran.), vol. 3&4, pp. 179-200.

Keputusan Mesyuarat Jawatankuasa Fatwa Kebangsaan (*Results of the National Verdict Committee Meeting*), Islamic Centre of Malaysia, Prime Minister Department, Kuala Lumpur, (Unpublished, no date).

Khumayni, Imam. 1373 AH, *Risalah Nowin*, Shirazi, `Abdu'l-Karim Bi Azar. (collector), Qum: Daftar Nashr Farhang Islami, vol. 4.

Lambton, A. K. S. "A Reconsideration of the Position of the Marja` al-Taqlid and the Religious Institution" in *Stvdia Islamica* xx, pp. 114-35.

Lammens, H. 1929, *Islam: Beliefs and Institution*, London: Methuen & Co. Ltd.

Latif, Danial. 1973, "Rationalism and Muslim Law" in *Islam and the Modern Age*, vol. 4, no. 4, pp. 43-70.

Levy, Reuben. 1962, *The Social Structure of Islam*, Cambridge: Cambridge University Press.

Lonsdale and Ragg, Laura. (eds. & trans. from Italian), 1980, *The Gospel of Barnabas,*. Karachi: Begum Aisha Bawani Waqf, 8th edition (1st edition: 1907, Oxford: The Clarendon Press).

Modern Islamic Political Thought. 1988, Austin: University of Texas Press.

Muslim, Abi'l-Husayn Muslim ibni'l-Hajjaji'l-Qushayri an-Naysaburi. 1983, *Sahih Muslim*, 5 vols., Beirut: Daru'l-Fiqr.

Mutahhari, Murtada. n.d. *Al-Harakat al-Islamiyyah fi'l-Qarni arrabi` `Ashara'l-Hijri*, Albany, California: Muslim Student Association (Persian Speaking Group).

Muzaffar, Chandra. 1987, *Islamic Resurgence in Malaysia*, Petaling Jaya: Penerbit Fajar Bakti.

Pasargadi, `Ala'uddin. (tran.) 1404 AH, "History and Human Evolution" in *Al-Tawhid*, vol. 1, no. 2, pp. 95-122.

Qadri, Anwar Ahmad. 1973, *Islamic Jurisprudence in the Modern World*, Lahore: Sh. Muhammad Ashraf (2nd rev. edition).

Qara'i, `Ali Quli. (tran.) 1986, "Glimpses of the Nahj al-Balaghah" in *Al-Tawhid*, vol. 3, no. 3, pp. 119-27.

Qara'i, `Ali Quli. (tran.) 1987, "The Role of Ijtihad in Legislation" in *Al-Tawhid*, vol. 4, no. 2, pp. 21-52.

Qara'i, A. Q. (tran.) 1988, "The Beginning of Shi`i Ijtihad" in *Al-Tawhid* vol. 1, no. 1, pp. 45-64.

Qara'i, Mahliqa. (tran.) 1984, "Islam and the Modern Age" in *Al-Tawhid* vol. 1, no. 2, pp. 60-80.

Qara'i, Mahliqa. (tran.) 1986, "Ijtihad in the Imamiyyah Tradition" in *Al-Tawhid*, vol. 4, no. 1, pp. 26-48.

Qara'i, Mahliqa. 1404 AH, "Sociology of the Qur'an: A Critique of Historical Materialism" in *Al-Tawhid*, vol. 1, no. 4, pp. 77-135.

Reza, Sayed Ali. (tran.) 1985, *Nahjul Balagha*, New York: Tahrike

Tarsile Qur'an, Inc. (4th rev. edition).

Sachedina, Abdulaziz Abdulhussein. 1988, *The Just Ruler (Al-Sultan al-'Adil) in Shi'ite Islam*, New York: Oxford University Press.

Schacht, J. 1964, *An Introduction to Islamic Law*, Oxford: The Clarendon Press, pp.70-71.

Shariati, Ali. 1981, *Man and Islam,* Marjani, Fatollah. (tran.), Houston: FILINC.

Shaykh al-Mufid. 1981, *Kitab al-Irshad, the Book of Guidance*, Howard, I. K. A. (tran.), Elmhurst, New York: Tharike Tarsile Qur'an.

Tabataba'i, Sayyid Muhammad Husayn. 1983, *Al-Mizan fi Tafsir al-Qur'an*, Beirut: Mu'assasah Al-'Alami li'l-Matbu'at, 21 vols.

Tabataba'i, Sayyid Muhammad Husayn. 1983, *Al-mizan*, Rizvi, Sayyid Saeed Akhtar. (tran.), Tehran: WOFIS, 3 vols.

Tyan, E. 1978, "Kadi" in *Encyclopaedia of Islam* (new edition) vol. 4, pp. 373-75.

Watt, W. W. Montgomery. 1974, "The Closing of the Door of Ijtihad" in *Orientalia Hispanica*, vol. 1, pp. 675-8.

Weiss, Anita M. 1986, *Islamic Reassertion in Pakistan*, New York: Syracuse University Press.

Zettersteen, K. V. and Pellat, C. H. 1960, "Ahmad Abu Du'ad" in *Encyclopaedia of Islam* (new edition), A-B, pp. 271.

Article 9

Marginalisation and Appropriation: Women and Mosques in Senegal

Kafia Cantone

Abstract

This paper aims to discuss the issue of women in the mosque, by looking at contemporary mosques in Senegal and their use of space, along with their justifications for the use of such space.

It is hoped that the material presented will draw attention to the non-monumental aspect of the mosque. This paper will then discuss the physical nature of mosque buildings. Our aim is to put forward some theoretical approaches derived from the methodology used in the field. We will briefly refer to the works of Western phenomenologists and Muslim anthropologists in order to open the discourse between Western academia and Muslim scholarship and to show the possible dialogue, and even the potential marriage, between the two discourses.

The paper will therefore consider the implications of the rise in female mosque attendance-particularly amongst the youth-in the chosen region in order to answer the broader question of whether women can or cannot frequent the mosque, from both a practical and legal perspective.

Introduction

This paper sets out to explore how space can be used to marginalise women from the mosque and how this notion is being challenged and re-interpreted by young women who are using distinctive dress for appropriating mosques in the contemporary setting of Senegal. Owing to the scarce documentation and archaeological evidence concerning the place allocated to women in the mosque at the time of the Prophet (saws), the focus of the paper will be the contemporary mosque as a building, viewed in its essential, non-monumental form. By non-monumental, I mean the humble origins of the primordial 'concept of mosque' at the time of the Prophet (saws), whose evolution through time and space has resulted in regional diversity or 'regionalism' - both in architectural or stylistic terms as well as in terms of religious practice, i.e. lived space.

I will be exploring this question mainly from a multi-disciplinary approach, focusing on various aspects related to women's mosque attendance. This includes contemporary religious movements as well as examples of contemporary mosque architecture from an area that has been largely neglected, Senegal. The reasons for such a choice are summarised below:

- A male, Western, non-Muslim bias in literature on Islam in general and Ethnocentrism in both Western and Muslim scholarship dealing with Sub-Saharan Africa, in particular: the need for Islamic Anthropology.

- The diversity of practices and extent to which Islam is practised in the region. This includes traditional forms of Islam represented by the Sufi *turuq*[1] and the phenomenon of 'Sunnification' and its contribution to the Islamisation of space. Women in mosques are marginalised by the *turuq,* in contrast to changing attitudes towards women praying in the mosque and their increasing presence in public places of worship as a result of the phenomenon of 'Sunnification'.

- The poor attention given to Islamic architecture, especially contemporary, in the area. This also includes a discussion of how regional variety epitomises a variety of practice.

- Other boundaries: the instance of non-spatial boundaries such as dress code to accentuate the differences in ideology, practice and segregation of the sexes in public spaces.

During my fieldwork in Senegal (November 2000-May 2001) I was actively engaging with women who frequent the mosque, getting them to fill in questionnaires as well as participating in interviews with me. This gave rise to a dynamic exchange between habitual users of a particular mosque and guest users, such as myself. As a Muslim, I was participating in the prayers and study

---

[1] Arabic, sing. *tariqa,* path or way.

circles as well as using these experiences to learn about how Islam is practised in Senegal.

Although this approach does not strictly fit into the categories of anthropology or ethnography, 'radical empiricism' in the works of Phenomenologists such as Michael Jackson and Paul Stoller as well as Muslim anthropologists such as Merryl Davies, have provided the basis of my methodology. These authors advocate the abolition of the 'classical' object (i.e. the studied) - subject (i.e. the one who studies) approach and the institution of the total participation and engagement between the person who studies and the people he/she is studying. Thus, by focusing on the commonalities and even the potential marriage between the two methodologies, it would be possible to open the dialogue between Western academia and Muslim scholarship. There is not necessarily a contradiction between being 'academic' in the Western sense and being a Muslim. Indeed, part of the motivation behind choosing this subject is to work towards a *rapprochement* between these two poles and eradication of some of the ethnocentrism described below. As Davies says,

> What the encounter with other people tells us about ourselves is often a significant learning technique, if used consciously (…) our own intellectual emotional biases are the stumbling blocks to understanding others. [2]

9.1   Marginalisation of Sub-Saharan Africa from the Ethnocentric View of the Muslim World

Up until recently, sub-Saharan Africa has been excluded from the areas traditionally associated with Islam: the Near East, North Africa and parts of Asia. Yet Islam's presence in Africa has been established for over a millennium, leaving a profound imprint on the social, economical, and political as well as cultural, linguistic

---

[2] M. W. Davies, *Knowing One Another: Shaping Islamic Anthropology*, London/NY: Mansell Publication, 1988, p. 7.

fabric of the societies it made contact with (Prussin: 1986).

Misconceptions of Islam in Africa have led to what has been referred to as 'ethnocentrism' - both in Western and Muslim scholarship. This is particularly surprising in contemporary Muslim authors, when from the Middle Ages onwards such authors as al-Idrisi, el-Bekri, Ibn Battuta, Ibn Khaldun, to mention only a few, proved to be a combination of anthropologists, ethnographers, geographers and historians doubtless inspired by the manifold references in the Qur'an that instigate the human race to get to know other members of its tribes and nations. Trans-Saharan trade also contributed significantly to the spread of Islam in the region in the early centuries of its development.

This is precisely what constitutes the foundation of Merryl Davies' argument for the establishment of an Islamic Anthropology, which could potentially be merged with new, positive trends in Western anthropology (Davies, *op. cit.*). Davies proposes finding commonalities with other people rather than seeing them as 'objects' of study or, for that matter, regarding them as inferior because they are non-Muslim or even a different denomination of Muslim. It is fundamental that such an attitude should be developed in Muslim scholarship if it is to be rid of the prevalent prejudice it receives from its ethnocentric Western counterpart. This does not mean that Muslims should strive to adopt their own version of being 'politically correct', but we should bear in mind that no dialogue is possible if the attitude of spiritual superiority and complacency is not removed from our attitudes.

Within the marginalisation discourse, whether it be of sub-Saharan Africa or Muslim anthropology, the main focus of the paper will be on the marginalisation of women from mosques in Senegal - i.e. spatial marginalisation. Formerly, the religious panorama of the region was dominated by the Sufi *turuq*. Although numerically they still make up the majority of the Muslim population, the rise of the 'Reformist' movement, which has gathered momentum in the last 10-15 years, has created an ideological shift or better a shift in ideological perspective, particularly amongst the youth. 'Young' women (that is, anyone below the age of menopause) who were previously deterred from going to the mosque by 'traditional' society[3], are now learning - often in the mosque itself - that they not only can frequent the mosque, but that the Prophet (saws) himself gave instructions for women not to be prevented from doing so. I have referred to this phenomenon as 'Sunnification'[4], that is the increasing emphasis on the Sunnah and its interpretation through the *ulema*, rather than through the intermediary of a *marabout* (religious leader/ intermediary in the context of the *turuq*) as this seems to be the best way to describe current trends in the region.

Since the 50s an increasing number of Senegalese students have travelled to the great centres of learning in the Arab world (especially North Africa and the Middle East, but also the Sudan), returning to their country to teach what they learned of 'pure' Islam. Today many of the 'propagators' of orthodox Sunni Islam are formed in Islamic studies as well as in classical Arabic within Senegal.[5]

---

[3] By this I mean the mainstream adherence to the Sufi *turuq*.

[4] Although there is an increasing trend to talk about 'Islamism' when referring to a resurgence in Islamic practice, it tends to be used as an umbrella term which often fails to reveal the nuances in the so-called Islamic movement. According to my own observations, I think it is possible to identify a general move towards the adoption of the Sunna, however, different groups have their own interpretations and justifications of their vision of the Sunna of the Prophet. Hence, in the case of Senegal, the group known as *Jamaatou Ibadou Rahmane* differs considerably from those who identify themselves with the Salafiyya, for instance: they both adhere with the principles of the Sunna as opposed to local (Sufi) expressions of Islam, but they in turn would totally disassociate themselves to a parallel 'Islamist' movement that adheres to Shi'ah principles. Hence the specific term of Sunnification.

[5] The city of Thiès is one such important training centre and headquarters of one of the most prominent Sunni organisations, the *Jamaatou Ibadou Rahmane*. Because they were amongst the first to put into practice the wearing of the veil for women and beards for men, the expression *Ibadou* has endured as a popular term to refer to those who practice the Sunna, rather than follow a *marabout*.

9.2   The Phenomenon of Sunnification and Increasing Women's Mosque Attendance: Islamisation of Space

Many of the returning students from the Arab world have set up their own classes, which may take place in the mosque or in the *madrasa*, or even in the student's homes. Several women I met chose the latter system as this meant being able to tailor the lessons according to their individual needs and levels.

It is in this way that both men and women learn about their rights and duties in Islam, which in turn strengthens their practice and consequently increases their attendance in the mosque. This increased attendance goes beyond the observance of the five daily prayers and Friday prayer, for Sunni mosques often offer classes in *tafsir, tajwid, narrations, fiqh* as well as Arabic and are open from dawn prayer to night prayers, rather than closing immediately after every prayer.[6] This phenomenon of returning to the 'open mosque' practice of the Prophet can be identified with the 'Islamisation of space:'

> ...Attempts to 're-islamicise' society by encouraging individuals to practice Islam in daily life and bridge the gap between religious discourse and practical realities through prayer, fasting, segregation of space between the two genders, veiling of women and so on. Thus, Islamisation from the 'bottom up' does not necessarily entail asking women to return to the home, but rather that the sexes are separated in public.[7]

The Islamisation of space may also involve the crossing of socially accepted boundaries. A case in point, in some mosques, is to allow menstruating women and/or women with children to attend the mosque. Such facilities - usually mats laid outside the back

---

[6] The custom amongst the Tijanis, for instance, is to turn off the lights as soon as the *maghrib* prayer is over and the men proceed to sit round a white sheet in a circle to recite the *wazifa*.

[7] Ask & Tjomsland, *Women and Islamization*, 1998, p. 2.

entrance to the mosque - mean that women could participate on a continuous basis, rather than having to interrupt their classes every month or for the first few months after their children are born. This marks a stark contrast to the *turuq* who do not admit women, as mentioned above, unless they have passed the age of menopause. However, not all Sunni mosques are this accommodating to women's needs. Again, theological interpretation may be at the root of the prohibition of women with periods or young children.[8]

9.3   Spatial Marginalisation and the Concept of Mosque

From a spatial perspective, the types of space that women are allocated and which they then appropriate are important in determining the transposition of ideology into practice. In other words, the articulation and 'genderisation' of space in the mosque reflects, microcosmically, what woman's space is on the macrocosmic level of society. First, however, let us define what a mosque is.

Etymologically, the word *masjid* designates only a place of prostration from the root *sajada*, to prostrate. A prostration can be made anywhere and not necessarily in a building. As the well-known narration of the Prophet (saws) states: *"wa ja'alte li el-ardh masjidan wa tahura"*.[9] There is, in fact, no real distinction between 'sacred' and 'secular' space in Islam because they are essentially inseparable. Whenever and wherever a Muslim takes off his or her shoes and makes ablutions in order to perform prayer, s/he has automatically entered into sacred space, which may measure no more than the prayer mat or the clean earth under his/her feet.

This being the case, one has to refer to prayer space as something not measurable or even necessarily tangible, but rather as a

---

[8] According to Abu Dawud (*Tahara*, bab 92:103) and Ibn Maja (*Tahara*, bab 117:123) menstruating women cannot attend the mosque: quoted in *Encyclopaedia of Islam* under *masdjid*.

[9] 'And we made the earth as your mosque (place of prostration)....' From *Bukhari*, p. 335 and others. Quoted in M. A. Lo, *Keifa nu'idu lilmasjidi makanatahu*, p.5.

conceptual/psychological/spiritual domain. In other words, Islam embraces both 'symbolic' space as well as 'designed' (physical or architectural) space, which is at once sacred and secular. Within the unified space of the mosque, there are 'locales', or the small spaces created by each individual worshipper who is at the same time linked to his neighbour by means of co-ordinated movements behind the leader or Imam of the prayer. The emphasis on the prayer is harmony, homogeneity and unity - a way of manifesting the multitude of mankind submitting their individual and collective wills to the Supreme Unity (Allah).

Furthermore, such functional simplicity contrasts with Christianity, for instance, because the Church can "rely on powerful visual symbols to help convey its message"[10] -whereas Islam relies on the Holy Book and rejects images. The 'puritanical' aspect of the mosque as a construction has filtered through to Reformist movements throughout the centuries. In West Africa, such was the case with the *jihadist* movements of the 19th century and can equally be perceived in contemporary 'orthodox' Sunni movements, as we shall see.

In Islam the mosque - or the concept of mosque as we shall refer to it henceforth - came to combine both secular as well as spiritual functions. Indeed, this combination is made explicit in the Friday congregational prayer. On Friday the requirement to gather the faithful for communal prayer arises, (*yawm ul-juma'a*) Friday, when the congregation literally gathers in '*jamaa'*. This would take place in a place of gathering (*majma'a*) or in the purpose-built (*masjid ul-jaami'*) or Main Mosque. It was, and still is, on this occasion that the sermon would be pronounced before the communal prayer commenced.

Nevertheless, even in such an atmosphere of unison, space is not entirely uniform. As we shall see, the issue of 'gendered space' can be the cause of this disunity. We need to return to the concept of

---

[10] M. Frishman, "Islam and the form of the Mosque" in *The Mosque*, 1997, p. 32.

mosque as conceived at the time of the Prophet (saws) for this contains the key to understanding the subsequent or resulting 'fragmentation' of the original homogenous space in the Prophet's mosque in Medina.

From the prototype of mosques, the Prophet's (saws) Mosque in Medina[11], we have an idea of how it was intended that space be used, and how it was used. As was mentioned above, the role of the mosque was not restricted to gathering the faithful for prayer, as it did not only serve liturgical purposes. The fact that the Prophet (saws) would pronounce sermons on Fridays, teach the religion to his followers, meet delegations, resolve disputes, as well as live in his quarters that bordered on the mosque – this combination of activities bestowed on the mosque something of a multi-functional arena combining politics, education, law, prayer and domestic life, all of which were diverse aspects of a unified space:

> In the Prophet's (saws) Mosque, from its very beginning, there was no separation of divine and earthly authority.[12]

As testified by the narration literature, women were just as much participants in the mosque as men. Jabir Abdullah reports that after the Friday sermon, the Prophet used to make a separate address to the female congregation.[13] And although the Prophet (saws) stated they could not be prevented from praying in the mosque[14], they had to occupy the back rows, i.e. those behind the men. Demarcation, let alone segregation, of this space was unheard of until well after

---

[11] "Although the Prophet's House can not have been the origins of the mosque, it remains possible that the Prophet's Mosque was the prototype of mosques in Islam." Johns, J. "The 'House of the Prophet' and the Concept of the Mosque" in *Oxford Studies in Islamic Art*, 1999, vol. 9, Part 2, p. 103.

[12] J. Johns, *op. cit.*, 1999, p. 93.

[13] *Bukhari*, vol. 2:42. Quoted in N. Awde, *Women in Islam: an Anthology from the Quran and Narrations*, 2000, pp. 75-76.

[14] Already under Umar's caliphate, women were being discouraged from attending the mosque but the *narrations* of the Prophet, "Do not prevent the female servants of God from the mosques of God" (*Bukhari*, vol. 2:10), prevented Umar from stopping them.

the death of the Prophet (saws). According to Muslim feminists[15] amongst others, most of the evidence points to the segregation of women (both in the mosque as well as in society) at the time of the Abbasids, in the 9th century. The issue of the mixing of the *mahram* and non-*mahram* men and women in public spaces was increasingly disapproved of in Muslim societies as a result of pre-Islamic practices, rather than being something emphasised by the Qur'an.

Be this as it may, what is clear from historical evidence is that women were increasingly marginalized from their legitimate space in the mosque. In accordance with three of the four main schools of Sunni thought (Hanafi, Maliki and Hanbali), the presence of women in the mosque is the cause of (*fitna*) evil.[16] Older women, however, may attend because they are less likely to cause (*fitna*) evil. The most extreme view is voiced by the Shafi'is who maintain that women can be prevented outright, seeing as they cannot make journeys unaccompanied by a *mahram*, the only exception being the pilgrimage to the Ka'abah.

> We are thus faced with what appears to be a discrepancy between the Prophet's practice and the Shari'ah recommendations.[17]

In the subsequent section, we shall see how regional interpretation and application of the rulings of the Sunni *madhahib* leads to different practices and corresponding spatial configurations.

9.4   Regional Variety: the Case of Senegal

Having looked at the broader panorama of the mosque and its function, we will now turn to the more particular, regional case-study in order to trace the interplay between 'idealised' or historical space and the particular or 'lived' space in Senegal. Our

---

[15] Laila Ahmed, Fatima Mernissi, Amina Wadud-Muhsen and others.

[16] Arabic for temptation, trial, charm, attractiveness, sedition.

[17] A. Sayyed, "Early Sunni Discourse on Women's Mosque Attendance" in *ISIM Newsletter*, vol. 7, no. 1, p. 10.

focus will be the examples of Senegalese mosques where space - formerly allocated to old women only - is being appropriated by young, veiled women who are turning to the Islamic sources (Qur'an and Sunnah) in order to claim their rightful place in the mosque and, by extension, in Muslim society.

Previously we saw how there is no demarcation between sacred and secular space in the mosque. The questions that should now be asked are: Where does the boundary of the mosque end and how far can it be expanded/extended through human agency? Does the building act as boundary or can this space be transcended? How do male-female dynamics fit into this paradigm?

In some Muslim countries, particularly during the 'peak season', such as during the holy month of *Ramadhan* or during *Eid-ul-Adha*, the familiar sight of worshippers praying on the tarmac around the mosque will not be unusual. I have personally experienced this in Senegal, where even the weekly Friday prayer can similarly spill out of bounds. Boundaries that are usually defined by built space are suddenly transformed into amorphous entities that barely seem to have a beginning or an end. What is interesting is that during these times of intense religious activity, boundaries between men and women appear to be relaxed. Herein lies the paradox.

In a society where, at least within the precincts of the mosques men and women are clearly separated (often in two separate buildings, or the men inside the mosque and the women in the courtyard), during the holy month of *Ramadhan*, for instance, the men's overflow may almost overlap with its female counterpart. We are thus faced with a situation where,

Boundaries may be marked or unmarked, clear or fuzzy, agreed or disputed, acknowledged by others or ignored, constant and consistent or variable.[18]

But whereas religious fervour reaches its zenith during the holy month of *Ramadhan* for the majority of Senegalese Muslims who are followers of various Sufi *turuq*, a very different case finds expression in the Sunni movement (also known locally as the *Mouvement Islamique*) whose recourse to the sources of Islam (the Qur'an and the Sunnah) result in different spatial cognition.

Sunni or *Ibadou Rahman* mosques, as they are known locally, have resorted to different ways of gendering the mosque. In some cases, there has been a conscious return to the practice of the Prophet (swas), i.e. where the women simply pray behind the men, unless there is not enough space for them; in other cases, a curtain has been placed between the men's area and the women's area; in yet others, if a separate building already exists, special arrangements are made, such as giving women visibility access previously denied to them.[19]

In other words, we are witnessing a process of re-evaluation of the existing Muslim tradition in the area and this process is making some of the formerly fixed boundaries a lot more porous and therefore flexible than they were in the past. Crucial in this process are the issues of visibility and audibility: can women hear as well as see what is going on in the main prayer hall? Are they able to participate equally in the lesson of the sermon as well as in the prayer?

When the men's building is separate from the women's, such

---

[18] A. Rapoport, "Spatial Organization and the Built Environment" in *The Encyclopaedia of Anthropology*, Tim Ingold (ed.), London: Routledge, 1994, p. 482.

[19] There may be a better definition of this. I am referring to ways of allowing women to participate visually as well as audibly to the prayer/sermon given in the men's section.

issues are essential if women are being considered as having equal access to the mosque. Yet for many centuries and in many parts of the Muslim world, including Senegal, this has not been the case. In some regions where women are relegated to the courtyard, they have to endure the boiling sun or the pouring rain. In others, separate outbuildings have only recently been fitted with often malfunctioning loudspeakers, and although these may provide some form of audible access to the main mosque, they certainly do nothing for the visual side.

This is now changing. Especially, though not exclusively, in Sunni milieus, the issue of visibility is becoming increasingly prominent: windows are being carved out of walls that previously acted as barriers, transparent instead of opaque curtains are being raised. Thus, ideological shifts are translated into spatial terms:

> By changing the rules governing the use of these buildings and by altering their semi-fixed feature elements, they can, of course, employ these spaces differently - that is, they can create new systems of settings within them.[20]

Those who pronounced themselves to be Salafis[21] -in my questionnaires- were generally more preoccupied with gender mixing than with other groups. This was manifested in the sexual segregation in the mosque. In the university mosque of Dakar, for instance, an opaque curtain screens off the female section. However, the question of visibility is being raised and the

---

[20] A. Rapoport, "Spatial Organization and the Built Environment" in *The Encyclopaedia of Anthropology*, Tim Ingold (ed.), London: Routledge, 1994, pp. 489-90.

[21]This term is used generically. The various groups in Senegal who identify themselves with the *Mouvement Islamique* are influenced by the *Islah* (Reform) movement based on the principles of the Salafiyya. There are, however, different currents, some of which adhere more literally to the teachings of the founders of the movement than others. Indeed, in data gathered in my fieldwork, some respondents would describe themselves simply as 'Sunni' (i.e. conforming to all four schools of Sunni thought), whereas others would specify adherence to the Salafiyya.

opaqueness of the curtain is being called into question. The Salafi mosque, by contrast, has very different ideas about segregation. This mosque, consisting of a simple roofed enclosure that literally sat astride the main road, uses this very road to separate the men from the women. If visibility is not totally impaired, the question of audibility with a busy main road acting as 'gender separator', cannot be much more inadequate.

9.5   Boundaries and Barriers: Islamicising Dress Codes

Barriers between men and women do not only take on the form of the built environment: they are also expressed through clothing. One of the most explicit manifestations of such a barrier is the *hijab*, whose role can be seen as a tool of Islamisation:

> Islamisation often includes the adoption of certain 'universal' Islamic cultural forms and practices, notably changes in the female dress code; donning the veil (Arabic hijab) by women is to Western eyes most conspicuous, and is often interpreted as an icon or return to orthodox Islamic narrations.[22]

Women in Senegal, despite the overwhelming majority of the population being Muslim, do not cover their heads or necks as a rule. Traditional dress, the *grand boubou*, a large square garment with a very low-cut neckline and wide sleeves, is worn in conjunction with a head-wrap and matching *seer*, a kind of petticoat. Nevertheless, those women who have decided to follow the Sunnah, often abandon traditional forms of dress and adopt what can best be described as an international Muslim dress code: scarf pinned under the chin, long-sleeved *jilbabs* or skirts. Furthermore, Salafi women wear an even more distinctive form of clothing: a large veil that comes down to the knees or even further down, a matching skirt and socks. They normally are clad in very sombre colours, such as dark blue, brown or black.

---

[22] K. Ask, & M. Tjomsland, (eds.), *Women and Islamization*, 1998, p. 3.

The message transmitted by any one of these women is explicit: non-Sunni or non-Salafi men know instantly that they are not to shake hands with such women. Thus the veil acts as a mnemonic device to communicate a certain code of behaviour that clearly goes against the custom of the majority of Muslims in Senegal, which involves physical contact between men and women as well as not being bound by an explicitly 'Islamic' dress code. At the same time, the veil - customarily demonized by Western academia as well as by Western-influenced Muslims - has now become a symbol which grants women access to previously barred public space.[23] Such a space is embodied in the mosque, especially in Senegal where the mainstream form of Islam, namely the *turuq*, marginalises young women. Ironically, although dress-wise followers of the *turuq* cover their heads only to pray, their regulations with regards to frequenting the mosque are intransigent. The *Ibadou's*, by contrast, are intransigent when it comes to covering, but considerably relaxed when it comes to frequenting the mosque.[24] Thus, the *hijab* carries both the negative connotation of 'barrier' (preventing physical contact between the two sexes, for instance) and the positive connotation of 'boundary'. The latter defines or marks out 'woman's space' and empowers women to access public space. If we were to analyse the segregation of space in the mosque from a phenomenological perspective, it would follow that:

> Spatial experience is not innocent and neutral, but invested with power relating to age, gender, social position and relationships with others.[25]

---

[23] *Ibid.*, p. 7.

[24] The 'Orthodox' Sunni interpretation of the same *narrations* relating to women frequenting the mosque, namely that it is not obligatory for women to attend the Friday prayer, leads to the conclusion that women (regardless of their age) are not to be prevented from going to the mosque provided that they meet the conditions of conduct and the appropriate dress-code.

[25] C. Tilly, *A Phenomenology of Landscape: Peace, Paths and Monuments*, 1994, p.11.

Somewhat of a paradox, however, is the fact that many young women have learned about their right to frequent the mosque from the mosque itself. Indeed, women often start wearing *hijab* at the same time as they start to frequent the mosque more assiduously and with the motivation of learning more about the religion. The inter-connection between education and 'reform' could not be more evident than in the case of women. Their external appearance, their conduct, the places they frequent – all act as differentiation markers from their non-Sunni counterparts, the majority of whom are intent on following the latest Western fashion, bleaching their skin and adding hair extensions. For such women -who practice the religion without observing the Islamic instructions on dress- the incompatibility of their lifestyle with the practice of the five daily prayers gradually leads to the realisation that fashion is secondary to the dictates of Divine law.

Conclusion

The paper has explored several aspects of marginalisation: Firstly, on a literary level, and how both Western and Muslim scholarship has tended to marginalise sub-Saharan Africa; and on the spatial and social level, in the case of 'traditional' expressions of Islam in Senegal, where we examined the marginalisation of women. Boundaries can take the form of both built and non-built forms: we saw how in the case of the so-called *Ibadous,* spatial segregation is being re-interpreted according to the practices at the time of the Prophet (saws) resulting in an 'Islamisation' of space, and that the veil acts as the tool with which to access this previously banned arena.

From a methodological perspective, it was suggested that there be further collaboration between Muslim and Western scholarship, particularly in the field of anthropology, in order to be able to analyse material as far as possible from an internal point of view. Radical empiricism and Islamic anthropology share the same ethos and they could therefore be used in conjunction to this end. Many of the issues brought up here need to be expanded upon, nevertheless, it is hoped that they can serve as a useful introduction to an area that has been little regarded: women's space in the mosque.

Bibliography

Ask, K. & M. Tjomsland, 1998, *Women & Islamization: Contemporary Dimensions of Discourse on Gender Relations*, Oxford: Berg.

Awde, N. 2000, *Women in Islam: an Anthology from the Quran and Narrations*, (*Narrations-s* taken from *Sahih Bukhari* translated by Nicolas Awde), Curzon.

Bourdier, J. P. 1993, "The Rural Mosques of Futa Toro" in *African Arts*, vol. 26, pp. 32-45.

Davies, M. W. 1988, *Knowing One Another: Shaping Islamic Anthropology*, London/NY: Mansell Publication.

Frishman, M. & H. U. Khan, 1997, *The Mosque: History, Architectural Development & Regional Diversity*, London: Thames & Hudson.

Johns, J. 1999, "The 'House of the Prophet' and the Concept of the Mosque" in *Oxford Studies in Islamic Art*, vol. 9, Part 2, pp. 59-112.

Lo, M. A. 1997(1418 AH), *Keifa Nu'idu Lilmasjidi Makanatahu*, Medina: Darul Khudeiri.

Prussin, L. 1986, *Hatumere: Islamic Design in West Africa*, London & Los Angeles: University Of California Press.

Rapoport, A. 1994, "Spatial Organisation and the Built Environment" in *Companion Encyclopaedia of Anthropology*, T. Ingold (ed.), London: Routledge, pp. 460-502.

Sayyed, A. "Early Sunni Discourse on Women's Mosque Attendance" in *ISIM Newsletter*, vol. 7, no. 1, p. 10.

Tilley, C. 1994, *A Phenomenology of Landscape: Places, Paths & Monuments*, Oxford: Berg.

Wehr, H. *Arabic-English Dictionary.*

Article 10

Polygamy: A Synopsis from the Book 'Woman's Rights in Islam' by Murtadha Mutahari

Ali Hussain Al-Hakim

Abstract

This paper will aim to examine the custom of polygamy in comparison with other forms of sexual institutions such as polyandry and sexual communism. The causes which gave rise to polygamy will be discussed and the opinions of Western intellectuals shall be criticised. The reasons why Islam did not abolish the practice of polygamy will be clarified, showing that under certain circumstances it is in fact the right of women. A detailed analysis into the main contributory factor to this, i.e. the outnumbering of men by women, will be provided, showing that this law in fact is a safeguard for women and the society as opposed to some chauvinistic establishment. Finally we will discuss the reasons which have impelled men and women to stand abjectly against this custom.

Introduction

Monogamy (the practice of being married to only one woman at a time) is the most common form of matrimony. The spirit of exclusive relationship or individual and private ownership prevails in it, although this ownership is different from that of wealth or property. In this system, the husband and wife each regard the feelings, sentiments and the sexual benefits of* the other, as exclusively belonging to him or to her.

The opposites of monogamy are polygamy (the custom of having more than one wife at the same time) and sexual communism. The latter, in a sense, may also be regarded as a form of polygamy.

10.1   Sexual Communism

Sexual communism means no exclusiveness. According to this theory, no man should exclusively belong to any particular woman, nor should any woman belong to any particular man. It amounts to complete negation of family life. History and the theories related to pre-historical times do not point to any period when man totally lacked family life and when sexual communism prevailed. What is claimed to have existed among certain barbarian tribes was a midway state between exclusive family life and sexual communism. It is said that among certain tribes it was the usual practice that several brothers jointly married several sisters, or several male members of a clan jointly married several women of another clan.

Will Durant in his book, *History of Civilisations*, vol. 1, writes that at certain places collective marriage was popular in the sense that several male members of a clan jointly married several female members of another clan. For example, it has been customary in Tibet that several brothers have an equal number of sisters as their wives. Nobody knows which sister is the wife of which brother. Every brother cohabits with any of the sisters he likes and a sort of sexual communism exists there. A similar custom existed in ancient England. The custom, which was prevalent among the Jews and some other people of the past and, according to which, after the death of a brother, another brother married his widow, was a remnant of this ancient custom.

10.1.1   Failure of Sexual Communism

In the case of sexual communism, a man cannot align himself with any particular woman, nor a woman with any particular man, and for this reason it could never become popular. Plato, who limited its scope to the ruling class or the 'philosopher-rulers' proposed it. But others did not find his suggestion agreeable and he was obliged to revise his opinion.

During the past century, Frederick Engels, the second father of communism, put forward this idea and strongly advocated it. But it was not accepted by the communist world. It is said that the Soviet Union tried to implement the family theory of Engels, but following some bitter experience ultimately had to recognise monogamy as the official policy.

Polygamy may be regarded as a matter of pride for man, but polyandry has never been and will never be a matter of pride for woman. The reason for this is that man wants the body of woman and woman wants the heart of man. So long as man controls the body of woman, it is immaterial for him if he loses her heart. That is why man attaches no importance to the fact that, in the case of polygamy, he is deprived of the love and devotional sentiments of woman, but for woman the main and the most important thing is the man's heart and his sentiments. If she loses them, she loses everything.

In other words, there are two important elements of matrimonial life, one material and the other sentimental. The material element of matrimony is its sexual aspect, which is at its height during youth and subsequently gradually declines. The sentimental element consists of mutual tender feelings and earnest devotion. It grows and becomes stronger with the passage of time. The nature of woman being different from that of man, she attaches more importance to the sentimental aspect of matrimony. But for man the material aspect is more important or, at least, both the aspects are of equal importance.

We will later quote a lady psychologist who is of the view that woman has a mental disposition of her own. The child develops and grows in her womb and is nursed on her lap. She badly needs the devotion and attachment of her husband in the capacity of the child's father. Only monogamy can meet this requirement.

10.2   Plato's View

It appears that, while enunciating his theory of 'philosopher-rulers', Plato has suggested in his book, 'The Republic', a sort of family socialism for this class. Several leaders of communism in the 19th century also made a similar suggestion, but, as reported by the author of the book, *Freud and the Prohibition of Consanguineous Marriage*, after some bitter experiences, several of the powerful communist countries officially recognised the law of monogamy in 1938.

10.3   Polyandry

Another form of polygamy is polyandry, viz. a woman having more than one husband at the same time. According to Will Durant, this custom is found among certain tribes of Tibet etc.

Al-Bukhari, in his famous corpus of narrations, as-Sahih, reports Aisha as having said that among the pre-Islamic Arabs there existed four kinds of conjugal relations. One of them was the proper marriage that is still being practiced. In this form a man proposes to a girl through her father and, after the fixation of a dowry, becomes responsible for her. There can be no controversy about the father of the children born in such wedlock. There was another kind of marriage, which was called *istibza'a*. To procure a better progeny for himself, the husband selected a man and asked his wife to allow him to have access to her for a fixed period. He himself kept aloof till the pregnancy of the woman. It was a marriage within a marriage and was indulged in with a view to improving the breed. According to another custom, a group of less than ten men established a liaison with a particular woman. On becoming pregnant, she called all of them, and true to the custom of the day, they had to respond to her call. She then selected one of the men to be father of her child out of those who were willing to take on that responsibility. The man, after being so chosen, could not decline to accept paternity of the child.

The fourth kind of conjugal relation was known as prostitution. The prostitutes flew a flag on the top of their houses which served as their distinguishing mark. Anybody could have access to these women. If such a woman gave birth to a child, she called all those who had intimacy with her, and with the help of a physiognomist, determined who was the father of the child. The man concerned had to accept the decision of the physiognomist and to own the child.

These were the forms of the conjugal relations which prevailed in pre-Islamic Arabia. The Prophet (saws) abolished all of them, except the one which is practiced today. This shows that the custom of polyandry also existed among the pre-Islamic Arabs. Montesquieu reports that the Arab globe - trotter, Abu Zahir al-Hasan, found this custom in India and China during his visit to these countries in the 9th century and regarded it as a form of debauchery. He also writes:

> On the coast of Malabar there lives a tribe called Nair. The male members of this tribe cannot have more than one wife, but the women are allowed to choose several husbands. Probably the reason is that the Nairs belong to a martial race and their profession is fighting and hunting. Just as we discourage the marriage of the soldiers in Europe so that it may not interfere with their profession of fighting, the Malabar tribes have also decided that, as far as possible, the male members of the Nair tribe should be excused from shouldering family responsibilities. As, owing to the tropical climate of the area, it is not possible to ban marriage totally, it has been decided that several men should have only one wife, so that they may not be heavily burdened with family responsibilities and their professional efficiency may not be affected.

10.3.1 Defects of Polyandry

The main and basic defect of the system of polyandry is that the paternity of the children practically remains uncertain. In this system, the relations between the child and the father are undetermined and that is the reason why it has not been successful. As sexual communism has not been able to take root anywhere, this system also has not been accepted by any society worthy of the name. As we have said earlier, family life, the building of a home for the future generation and the definite connection 'between past and the future generations are some of the demands of the human instinct. The exceptional cases of the existence of plurality of husbands, among certain sections of society, do not prove that the desire of the formation of one's own family is not an instinct of man. Similarly, perpetual celibacy or complete abstinence from conjugal life, as practised by a number of men and women, is also a sort of deviation. Polyandry is not only inconsistent with man's monopolistic nature and his paternal love, but it is also opposed to the nature of woman. Psychological investigations have proved that woman wants monogamy more than man.

It is thus a grave mistake to compare polyandry with polygamy and to say that there is no difference between them. It is also wrong to say that polygamy became popular in certain parts of the world because man belonged to the stronger sex, and polyandry could not do so because woman belonged to the weaker sex. A contemporary woman writer says:

> We can say that as man can have four wives, woman also should have a similar right, for both are human beings. This logical conclusion is most appalling to men. They are enraged on hearing such an argument and shout: "How can a woman have more than one husband?" In reply we quietly say: "How can a man have more than one wife?"

She further says:

> We do not want to promote immorality or to belittle the importance of chastity. We only want to make men understand that the views held by them, about women, are not based on any solid ground. Man and woman are equal as human beings. If man has the right to have four wives, woman also must have the same right. Even if it is granted that woman is not intellectually superior to man, it is certain that spiritually and mentally she is not weaker than he is.

As you might have observed, the above statement makes no distinction between polyandry and polygamy, except that man, being the stronger sex, has adopted polygamy to his own advantage, and woman being the weaker sex was not able to do so.

The above writer further says that man regards woman as his property, and that is why he wants to have several wives. In other words, he thus wants to acquire as much property as practicable. Woman, being in the position of a slave, cannot have more than one master.

Contrary to the views of this writer, the fact that the system of polyandry has never been accepted by any large section of people proves that man does not regard his wife as his property, for, as far as property is concerned, it is a common practice all over the world to own it jointly and to be benefited by it jointly. Had man considered woman to be his property, he certainly would have had no objection to sharing her with others. There is no law in the world restricting the ownership of a property to only one owner.

It is said that the husband is one individual and the wife is another individual. They should have equal rights. Why should the husband have the right of enjoying polygamy and why should the wife not have the right of enjoying polyandry?

We say, here lies the mistake. You presume that polygamy is a part of the rights of the husband and polyandry a part of the rights of the wife. The fact is that polygamy is a part of woman's rights and polyandry is neither a part of man's rights nor of woman's rights. It is against the interests of both man and woman. We shall prove later that Islam has laid down the system of polygamy with a view to safeguarding the interests of woman. Had the intention been to be partial to man, Islam could have allowed the husband to have extramarital affairs with a woman other than his wife and would have laid no responsibility on him with regard to his legal wife and legal children.

10.3.2   Causes for the Failure of Polyandry

The main cause for the failure of polyandry is that it neither suits man's nature nor that of woman. It does not suit man's nature, because firstly, it does not conform to his monopolistic spirit and, secondly, because it is not in agreement with the principle that a father should be confident of his paternity. It is human nature to have an attachment with one's children. Every human being is, by nature, keen to beget children and wants his relationship with his past and future generations to be definite and satisfactory. He wants to know whose son and whose father he is. Polyandry does not agree with this instinct of man. On the other hand, polygamy creates no such problem, either in the case of man or in that of woman. It is reported that about forty women once came to Imam Ali (as) and asked him why Islam had allowed men to have several wives, but had not allowed women to have several husbands. They asked whether it was not a case of undue discrimination.

Imam Ali (as) ordered some cups of water to be brought in and gave one cup to each woman. Then he ordered them to pour all the water into a big utensil, which was placed in the middle of the room. When the order had been carried out, he asked them to fill their cups again, but only with the water, which they originally contained. The women said that it was not possible, as the whole water had mixed. Imam Ali (as) said that if a woman had several husbands, they would naturally have sexual connections with her. If she became pregnant and gave birth to a child, it would not be possible to determine as to who was the father of that child.

As far as woman is concerned, polyandry is neither in her interest nor does it conform to her nature. Woman does not want a husband to only satisfy her sexual instinct. Had it been so, it could be said: 'the more, the better'. Woman wants a man whose heart she may control, who may be her protector and defender, who may make sacrifices for her and who may work hard and bring money for her. The money which a woman earns through her own work and labour neither meets her requirements nor has the same value as that which is given to her by the man who loves her. A husband meets the financial needs of his wife with the spirit of sacrifice. The wife and children are the best and strongest incentives for man to work.

On the other hand, polyandry has never been in the interests of woman; it is not a right of which she has been deprived. The writer whose views we have quoted has said:

> We want to make men understand that the views held by them about women are not based on any solid ground.

Coincidentally, that is what we also want to do. In the following chapters we propose to explain the basis of the Islamic views regarding polygamy.

In the case of polyandry, woman cannot also claim the love, devotion and sacrifice of any man. That is why, like prostitution, it has always been abominable to woman. Hence polyandry neither conforms to the wants and the leanings of man, nor to those of woman.

We invite all thinking people to look into it and see whether the Islamic views are based on any solid ground. We give our word of honour that we shall withdraw everything if it is proved by anybody that the basis of the Islamic viewpoint is defective.

10.4   Polygamy

Another form of polygamy is plurality of wives. It has been more commonly and successfully practised than polyandry and sexual communism. It has not only existed among the barbarian tribes, but has also been practised by many civilised people. Apart from the Arabs, the Jews, the Iranians of the Sassanid period and others have practised it. Montesquieu says that in Malaya it was permissible to have three wives. He also says that the Roman Emperor, Valentinian II, had by an edict allowed the subjects of the Empire to marry several wives, but as this law was not suited to the climate of Europe other emperors, like Theodore etc, repealed it.

10.5   Polygamy in the West

We deem it necessary to give a brief account of polygamy in Europe during the Middle Ages, as described by an eminent Western historian. This account should convince those who criticise the East for polygamy that in spite of all its defects it is much more dignified than what existed in Europe.

Will Durant in his book, *History of Civilizations*, vol. 17, gives an interesting account of the state of morality in Italy during the Renaissance. We give below a summary of what he has said under the heading 'Morals in Sexual Relations'.

In the course of his brief introduction, he says that before describing the morals of the laity it may be pointed out that by nature man is polygamous. Only strict moral restrictions, an adequate amount of hard work and poverty, and a continuous vigilance by the wife can compel him to maintain monogamy.

Then he says that adultery was not uncommon during the Medieval Ages, prior to the Renaissance. As during the Middle Ages the guilt of adultery was extenuated by chivalry, similarly, during the Renaissance period, it was watered down among the educated classes by the craving for the polished manners and the refined spirit of the females. Girls belonging to respectable families were, to a certain extent, kept segregated from the males not connected with their own family, and were taught the merits of pre-marital chastity. Sometimes these instructions were exceptionally effective. It is reported that a young woman, after being assaulted, drowned herself. That must have been an exceptional case, because a bishop took the trouble of installing a statue of her, after her death, to commemorate her chastity.

The number of premarital affairs must have been considerable, because there were innumerable children born of illegitimate relations in every town in Italy. It was a matter of pride not to have an illegitimate child, but to have one was not a matter of shame. Usually a husband persuaded his wife at the time of the marriage to bring her illegitimate child with her, to be brought up along with his children. Illegitimacy was not a slur on the reputation of anyone. Furthermore, a certificate of legitimacy could easily be obtained by bribing a clergyman. In the absence of other lawful or eligible heirs, an illegitimate son could inherit property and even a crown, as Frante I, succeeded Alfonso I, King of Naples. When in 1459 Plus-II came to Bavaria, seven princes, all of whom were illegitimate, received him. Rivalry between the legitimate and illegitimate sons was a significant factor of a long series of commotion during the Renaissance period.

As far as homosexuality is concerned, it was only a revival of the ancient Greek tradition. San Bernardino found this sort of perversion so common in Naples that he thought it to be threatened with the fate of Sodom. Antino found the perversion equally prevalent in Rome. The same thing can be said about prostitution. In 1490, out of a total population of 90,000, there were 6,800 registered prostitutes in Rome. Of course, this figure does not include clandestine and unofficial prostitutes. According to the statistics of 1509, out of a population of 300,000 of that city, there were 11,654 prostitutes. In the 15th century, a girl who had reached the age of 15 without having a husband was regarded as a slur on the fair name of her family. In the 16th century, the 'age of disgrace' was extended to 17 years to enable the girls to receive higher education. Men, who enjoyed all the facilities provided by widespread prostitution, were attracted to marriage only if the woman concerned promised to bring a considerable dowry. According to the system of the Middle Ages, husband and wife were expected to love each other and share each other's joy and grief. Apparently in many cases this expectation came true, but still adultery was rampant. Most of the marriages of the upper classes were diplomatic unions contracted for political and economic gains. Many husbands regarded it as their right to have a mistress. The wife might feel dejected, but usually condoned the situation.

Among the middle classes, some people thought that adultery was a lawful pastime. Machiavelli and his friends apparently did not feel uneasy about the stories of their unfaithfulness, which they exchanged with each other. When in such cases the wife followed the example of her husband to seek revenge upon him; he usually accepted her behaviour and did not feel jealous or perturbed.

This was a specimen of the life of the people who regarded polygamy as an unpardonable crime of the East and have occasionally blamed its climate for this supposedly inhuman custom. As far as their own climate is concerned, it does not allow them to be unfaithful to their wives and to exceed the limits of monogamy!

In addition, it should be remembered that the absence of lawful polygamy among the Europeans, whether good or bad, has nothing to do with the religion of Christ, who never prohibited it. On the other hand, it confirms the rules of the Old Testament, which expressly recognises polygamy. Thus we can say that, in fact, the religion of Christ allows polygamy, and the ancient Christians have actually practiced it. Hence, the legal abstinence of the Europeans from it must have some other reason or reasons.

10.6   Islam and Polygamy

In contrast to polyandry, Islam has not totally abolished polygamy, but has restricted it. On the one hand, it has fixed the maximum number of wives, which one can have, to four, and on the other it has stipulated certain conditions, and has not allowed everyone to indulge in having several wives. We shall discuss the conditions stipulated by Islam later and will explain why Islam has not banned polygamy.

It is surprising that during the Middle Ages, when anti-Islamic propaganda was at its peak, the opponents of Islam used to say that it was the Prophet of Islam (saws) who, for the first time, invented the custom of polygamy. They claimed that this custom was the basis of Islam and the rapid spread of Islam among the various people of the world was due to it. At the same time, they claimed that polygamy was the cause for the decline of the people of the East.

Will Durant in his *History of Civilisations,* vol. 1, says that the ecclesiastics of the Middle Ages believed that polygamy was an invention of the Prophet of Islam (saws), whereas this is not a fact. As we know, the matrimonial life in most of the primitive societies proceeded according to this system. There are many causes for its emergence. In primitive societies men were mostly busy hunting and fighting and the rate of mortality among them was naturally high, and as the number of women exceeded the number of men it became essential to adopt this system. It was not possible to allow some women to remain unmarried, for the rate of mortality being high in the primitive societies required every woman to procreate children. There is no doubt that this system suited those societies, not only because of the excess of women over men, but also because it strengthened them numerically. In modern times the most strong and healthy men usually marry late in life and beget only a few children. But in the olden days the strong men could have the best wives and could procreate a large number of children. That is why this practice continued to exist for a very long time, not only among the primitive people but also among the civilised ones. It is only recently that it has gradually begun disappearing from the countries of the East. Agriculture has stabilised the life of men and reduced the hardships and perils of the ancient times, with the result that the number of men and women has almost equalised. Now polygamy, even in primitive societies, has become a privilege of a small wealthy minority and the masses have to be content with only one wife and, as an additional enjoyment, they can only indulge in adultery, whenever possible.

Gustav Leobeon in his book, *History of Culture*, says that no Eastern custom is so infamous in Europe as polygamy, nor has Europe misjudged any other custom to the extent that it has misjudged this. European writers have believed polygamy to be the basis of Islam and the main cause of its spread.

They also hold this custom to be mainly responsible for the decline of the Eastern people. Other objections apart from these, showing sympathy with the women of the East, are raised alleging that these ill-fated women are detained within the four walls of their houses, under the hardhearted eunuchs. They further say that the slightest action on their part, which may displease the head of the household, renders them liable to be put to death. Such notions have no basis at all. Unbiased Europeans should know that it is the custom of polygamy that has strengthened family relations and uplifted the moral spirit of those people among whom it is prevalent. It is due to this custom that a woman in the East enjoys more respect than she does in Europe. Before proving this point, we must make it clear that this custom is in no way related to Islam. Even prior to Islam, all the people of the East, including the

Jews, the Iranians, and Arabs etc, practiced it. The people who embraced Islam in the East did not derive any benefit in this respect. So far, no such mighty religion has appeared in this world as could invent or abolish such a custom as polygamy. It has not been introduced by any religion. It is the creation of the climatic and the racial characteristics and other causes related to the way of life in the East. Even in the West, where the climate is not congenial to the existence of such a custom, monogamy is a thing which is found only in law books. In actual life there is no trace of it. It is not known how and in what way the lawful variety of polygamy found in the East is inferior to the clandestine polygamy of the people of the West. Apparently, the former is better and more dignified than the latter. The people of the East, when they visit a European country and are confronted with the European criticism of their custom, are naturally bewildered and feel offended.

It is a fact that Islam has not invented polygamy. It has only restricted it. It has prescribed a maximum limit for it and has laid down strict conditions for it. This custom already existed among most of the people who accepted Islam. They were only compelled to comply with the conditions laid down by Islam. In his book, *Iran during the Sassanid Period*, Christenson writes:

> Polygamy was considered to be the basis of the family. Practically, the number of wives which a man could have, depended on his means. The poor people apparently could not afford to have more than one wife as a general rule. The head of the family had special rights as such. One of the wives was regarded as the favourite wife and enjoyed full rights. Some other wives were treated as servants only. Legal rights of these two categories widely differed. The slave girls were included among the servant wives. It is not known how many favourite wives a man could have. But there has been a mention of two favourite wives in the course of several legal discourses. Each of them was called the lady of the house. Apparently they lived in separate houses. The husband was bound to maintain the favourite wife so long as she lived. Every son till he reached the age of puberty,

and every daughter till she was married, had the same rights. But only the male children of the servant-wives were admitted to the paternal family.

In his *Social History of Iran from the fall of the Sassanians to the fall of the Omayyads,* the late Sa'id Nafisi writes:

> The number of women whom a man could marry was unlimited and at times it is observed in the Greek documents that one man had hundreds of women in his house.

Montesquieu, quoting a Roman historian, says that several Roman philosophers, who were being tortured by the Christians because they refused to embrace Christianity, fled from Rome and took refuge in the court of the Iranian King, Khusro Parviz. They were astonished to see that not only was polygamy legal there, but the Persian men also had intimacy with the wives of others.

It may be pointed out here that the Roman philosophers took refuge in the court of the Iranian king, Anushirwan, and not in the court of Khusro Parviz. Montesquieu has mentioned the name of the latter owing to some misunderstanding.

During the pre-Islamic period, the Arabs could have an unlimited number of wives. It was Islam that prescribed a maximum limit. This naturally created a problem for those who had more than four wives. In exceptional circumstances, some even had ten. They had to part with six of them.

From the above it is evident that polygamy is not an invention of Islam. Islam only restricted it. Certainly, it did not abolish it totally. In the following chapters we shall discuss the causes, which gave rise to this custom and shall explain why Islam did not do away with it. We shall also discuss the reasons which, in modern times, have impelled both men and women to rise against this custom.

10.6.1   Historical Causes for Polygamy (I)

What are the historical and social causes for polygamy? Why have many nations of the world, especially the Eastern nations, accepted this custom, and why have other nations, such as the Western nations, never practised it? How is it that out of the three forms of polygamy only plurality of wives could gain considerable popularity? Polyandry and sexual communism either have never been practised or have been practised rarely, and only in exceptional cases.

Unless we look into these questions, we cannot discuss the question of polygamy from the point of view of Islam, nor can we study it from the viewpoint of modern human requirements.

If we do not take into consideration the ample social and psychological studies made in this respect, we too, like many superficial writers, may repeat the same argument and say that the causes of polygamy are obvious. That is, that this custom has come into existence as a result of the high-handedness and the domination of man and the subjugation of women; it is an outcome of the patriarchal system. As man has dominated woman and has ruled over her, he has adopted the laws and the customs to his own benefit. That is how he enforced this custom, which is beneficial to him and harmful to woman, and he has been practising it for centuries. As woman was suppressed, she could not put polyandry into practice. As the age of the high-handedness of man is now over, the privilege of polygamy should, like many other false privileges, make room for equal and reciprocal rights of man and woman.

This way of thinking is very superficial and puerile. Neither is the cause of polygamy the oppression by man, nor the failure of polyandry the suppression of women. If the custom of polyandry has practically come to an end, that is not because the age of man's high-handedness is over. Man has lost no privilege; he has actually gained an advantage over woman.

We do not deny the factor of oppression as one of the factors which give a particular turn to history. Neither do we deny that man has, throughout history, misused his domination over woman. But we believe that it is sheer short-sightedness to explain family relations on the basis of the oppression factor only.

If we admit this view, we must also admit that during the period when polyandry was popular among the pre-Islamic Arabs or, as reported by Montesquieu, among the Nairs on the Malabar Coast women had an opportunity to dominate man and impose polyandry over him. It also would also have to be admitted that that period was the golden period of woman. But we know for definite that the pre-Islamic period of Arabia was one of the darkest periods in the life of women. Earlier we have quoted Montesquieu as saying that the custom of polyandry among the Nairs was not due to the domination or respect of woman, but was the result of the decision of society to keep the soldiers free from the burden of family responsibilities.

Further, if patriarchy is responsible for polygamy, how is it that this system did not gain popularity in the West? After all, the patriarchal system is not confined to the East. Have the people of the West been, from the beginning, pious Christians believing in the equality and reciprocity between man and woman? Has the factor of domination worked to the benefit of man in the East and for the promotion of justice in the West?

Until half a century ago, Western woman was among the unluckiest in the world. Her husband controlled even her own property. The Europeans themselves admit that during the Middle Ages the position of the Eastern woman was far better than that of her counterpart in the West. Gustav Leabeon says that Islam, in its early days, gave the woman exactly that position which the European woman would not achieve until much later; that is, after the chivalry of the Arabs of Andalusia was transmitted to Europe. Courteous behaviour towards woman is the main component of the chivalry, which the Europeans learnt from the Muslims. It was Islam, and not the religion of Christ, as is commonly believed, that enhanced the position of woman. During the Middle Ages the chiefs and barons, although Christians, never held woman in respect. A study of ancient history leaves no doubt that the behaviour of the dukes and barons of Europe towards woman was most barbaric.

Other European authors have also given a more or less similar description of the position of women during the Middle Ages. Though patriarchy prevailed in Europe during that period, polygamy did not become customary.

The fact is that polyandry (wherever it was practised) was never due to the power and domination of woman, nor was its ultimate failure due to her weakness and suppression. Similarly, polygamy in the East is neither due to the oppression and high-handedness of man, nor is it unpopular in the West owing to the existence of equality between man and woman.

10.6.2 Historical Causes of Polygamy (II)

Man's lust for indulgence in sensual pleasure and his unrestricted domination alone are not a sufficient cause for the emergence of polygamy. There must also be some other contributory causes for a licentious man to satisfy his taste for variety. It is easier and less cumbersome to indulge in free love instead of having a woman of his choice as his legal wife and shouldering the responsibility of the maintenance of their possible future children. Plurality of wives gains popularity only in the societies where there are moral and social restrictions on free love, and a voluptuary has to pay the price for seeking variety by accepting the woman concerned as his legal wife, and by shouldering the responsibility of fatherhood of their children.

Now let us see whether there is any contribution of geographical, economic or social factors in this respect.

10.7   Geographical Factors

Montesquieu and Gustav Leobeon insist that climatic conditions are the main cause for the development of polygamy. These intellectuals believe that the climate of the East is such that this custom is inevitable there; in Eastern countries, puberty and old age in females commence earlier, and therefore a man requires a second and a third wife. Moreover, they think that one woman cannot satisfy the sexual needs of a man brought up in the Eastern climate. Gustav Leobeon in his book, *History of Islamic and Arab Culture* says:

> The custom of polygamy was not introduced by religion. It is an outcome of the climatic conditions, the racial characteristics and other causes related to life in the East. It need not be emphasized that these are very strong and effective factors. Furthermore, their physical and temperamental traits, their nursing of children and their ailments and diseases often force the women of the East to keep themselves aloof from their husbands. As the climatic conditions and the national characteristics of men in the East are such that they cannot bear even temporary separation, polygamy has become customary.

Montesquieu in his book, the *Spirit of Law* says:

> In tropical countries women attain puberty at the age of eight, nine or ten years and after being married, soon become pregnant. It may be said that in tropical countries, pregnancy immediately follows marriage.

Predo, giving an account of the life of the Prophet of Islam (saws), states that he married Khadija, at the age of five and consummated the marriage at the age of eight. Because of a very early marriage, women in the tropics become old at the age of twenty. He says that before they become mature, they are already old. In the countries having a temperate climate, women retain their charm and beauty for a long time. They attain puberty at a later age, and they are more mature and experienced at the time of their marriage. They have children at a comparatively advanced age, and the husband and the wife become old almost at the same time. That is how equality between man and woman is established, and men do not need to have more than one wife. Thus it is because of the climatic conditions that the law prohibits polygamy in Europe and allows it in Asia.

The above explanation is in no way correct. The custom of polygamy is not confined to tropical regions in the East. During the pre-Islamic period this custom was common in Iran, where the climate is temperate. It is purely fictitious to say that in the tropics, women get old at the age of twenty, as alleged by Montesquieu. It is even more fantastic to say that the Prophet of Islam married Khadijah (as) at the age of five and consummated the marriage at the age of eight. Everyone knows that at the time of their marriage Khadijah was forty and the Prophet (saws) was twenty-five.

Secondly, if it is accepted that the early onset of old age in women and the intense virility in men are the causes of this custom, why did the people of the East not adopt the practice of free love and debauchery, as did the people of the West, both during the Middle Ages and in modern times. In the West, as Gustav Leobeon has pointed out, monogamy is found only in the legal books and there is no trace of it in daily life.

Again, in the East, polygamy exists in its legal form. The man has to accept the woman as his legal wife and has to bear the responsibility of their children. In the West, it exists in an illegal and clandestine form. Man indulges in free love and escapes all matrimonial responsibility.

10.8   Menses

Some others attribute polygamy to a woman's menstrual periods and her aversion to sex during that time as well as to her exhaustion after childbirth and her desire to avoid sexual intercourse during the nursing period.

Will Durant says that in primitive societies women grow old quickly. That is why, in order to be able to nurse their children for a longer period, to lengthen the interval between their own pregnancies, without interrupting the husband's desire to have children, and to enable him to satisfy his sexual urge, they encourage their husbands to have a new wife. It has been often observed that the first wife, with a view to making her own burden lighter, has persuaded her husband to contract another marriage in order to have more children and to acquire more wealth.

There is no doubt that a woman's menstrual periods and her exhaustion resulting from childbearing place man and woman, sexually, in dissimilar positions.

These reasons often make men turn to another woman, but they alone cannot be a sufficient cause of polygamy, unless some social or moral impediment exists, preventing man from indulging in free love. The above factors can be effective only when man is not free in the pursuit of his sexual desires.

10.9   Limitation of the Period of Fecundity in Females

Some believe that the limitation of the period of fecundity of a woman, and her menopause are one of the causes which gave rise to polygamy; for it may happen that a woman reaches this age without being able to bear enough children. It is also possible that her children may not have survived.

In such cases, if the husband does not wish to divorce his first wife and at the same time wants to have more children, he has no alternative but to have a second, or sometimes even a third wife. Similarly, the sterility of the first wife may be another reason for the husband contracting a second marriage.

10.10   Economic Factors

Some economic factors have also been mentioned as the cause for polygamy. It is said that in ancient times, several wives and a large number of children were regarded as economic assets. Man extracted work from his wives and children, and treated them like slaves. Sometimes he even sold them. Most slaves were not captured in battles but were sold by their fathers.

This may be a cause of polygamy, because man can have children only by accepting the woman as his legal wife. Free love cannot ensure this advantage. However, this cause cannot explain all the cases of polygamy.

Some primitive people had several wives with this idea in mind. But this was not the case with everyone. In the ancient world polygamy was customary among the classes which lived with dignity and decorum. The kings, princes, chiefs, the divines and the merchants had several wives. As we know, these classes never exploited their wives and children economically.

10.11   Number of Members in a Family

Interest in the numerical increase of the children and the expansion of the family has been another cause of polygamy. The position of a man and a woman with regard to the number of children each of them can have is different. The number of children a woman can bear is very limited, whether she has one husband or several husbands. But the number of children a man can beget depends on the number of women he has at his disposal. It is theoretically possible that a man may have thousands of children by hundreds of wives. Unlike the modern world, in the ancient world the number of family members was counted as an important social factor. The tribes and the clans did all they could to increase their numbers. It was a matter of pride for ancient people to belong to a large tribe. It is obvious that polygamy was the only means of achieving that end.

10.12   Numerical Superiority

The last and the most important factor which has contributed to the emergence of the custom of polygamy is that women have always outnumbered men. It is not that the birth rate of females is greater than that of males. If occasionally in certain places more females are born, in other places more males are born. But still the number of women eligible for marriage is always higher than the number of men. The reason for this is that the mortality rate among men has always been higher. And therefore it follows that, were monogamy to be enforced strictly, a large number of women would go without having legal husbands, legal children or any kind of domestic life.

There can be no doubt that at least in primitive societies this was the position. We have already quoted Will Durant, who says that in primitive societies the life of man was constantly in danger because he was always busy with hunting and fighting, and that is why the rate of mortality among men was higher than among women. As the number of women increased, there were only two alternatives: either to adopt polygamy or to force a large number of women to pass their entire life as spinsters.

10.13   Recapitulation

We have described above all the causes which can be presumed to be the reason for polygamy. As you must have observed, some of these causes, such as climate, are actually not causes at all. Hence we ignore them. Other causes can be classified into three categories. The first category includes those causes which might have been effective in persuading man to adopt polygamy, but which provide no justification for his action. They have an aspect of oppression, high-handedness and cruelty. Economic causes fall under this category.

It is evident that the sale of children is one of the cruellest and most barbaric human acts. To resort to polygamy for this purpose is as unlawful as this act itself.

The second category includes those causes which may be regarded as justification as far as the husband or society is concerned. Sterility of the first wife, her reaching the age of menopause while the husband still requires a child, or the need for a large body of people by the tribe or the country are among such causes. As a general rule, all causes, which emanate from the dissimilarity between husband and wife as regards their sexual needs or procreation power, have a justifying aspect.

The third category consists of a cause which, if it is admitted that it ever existed or still exists, not only provides a justification for polygamy, but also makes it obligatory. In this case, polygamy is a woman's right which man and the society must discharge. This cause is the numerical superiority of women over men. In the case of the number of women eligible for marriage being larger than the number of such men, polygamy becomes an obligation on men and a right of women; for in the case of legally enforced monogamy, a number of women are bound to be deprived of their right of family life.

The right of marriage is a basic human right and no one can be deprived of it under any pretext. Society cannot take any action which may deprive a section of the people of this right.

The right of marriage is as natural a right as the right of freedom, the right to work, and the right to get food, shelter and education. Hence, the law of monogamy is repugnant to the natural human rights in the case of the existence of a larger number of women eligible for marriage than the number of available men.

This, at least, has been the case in the past. In the next chapter we shall see whether there still exist circumstances which not only justify polygamy, but also create a woman's position of this right vis-à-vis the right of the first wife.

10.14   Rights of the Woman in a "More-than-One" Marriage

We have explained the causes for the failure of polyandry and the prevailing of polygamy and have shown that multifarious causes have contributed to the origin of the latter custom. Some of the causes originated from the man's spirit of oppression and domination and others from the disparity between man and woman as regards the duration of their power or procreation and the number of children which each of them can beget. The latter type of causes can be regarded as a justification for polygamy. But its main cause, throughout history, has been the numerical superiority of women eligible for marriage over such men. This cause leads to the creation of a right for woman and an obligation of man.

To avoid a lengthy discussion, we will skip over those causes which can be regarded merely as a justification for polygamy and confine our attention to its main cause which, when in existence, turns it into a right of the fair sex.

To prove the case, two preliminary points have to be established. First it is to be proved that, according to reliable statistics, women eligible for marriage actually outnumber men. The second point to be proved is that the actual existence of circumstances creates a right which married men and women owe to the women who have been deprived of marriage.

As for the first point, fortunately, almost authentic statistics exist in the modern world. A census is taken in every country periodically. In the advanced countries not only are the total figures of males and females collected, but the number of men and women in various age groups is also shown. These figures are regularly published by the United Nations in its annual report on world population.

It may be pointed out that for our purpose it is not enough to know the total number of males and females in any given country. Simultaneously, we should also know the ratio between the number of men and the number of women eligible for marriage. In most cases this ratio is different from that which exists between the total population of males and the total population of females. There are two reasons for this difference. One is that the onset of puberty in females is earlier. That is why in most countries the legal age of consent in the case of girls is lower than in the case of boys. In practically most of the countries of the world the husband is on average five years older than the wife.

The other and the more important reason is that the mortality rate among boys is higher than among girls, with the result that during marriageable age the balance between them is upset. Sometimes the disparity becomes very marked. It may be that the total number of males and females in a country is almost equal, or even that the number of males is higher; however, girls of marriageable age still far exceed boys of the corresponding age group.

The United Nations Population Report for the year 1964 bears witness to this fact.

For instance, according to this report, the total population of the Republic of Korea is 26,277,635 people. Out of this total 13,145,289 are males and 13,132,346 are females. Thus the number of males is 12,943 more than that of females. This ratio is maintained in children of less than one year, of 1 to 4 years, of 5 to 9 years, of 12 to 14 years and of 15 to 19 years.

Statistics show that in all these age groups the number of males is larger than that of females. But in the age group of 20 to 24, the ratio changes. In this age group the total number of males is 1,083,364 and the total number of females is 1,110,051. In all the higher age groups, which are the groups of marriageable age, the number of females is greater.

Still, the case of the Republic of Korea, where the total number of males is greater than females, is exceptional. In almost all other countries, not only in marriageable age groups but also in the total population, the females outnumber the males. For instance, the total population of the Soviet Union is 216,101,000 and out of this total 97,840,000 are males and 118,261,000 are females. This disparity is maintained throughout all age groups, pre marriageable as well as marriageable, that is from 20 years to 24 years, from 25 years to 29 years, from 30 years to 34 years and even from 80 years to 84 years.

The same is the case with other countries, such as England, France, West Germany, East Germany, Czechoslovakia, Poland, Rumania, Hungary, U.S.A., Japan etc. Of course at certain places, such as West Berlin and East Berlin, the disparity between the number of males and the number of females is abnormally large.

In India, in the marriageable age group, the number of men exceeds the number of women. Only in the age group of 50 and above is the number of women greater. Apparently, the supposed paucity of women is due to the fact that many people in that country do not like to mention the names of their young wives and young daughters at the time of census.

According to the figures of the last census, Iran is one of the exceptional countries where the number of males exceeds the number of females.

It is surprising that some critics insist that the law allowing polygamy should be abolished at least in those countries where the number of men exceeds the number of women. In the first instance, this law is universal. It is not meant for any particular country. Secondly, it is not enough to know the ratio of males and females in the total population. We have seen that in the Republic of Korea, though the number of males is greater in the total population, there are more females in the marriageable age group. Furthermore, the census figures are not very reliable in many countries. For example, we know for a fact that although polygamy has been customary in Iran, either in the urban and the rural areas, a shortage of would-be brides has never been felt there. This fact speaks louder than the census figures.

Ashley Montague, in his book, *Woman -the Superior Sex*, admits that throughout the world the number of women of marriageable age exceeds the number of men.

The statistics of 1950 show that the number of women of marriageable age in America exceeded the number of men by about one million four hundred and thirty thousand.

Bertrand Russell in his book, *Marriage and Morality,* says that, in present day England, women exceed men by two million. Consequently, if they follow traditional morales they will remain childless, which is a big privation for them.

Some years ago, a news item appeared in the press, saying that following considerable pressure from those German women who, owing to the huge number of German casualties resulting from the Second World War, were unable to find husbands and secure family lives, the German Government had approached Al-Azhar University to provide it with the formula for polygamy. It was later learnt that, following serious opposition by the Church, the proposal had to be dropped. The Church preferred the privation of women and the spread of licentiousness to the system of polygamy, because this system is Eastern and Islamic.

10.15   Why are there more Women of Marriageable Age than Men?

Although the birth rate of girls is not higher than that of boys, there are more women of marriageable age than men. The reason is clear. The mortality rate of men is higher. Deaths usually occur at the age when man should normally be the head of a family. If we take into consideration the deaths which occur following accidents such as wars, drowning, falls, motor collisions etc. we shall find that most of the victims are men.

It is seldom found that a woman is among the victims. Whether it is a case of a clash between human beings or between man and nature, most of the victims are adult males. To know why the balance between men and women of marriageable age is upset it is enough to realise that, since the beginning of human history, there has not been a single day when wars have not been waged and men have not perished.

The casualties resulting from wars in the industrial age are a hundred times more than those which occurred during the hunting age or in the age of agriculture. During the Second World War, the casualties numbered about seven million. You will agree with us, if you calculate the casualties of regional wars in the Far East, the Middle East and Africa during the past decade alone.

Will Durant says that several factors have contributed to the decline of the custom of polygamy. Stable agricultural life has lessened the hardships and perils of the life of men, with the result that the number of men and women has almost equalised.

What Will Durant has said is quite amazing. Had the losses of human life been confined to the struggle of men against nature, there would have been a difference between the hunting age and the agricultural age. But wars have taken a greater toll of men's lives and the number of war casualties has decreased the numbers of men in any age. Furthermore, the main reason why women have suffered fewer casualties is that men have always protected them and have, themselves, undertaken the most dangerous jobs. Thus, like in the hunting age disequilibria has continued during the agricultural age also.

Will Durant has not uttered a word about the industrial age, though this is the period which has witnessed the greatest killing of men and during which the balance was greatly upset.

10.16 Woman has a Greater Power of Resistance against Disease

It has lately been discovered that man possesses fewer powers of resistance against disease than women. This is another reason why the mortality rate among men is higher.

Some years ago, the French Bureau of Statistics reported that in France, 105 boys were born against every 100 girls and the number of women exceeded the number of men by one million, seven hundred and fifty-eight thousand. It attributed the difference to the female power of resistance against disease.

Not long ago an article was published in Courier, the illustrated UNESCO magazine, according to which, woman is intellectually superior to man. Her average longevity is more. Usually, she is healthier than man and has a greater power of resistance against disease, and is cured easier. Against one stammering woman there are five stammering men. Against one colour-blind woman there are 16 colour-blind men. Haemorrhage is almost confined to men. Women are more resilient in accidents. During the Second World

War it was proved that, in similar circumstances, women could bear the hardships of blockades, prisons and concentration camps better than men. In almost all countries the cases of suicide by men are three times those by women.

Ashley Montague has mentioned his theory of woman's greater power of resistance against disease in his book, *Woman -the Superior Sex.*

If, by chance, one day man decides to wreak his vengeance upon woman and succeeds in plunging her into the most dangerous and fatal jobs or pushes her into the battlefield to face the guns and the bombs, even then the balance between men and women will not be restored, because she has a greater power of resistance against disease.

This much is about the first point viz. numerical superiority of women of marriageable age over men of marriageable age. We know that this superiority is an actual fact. We also know its causes, and its cause or causes from the beginning of human history still exist.

10.17   Rights of Women in Polygamy

The second point is that the numerical majority of women of marriageable age not only creates a right for them but also an obligation for men and married women.

There is no denying the fact that marriage is one of the most natural and most basic rights of human beings. Everybody, whether man or woman, has the right to lead a family life and have children. This right is similar to that of doing work, having a house, receiving education, utilising the health services and enjoying freedom and security.

It is the duty of the society not to place any obstacles in the way of the enjoyment of this right. On the other hand, it should provide all possible facilities for this purpose.

In our opinion it is a big drawback of the Universal Declaration of Human Rights, that it has not paid any attention to this right of approaching competent national tribunals, the right of right. It has recognised the right of liberty and security, the right to have and to change one's nationality, the right to marry without any limitation of race or religion, the right to own property, the right to form an assembly, and the right to have rest and leisure, but it does not mention the right of leading a legal family life.

For a woman this right is of utmost importance, for she needs a family life more than a man. As we have already said, the material aspect of marriage is more important to a man, and to a woman its spiritual and sentimental aspect is more important. If man has no family, he can at least partially fulfil his needs by indulging in free love and debauchery. But to a woman, a family has a greater importance. Debauchery cannot even partially fulfil her material and sentimental needs.

To a man, the right of having a family means the right to satisfy his lust, the right to have a partner in life and the right to have legal children. But to a woman it also means the right to have a protector and patron and one from whom she may draw moral support.

After the establishment of the two premises, viz. the number of women eligible for marriage is larger than the number of men, and the natural human right is to have a family life, it is easy to draw the conclusion that if monogamy is regarded as the only legal form of marriage, a large number of women are bound to be deprived of their natural right and only polygamy, along with specific conditions, can restore it.

It is the duty of liberal-minded Muslim women that, in the name of defending the just rights of women at large, in the name of protecting morality and in the name of protecting the human race, they call upon the UN Commission for Human Rights to officially recognise the Islamic system of plurality of wives as a human right, and thus render a great service to the fair sex and to morality.

10.18   Russell's Theory

As pointed out earlier, Bertrand Russell was conscious of the fact that in the case of monogamy being the sole form of marriage, a large number of women would be deprived of their right. He has suggested a very simple solution to the problem. He wanted women to be allowed to entice men and bear fatherless children. As the father usually supports the children, the government should take his place and give a subsidy to the unmarried mothers.

Russell says that at present there are more than two million surplus women in Britain, who cannot ever hope to have children because of the law of monogamy. This is a big privation. He says that the system of monogamy is based on the presumption of approximate numerical equality between men and women, but where no such equality exists it gives a raw deal to those women who, in accordance with mathematical law, are doomed to remain unmarried. Besides, if it is desired to increase the population, such a raw deal is not even in the public interest, let alone in the private one.

This is the solution of this social problem as suggested by a great philosopher of the 20th century. But, according to Islam, the whole problem is solved if an adequate number of men, having the necessary financial, moral and physical qualifications, agree to bear the responsibility of more than one legal wife, showing no distinction between her, and his first wife, and between the children of both of them. The first wife should accept the second one cheerfully with the spirit of doing a social duty, which is most necessary and the best form of morality.

Contrary to the Islamic mode of thinking, this philosopher advises the deprived women to steal the husbands of other women and call upon the government to support the children borne of such illicit connections.

It appears that this philosopher of the 20th century maintains that woman needs marriage only for three reasons:

To satisfy her sexual needs, to get children and to meet her economic requirements. The first two needs can be met clandestinely. As for the third one, the government should look after it. He forgets that woman also has some sentimental needs. She wants to be under the protection of a loving husband and that her contact with him should not be merely of a sexual nature. Another point to which this philosopher attaches no importance is the position of the children born of illicit connections. Children need to be acknowledged by their parents and enjoy their sincere love and affection. Experience has shown that the mother seldom shows affection to that child of hers whose father is not known. How can the lack of this love be compensated? Can the government do anything in this respect?

Lord Russell regrets that a large number of women will have to remain childless unless his proposal is given a legal form. But he should have known that British women could not wait for any law. They themselves have already solved the problem of maidenhood and the fatherless child.

In the annual report for 1958, prepared by Dr. Z. A. Scott, Head of the Medical Department of the London Council, it was pointed out that out of every ten children born in the previous year one was illegitimate. The report further said that illegitimate births were constantly on the increase. The figures of illegitimate births shot up from 33,838 in 1957 to 53,433 in the following year.

It appears that the British people have solved their problem without waiting for the enactment of Lord Russell's suggestion.

10.19   Polygamy Prohibited, Homosexuality Permitted!

Instead of acting upon the advice of Lord Russell and solving the problem of unmarried woman, the British Government has taken a step in the opposite direction. It has more than ever, deprived woman of the male sex by legalising homosexuality. At present, polygamy is prohibited in Britain, but homosexuality is lawful.

In the eyes of the British people it is inhumane to have a woman as a second wife. However if the second "wife" happens to be a male, then there is no harm. They regard homosexuality to be a dignified act in conformity with the requirements of the 20th century. According to the verdict of the British authorities, plurality of wives is not objectionable provided the wives other than the first one have whiskers. It has been said that the Western world has solved sexual and family problems, and that we should follow its example. This is how it has solved them.

This Western action is not surprising in the least, for it is a logical outcome of the way the West is going.

What is surprising is that our people, especially the educated young men, have lost their power of independent thinking and analysing problems. They have lost their personalities. They are too credulous. If they have a diamond in their hand and the people from the other side of the world say it is a walnut, they throw it away. But if they see a walnut in the hand of an alien and are told that it is diamond, they readily believe it.

10.20   Is Man Polygamous by Nature?

You would be surprised if you are told that psychologists and social philosophers in the West believe that man is born polygamous and that monogamy is against his nature.

Will Durant, explaining the present day moral chaos, says that much of it is due to our incurable interest in variety. Man by nature, cannot be content with one woman.

He says that by nature man is polygamous. Only the strongest moral restrictions and an appropriate amount of poverty and hard work, along with the external vigilance of the wife, can impose monogamy on him.

The German professor, Schmidt, says that throughout history man has been unfaithful to his wife. There are indications that, even during the Middle Ages, the young men changed their sweethearts again and again, and 50% of married men were unfaithful to their wives. Robert Kinsey in his report, known as the Kinsey Report, says that American men and women surpass all other nations in unfaithfulness. In another section of the report he says that, unlike man, woman dislikes diversity and that is why she often does not submit to his overtures, but man regards diversity as an adventure. What is more important is that he is more interested in physical pleasure than in the spiritual and sentimental variety. Man pretends to have a purely sentimental and spiritual relation only for so long as he does not get an opportunity to have physical contact. A famous physician told Kinsey that obviously man was polygamous and woman monogamous, because millions of sperm developed in man while one ovum was produced in the ovary of woman during each period of fecundity. Apart from the theory of Kinsey, it would not be a bad idea if we ask ourselves whether it is difficult for a man to be faithful.

A French sociologist, answering this question, says that for a man to be faithful is not merely difficult but is well nigh impossible. One woman is born for one man, but one man is born for all women. If a man is unfaithful and betrays his wife, he is not to blame. It is the fault of nature, which has put all the forces of unfaithfulness in him.

A French magazine under the heading, *French Way of Love and Marriage*, writes that French couples have solved this problem. They know the rules of the game. So long as the husband does not exceed the limits, his occasional affairs with other women are of little importance. As a rule, a husband can in no case remain faithful after two years of married life. It is somewhat different in the case of women and fortunately they are aware of this difference. In France, a wife does not feel offended when her husband commits adultery. She consoles herself by saying that he might have taken his body to another woman, but his soul and sentiments continue to be hers and hers alone.

Some years ago, there was a controversy concerning the views expressed by a biologist named Dr. Russel Lee. He was of the view that a man's contentment with one wife weakened his progeny and hence this action amounted to an act of treachery against the human race. He thought that the system of multi-relations made the children healthy and strong.

We believe that the above description of the nature of man is not correct at all. These thinkers appear to have been inspired by the particular atmosphere prevailing in their own part of the world.

Anyway, we believe that both biologically and psychologically man and woman are dissimilar to each other and nature has purposely made them so. Therefore, the equality of their rights should not be used as a pretext for the uniformity of their rights. Even from the viewpoint of those who support monogamy, the spirit of woman is different from that of man. Woman is monogamous by nature. Polyandry is against her spirit and does not conform to what she expects of her husband. But man is not monogamous by nature in the sense that polygamy is not against his spirit and is not inconsistent with what he expects of his wife.

But we do not agree with the view that the spirit of man does not conform to monogamy. It is absolutely incorrect to say that his passion for diversity is incurable. We also do not believe that man cannot be faithful, or that one woman is born for one man and one man is born for all women.

To our belief, the causes of man's unfaithfulness are related to the social atmosphere and man's nature is not responsible for it. Factors causing unfaithfulness stem from that atmosphere which, on the one hand, encourages woman to employ all sorts of temptations and seductions to lead a stranger astray, and on the other hand, deprives millions of women of their right of marriage by enforcing the law of monogamy.

In the Muslim East, prior to the introduction of Western ways and manners, 100% of the men adhered to monogamy in the real sense. They neither had more than one legal wife nor did they indulge in concubinage.

10.21   Polygamy as the Factor Saving Monogamy

You will be surprised if we say that polygamy was the most important factor, which served monogamy in the East. It's legality is really the biggest saving factor, in case the number of women requiring marriage exceeds the number of men eligible for it, because if the right of the surplus women for marriage is not recognised and the morally, financially and physically well qualified men are not allowed to have more than one wife, free love and concubinage are bound to become rampant, destroying the very basis of real monogamy.

In the Muslim East, on the one hand, polygamy was permissible, and on the other temptations and provocations to immorality did not exist. Therefore, true monogamy prevailed in most families. Concubinage never developed to the extent that gradually a philosophy had to be invented to justify it. In the East, it was never claimed that man was born polygamous and could not at all adhere to monogamy.

It may be asked what alternative a man has when polygamy is legally prohibited and, as the intellectuals say, man is polygamous by nature.

According to the thinking of these gentlemen, the answer is quite clear. Man should be legally monogamous and practically polygamous. He should not have more than one legal wife, but he should be free to cohabit with any number of women he likes. Concubinage is the natural right of man. It is unchivalrous to restrict him to one woman.

We believe that the time has come when readers should have a clear idea of the problem and should know what the question really is. It is not a question of whether polygamy or monogamy is better. There is no doubt that monogamy is preferable, for monogamy means an exclusive family life. In this system, the body and the soul of each of the husband and the wife belong exclusively to the other. It is obvious that the spirit of marriage is the union of hearts, which manifests itself better in an exclusive marriage. Humanity does not have to choose between monogamy and polygamy.

The only problem is that absolute monogamy is not practical in certain social circumstances, especially when the number of women in need of marriage is greater than the number of eligible men. Absolute monogamy pervading every family is only fiction. There are only two alternatives: either to officially recognise polygamy or to encourage unrestricted concubinage. In the case of the first alternative only a small percentage of married men, in no case more than 10% will have more than one wife and all women in need of a husband will be able to secure a home and family life. In the case of the second alternative every woman having no legal husband will have sexual relations with several men, and thus almost all married men will become practically polygamous.

This is the correct picture of polygamy. But the partisans of the European way of life are not prepared to present the true picture of the problem. They do not want to tell the truth openly. In reality they defend concubinage. They regard the legal wife as a burden and a stumbling block in their way. To them even one wife is too much; let alone two, three or four. They pretend to be supporters of monogamy, but, in fact, complete freedom from matrimonial restrictions is what they would like to have.

10.22   Wiles of the 20th Century Man

The 20th century man has succeeded in fooling woman on many questions related to family rights. He uses the high-sounding words of equality and liberty to reduce his own commitments and to add to his opportunities for enjoyment.

But there are a few questions in respect of which he has been so successful as in disparaging polygamy.

Occasionally, we come across writings that make us wonder whether their authors are simpletons or rogues. One writer says: At present, in the advanced countries, relations between husband and wife are based on a system of reciprocal rights and obligations, and for that reason it is as difficult for a woman to recognise polygamy in any form, as for a man to bear the existence of rivals in the field of his conjugal relations.

We do not know whether that is their conception of the problem, or whether they really do not know that polygamy has resulted from a social problem, which puts a heavy responsibility on the shoulders of married men and women, and for which no solution other than polygamy has, so far, been discovered. Shutting the eyes to the real problem and raising the slogans of 'long live monogamy' and 'down with polygamy' can serve no purpose.

Do they not know that polyandry is neither a part of woman's rights nor a part of man's rights. It has nothing to do with their reciprocal needs.

It is ridiculous to say that it is as difficult for woman to agree to polygamy as it is for a man to tolerate the existence of rivals in the matter of conjugal relations. Apart from the fact that such a comparison is wrong, it appears that these gentlemen do not know that the present-day Western world, by the glitter of which they are so greatly dazzled, actually requires the husband to respect the love-affairs of his wife and tolerate the existence of rivals. It deprecates any interference on the part of the husband as jealousy and fanaticism. We wish that our young men had a deeper knowledge of what is going on in the West.

As polygamy is the outcome of a social problem and is not man's instinct, it is obvious that in a society where women are not in a numerical majority, it should automatically disappear or at least its incidence should be minimised. But it will not be proper to ban it even in such circumstances, if such circumstances exist at all. The legal prohibition of polygamy is neither sufficient nor something correct. There are certain prerequisites to achieve this end. First of all, social justice should be ensured and adequate opportunities of suitable employment made available for every man, so that everyone eligible for marriage should be in a position to have a family life. The second condition is that every woman should be free to choose her husband and should be under no compulsion by her guardians or anyone else to marry any particular person of their choice. It is obvious that a woman who has a chance to marry a bachelor would never like to marry a man who has a wife. It is only their guardians who sell women for the sake of money and give them in marriage to the moneyed people.

The third condition is that there should not be too many temptations which seduce even women who have husbands, not to mention women who have no husbands.

Should society be earnestly interested in reformation and in enforcing true monogamy, it should endeavour for the fulfilment of the above three conditions. Otherwise, a legal ban on polygamy will only lead to moral depravation.

10.23   Crisis resulting from the Privation of Women having no Husbands

If the women in need of marriage outnumber such men (bachelors), the prohibition of polygamy is a treachery to humanity. It is not merely a question of suppressing the rights of some women only. Had this been the case, it could have been tolerated to a certain extent. The crisis which society faces, as a result of legally enforced monogamy, possesses a bigger danger than any other crisis, for the family organisation is more sacred than any other organisation.

A woman who is deprived of her natural right is a living being, prone to all the reactions of a living being such as in the case of privation. She is a human being who is susceptible to psychic disorders and complexes. She is an Eve armed with the weapons for seducing men.

She is not wheat or barley, the surplus stock of which can be dumped into the sea or stored for any future emergency. She is not a house or a room, which, if not acquired immediately, can be locked. She is a living person. She is a human being. She is a woman. She has marvellous potentialities. If she is frustrated she can ruin the society. She cannot be an idle onlooker while others enjoy life. Her privation will give rise to complexes and malice. If malice and instinct join hands, the consequences can only be catastrophic.

The women deprived of family life will do their utmost to seduce men and to exploit their weakness in this respect. Even then the matter will not end. The wives, who will find their husbands to be unfaithful, will think of taking revenge upon them and thus will become unfaithful. About the final result, the less said the better.

This final result has been summarised in the well know Kinsey Report in one sentence: 'The men and women of America have surpassed all other nations in unfaithfulness'.

It is to be noted that the matter does not end with the corruption and perversion of men. The conflagration in the end also engulfs the women having husbands and families.

10.24   Various Reactions Concerning the Excess of Women

The phenomenon of the comparative superabundance of women has always existed in human history, but the reactions to this phenomenon, which create difficulties for the society, have not been the same in all societies. The people, who were more attached to the spirit of piety and chastity and were guided by the teachings of the great heavenly religions, solved the problem by adopting the system of polygamy. Other people who were not so greatly attached to this spirit used the phenomenon as a means of indulging in debauchery.

Neither was polygamy in the East introduced by Islam, nor its prohibition in the West in any way related to the religion of Christ. This custom existed in the East before the inception of Islam and was sanctioned by the Eastern religions. Even in the Bible, it has not been expressly prohibited.

A greater blow has been given to monogamy by the nations which have taken to debauchery than by those, which have adopted polygamy.

Dr. Mohammed Husayn Haikal, author of the book, *Life of Mohammed*, after quoting several verses of the Holy Qur'an on the question of polygamy, says: These verses favour adherence to monogamy. They say that if you fear that you will not be able to do justice to more than one wife, then have only one. Incidentally, they emphasise that absolute justice is not possible. Anyhow in view of the fact that there may be occasions when polygamy is unavoidable, they allow it conditionally. The Holy Prophet (saws) himself contracted several marriages when a large number of Muslim women lost their husbands during the early battles of Islam. Is it possible to say that following wars, epidemics and disturbances, which take a toll of thousands and sometimes millions of people, it is still preferable to adhere to monogamy rather than to adopt polygamy as an exceptional case and with the condition of doing justice to their wife or wives? Can the people of the West claim that after the World War the law of monogamy has been enforced in the same way in which it now exists in name?

10.25   Drawbacks and Defects of Polygamy

A happy married life depends on sincerity, tolerance, sacrifice and unity. All these things are endangered in the case of polygamy. Apart from the unenviable position of the wives and the children in a plural marriage, the responsibilities of the husband himself are so heavy and crushing that it is no fun to shoulder them.

Most of the men, who are happy and satisfied with polygamy, are those who practically evade their legal and moral responsibilities. They turn all their attention to one wife and ignore the other, whom they leave, in the words of the Holy Qur'an, 'hanging'. What such people call polygamy is in reality a sort of monogamy coupled with high-handedness, tyranny and criminal injustice. There is a proverb current among the common person, which says: 'One God, One Wife'.

That has been and is the belief of most of the people and, if we measure the problem by the standard of individual happiness, it is correct. The rule of monogamy, if not applicable to all men, is certainly applicable to most of them.

If someone thinks that polygamy, with all the legal and moral responsibilities it entails, is a bed of roses, he is sadly mistaken. From the angle of personal comfort and happiness, monogamy is definitely preferable.

10.26   Correct Appraisal

In any case, comparing it with monogamy cannot make a correct appraisal of the system of polygamy, which emanates from personal and social needs. The right way of evaluating such a system is to give consideration to the causes which give rise to it, to see what evil consequences will follow if those causes are overlooked, and at the same time to give a thought to the defects and drawbacks of the system itself. It is only after fully weighing all the pros and cons of a system that we can arrive at the right conclusion. To illustrate the point we give an example. It we look at the system of conscription only from the angle of the interests and inclinations of a family, to which a recruit belongs, there can be no doubt that the law of conscription is not a good law. It would have been much better if there had been no such law, and no darling of a family had been snatched from his family, and occasionally sent to the warfront.

But this is not a correct evaluation of the question. Along with the separation of a son from his family, we should also take into consideration the defence requirements of the country. If we do that, it will appear perfectly reasonable and logical that an adequate number of citizens should always be kept ready for the defence of the country and their families should willingly put up with the inconveniences caused by compulsory military service.

Earlier, we referred to some individual and collective needs which sometimes justify polygamy. Now, to prepare the ground for an overall judgement, let us discuss the defects and drawbacks of this system. We admit that it has certain demerits, but we do not believe that all that is said against it is valid. Anyway, we propose to discuss its defects from various angles.

10.27   From the Psychological Angle

The conjugal relations are not confined to such material and physical matters as bodily contact and financial support. If they had been so confined, it would have been easy to justify polygamy, for material and physical matters are divisible between several people, each having a share.

The basis of conjugal relations is emotional and psychological. They are based on such things as love, emotions and feelings. Married life means the union of hearts. Like all metaphysical things, love and feelings are not divisible. They cannot be rationed among several people nor can a definite quota thereof be allotted to any one. A heart cannot be divided between two people. Love and worship are concomitant. They do not admit a rival. Love cannot be measured and distributed like wheat and barley. Furthermore, feelings cannot be controlled.

The heart dominates the head. The spirit of marriage, that is, its human aspect, which distinguishes the relations between two human beings from the purely instinctive relation between two animals, is neither divisible nor controlled. Hence, polygamy should not be permitted.

To our belief, the above statement is exaggerated. It is true that emotions and feelings constitute the spirit of marriage.

It is also true that feelings are not controllable. But it is pure fancy, rather a fallacy, to say that feelings are not divisible.

It is not a question of dividing and distributing feelings in the same way as a material object is divided and distributed. It is a question of the mental capacity of man, which is not too limited to accommodate relations with two people. A father having ten sons loves all of them to the extent of worship and makes sacrifices for them.

Anyhow, one thing is definite. Love cannot be as intense in the case of several wives as it can be in the case of one. Intense love is not consistent with plurality, but it is not consistent with reason too.

In his book, *Marriage and Morality*, Russell says that many people today regard love as a fair exchange of feelings. This argument alone, irrespective of all other arguments, is enough to condemn polygamy.

If it is only a question of the fair exchange of feelings, we wonder why the exchange should be monopolistic. A father having several children loves them all, and they all reciprocally love him. Is not the exchange of feelings between them fair? Incidentally, even in the case of several children, a father's love for each child is always greater than the love of each child for the father. The most amazing part of the above statement is that, it has been made by a person who advises the husbands to respect their wives' love affairs with strangers and not to interfere in them. He also gives the same advice to the wives. Does he believe that the exchange of feelings between a husband and a wife will still be fair?

10.28   From the Angle of Behaviour

In the case of polygamy, the relations between co-wives are proverbially notorious for incongruity. A woman usually regards the co-wife as her worst enemy. Plurality often induces wives to take action against each other and occasionally against the husband too. It creates malice and turns the family atmosphere, expected to be an atmosphere of sincerity and serenity, into a veritable battlefield. Enmity and rivalry, existing between the mothers, passes on to their children and two or more blocks are formed. The family atmosphere, instead of being the first school of moral training for the children, turns into a school of dissension and inhuman behaviour.

There is no doubt that polygamy has all these evil effects. But one point must not be overlooked. We have to see whether they are the natural effects of plurality or the product of the unreasonable attitude of the husband and the second wife. We believe that most of the evil effects are not the direct result of plurality, but are the consequences of its wrong implementation.

Suppose a husband and a wife live together and lead a normal life. In the meantime the husband comes across another woman and takes a fancy to her. After a secret understanding between the two, the second woman raids the house and takes undue advantage of the husband, and challenges the authority of the first. It can be easily imagined what the reaction of the first wife would be. There is nothing more disturbing to a woman than the impression that her husband despises her. To be unable to retain the affection of her husband is the biggest failure of a wife. When the husband takes to arrogance and licentiousness, and the second wife plays the role of a freebooter, it is useless to expect the first wife to be patient.

But things will be different and the internal conflict will be greatly reduced if the first wife knows that her husband is justified in having a second wife and that he is not fed up with her. The husband also must not assume arrogance nor should he indulge in sensuality. After having a second wife, he should more than ever be kind to his first wife, and should more than ever respect her feelings. The second wife also should remember that the first wife has certain rights, which are to be respected. In short, all the parties concerned should remember that they have taken a step to solve a social problem.

The law of polygamy is a progressive solution of a social problem and is based on the broader interests of the society. Those who execute it should possess a standard of high thinking and should be well trained in the Islamic ways.

Experience has shown that if the husband is neither licentious nor arrogant, and the wife is convinced that he needs a second wife, she, herself, volunteers to arrange the second marriage of her husband. In such cases the aforementioned troubles do not arise, as most of them result from the misbehaviour of the husbands.

10.29   From the Moral Angle

It is said that polygamy means indulgence in sensuality. Morality demands that the gratification of sexual desire is minimised, for the nature of man is such that the more he indulges in sex, the more intense his yearning for it becomes.

Montague in his book, *Spirit of Laws*, while dealing with the question of polygamy, says that the King of Morocco has, in his harem, women of all races including white, yellow and black. Even if this man had twice as many women as he has, he still would have craved for more. Sensuality is like miserliness. The more it is practiced, the more intense it becomes. As the collection of more and more gold and silver intensifies greed and avarice, indulgence in polygamy promotes vicious and unnatural ways of love making, for, in the field of sensuality, every act which exceeds the limit, encourages perversion. When disturbances broke out in Istanbul, not a single woman was found in the harem of the ruler, because he indulged in unnatural lovemaking (homosexuality).

This objection can be looked at from two angles. Firstly, it has been claimed that sexual acts are repugnant to pure morality and that sexual desire should be controlled to the utmost extent. Secondly, it has been asserted that human nature is such that the more a man indulges in sex, the more intense his yearning for it becomes.

As regards the first view, it may be said that unfortunately it represents a wrong way of thinking. It has been inspired by Christian, Hindu, Buddhist and Cynic ideas of morality based on renunciation. From the Islamic point of view, it is not correct to say that the less the gratification of sexual desire, the more moral it is. (Perhaps, according to this theory, perfect morality means no gratification at all). It is only excessive indulgence, which is regarded by Islam as repugnant to morality.

To ascertain whether polygamy means excessive indulgence let us see whether man is, by nature, monogamous or not. As stated earlier, nobody now believes that man is purely monogamous or that polygamy is an act of perversion. To the contrary, many sociologists are of the view that man is, by nature, polygamous and monogamy is as unnatural as celibacy.

Though we do not believe that man is polygamous by nature, we also do not believe that he is purely monogamous and that polygamy is unnatural, and a sort of perversion, like homosexuality.

Those who, like Montesquieu, regard polygamy tantamount to licentiousness, have harems in their mind. They think that Islam, by allowing plurality, wants to provide an excuse for the harems of the Abbasid Caliphs and the Ottoman Sultans. But in fact Islam is totally opposed to such a thing. The terms and conditions laid down by Islam in respect of puerility are such that the chances of licentiousness are absolutely eliminated.

As for the second point that the more the natural desires are satisfied, the more they grow, and the more they are suppressed, the more they are pacified; it is diametrically opposed to the current Freudian theory.

According to the Freudists, instinctive desires are pacified if they are satiated, but if they are suppressed, they become violent. That is why the Freudists advocate complete freedom and the violation of all traditional restrictions and restraints in sexual matters. I wish that Montesquieu had been alive today and had seen how his theory is being ridiculed by the Freudists.

From the Islamic point of view, both the theories are false. Human nature has its own laws and limits, which must be recognised. It becomes passionate both as a result of privation as well as unrestricted freedom.

Anyway, neither is polygamy immoral and disturbing to spiritual peace, as Montesquieu and the like presume, nor is it against human nature, to be content with one or more legal wives as the Freudists claim.

10.30   From the Legal Angle

By virtue of a marriage contract, both the husband and the wife belong to each other, and each of them has a right to enjoy the other. As far as marital benefits are concerned, the marriage contract creates a sort of proprietary right. In the case of polygamy, it is the first wife who has the first claim to the marital benefits, and as such any transaction between the husband and another wife is ultra vireos, for the goods under transaction, as marital benefits may be called, have already been sold to the first wife. Hence no subsequent transaction can be valid without her consent. As such, if polygamy is to be allowed, its validity must depend upon the consent and agreement of the first wife. She should have the right to decide whether she can or cannot allow her husband to have another wife.

This means that to have a second, third and fourth wife is just as if a person had sold his property to a person and then resold it to a second, third and fourth customer. The validity of such a transaction will depend on the consent of the first, second and third buyers respectively. If the vendor actually delivers the property to the subsequent buyers without such consent, he is liable to prosecution.

This objection is based on the presumption that the legal nature of marriage is that of the exchange of benefits, and that each of the husband and the wife owns the marital benefits accruing from the other. Though this presumption is not sound, for the present we do not want to dispute it. Let us presume the position to be actually so. However this objection can be valid only in the case that the husband takes another wife just for pleasure. Obviously, if it is admitted that the legal nature of marriage is that of the exchange of marital benefits, plurality of marriage is not justifiable, so long as the wife can, in every respect, meet the lawful needs of her husband. But if there exists any of the justifying causes mentioned earlier, the objection becomes void. For instance, if the wife is barren or has attained the age of menopause and the husband is still in need of a child, or the wife is sick and not fit for cohabitation, the right of the wife will be no bar to plurality of marriage.

This is the position in case polygamy is only a personal requirement of the husband. But if it is a social requirement, for example, if women outnumber men in a society or the society needs a larger population, then the case is quite different. In such cases, plurality is a duty, which is to be performed by an adequate number of men. It is a duty to be carried out to save the society from corruption and prostitution or to increase the population of the community. When it is a question of social duty, obviously the question of the consent and permission of the wife does not arise. Suppose in a society women outnumber men or the society needs a larger population, then a social duty devolves on all married men and women which should be carried out by an adequate number of them in the spirit of self sacrifice. This is exactly like the case of conscription. The defence of the country devolves a duty on all families to send their dear ones to the front for the sake of the society. In such cases there is no question of the consent of the parties concerned.

They, who maintain that justice demands that polygamy must depend upon the consent of the existing wife, look at the question from a narrow angle. They think that a husband always wants to have more than one wife only for pleasure and variety. They forget that there can also be other individual and social needs. Basically, plurality of marriage should not be acceptable even with the consent of the existing wife, if no individual or social need is involved.

10.31   From the Philosophical Angle

The law of polygamy is repugnant to the principle of equality between men and women as human beings. As man and woman both have equal rights, either both of them should be allowed to practice polygamy or neither of them. It is a pure and simple discrimination to allow man to have several wives and not to allow woman to have several husbands. To allow man to have up to four wives means that the value of a woman is only one-fourth that of man. This position is derogatory to woman and is not even in keeping with the Islamic view in respect of inheritance and evidence. In respect of giving evidence, two women are regarded as equal to one man.

This is the most flimsy objection. It seems that the critics have paid no attention to the individual and the social causes of polygamy. They think that it is only a question of passion. Hence man and woman should be treated equally. We have already discussed the cases in which polygamy is justified. We have also pointed out the circumstances in which a duty in respect of a husbandless woman devolves on all married men and women. Hence, it is not necessary to dwell on this question any more.

It is enough to say that if the teachings of Islam in respect of polygamy, inheritance and evidence had been due to any apathy towards woman's rights, and had Islam discriminated between man and woman as human beings, it would have held a uniform view on all relevant questions. In the case of inheritance it would not have allowed woman only a half of the share of man in some cases and an equal share in others. Similarly, in the case of evidence there would not have been different rules in different cases. All this shows that Islam has some other philosophy. We have already explained the question of inheritance in a preceding chapter. We have also pointed out elsewhere that from the Islamic point of view the question of equality between man and woman as human beings is a part of basic human rights. In any case, while dealing with family rights, Islam has also taken into consideration certain other aspects which are more important than the question of mere equality.

10.32   Role of Islam in the Development of Polygamy

Islam neither invented polygamy (for it had been in existence for centuries before the inception of Islam), nor did it abolish it, for there existed no other solution for certain social problems. Islam only reformed this ancient custom.

10.32.1 Limitations

Before Islam, one could have an unlimited number of wives and could form a harem. Islam prescribed a maximum limit. It did not allow anyone to have more than four wives. Those who had more than four wives at the time of embracing Islam were required to release the extra wives.

We come across the names of several such people in the early history of Islam. A man named Ghaylan bin Aslamah had ten wives. Another man named Nawfal bin Mu'awiyah had five. The Holy Prophet (saws) ordered them to part with their extra wives.

The Shi'ah narrations report that during the days of Imam Sadiq (as) a Zoroastrian embraced Islam. He had seven wives. The Imam (as) was asked as to what that man should do with his wives. The Imam (as) said that he must part with three.

10.32.2 Justice and Equal Treatment

Another reform introduced by Islam was the condition of giving equal treatment to all the wives. Islam does not allow any discrimination between the wives or between their children. The Holy Qur'an expressly says:

> If you fear that you will not do justice (to them) then have one only.
> (Qur'an, 4:3)

The Pre-Islamic world observed equality neither between the wives nor between their children. We have already quoted Christenson and others who say that during the Sassanid period polygamy was customary in Iran. One or more wives were called favourite wives and they enjoyed full rights and others, known as servant-wives, had lesser legal rights. Only the male children of the servant-wives were recognised to be the members of the paternal family.

Islam abolished all such customs and usages. It does not allow any wife or her children to be regarded as inferior to the other wife or children of her husband. Will Durant in his book, *History of Civilisations*, vol. 1, writes:

> When a person accumulated wealth he feared that if it would be divided among all his children, each one of them would receive only as small portion of it. So he felt anxious to make a distinction between his real and favourite wife and other mistresses to enable the children of the real wife only to inherit from him.

This shows that in the ancient world discrimination between the wives and between their children was common. Anyhow, surprisingly enough Will Durant adds:

> Till recently this continued to be the case in Asia. Gradually the real wife took the position of the sole wife. Other wives either disappeared or became clandestine mistresses.

Will Durant did not take notice of the fact, or he did not want to do so, that 14 centuries ago Islam abolished discrimination between the children. To have one real wife and several secret concubines is a European and not an Asian custom. It has only lately infiltrated into Asia.

Anyhow, the second reform, which Islam introduced in the domain of polygamy, was the abolition of discrimination between the wives and between their children. No form of favouritism with any particular wife is permissible. Almost all jurists are unanimous on this point. Only a few minor juristic schools have interpreted the rights of women in a way that appears discriminatory. But there is no denying the fact that their view is in contradiction with the correct interpretation of the Qur'anic passage. The Holy Prophet (saws) is reported by both the Shi'ah and the Sunnis to have said:

> He who has two wives but does not treat them equally and shows leaning towards one of them, will be raised on the Day of

Resurrection in such a state that one side of his body will be dragging
along the ground. He will eventually go to Hell.

Justice is the greatest moral virtue. To prescribe the condition of
justice and equal treatment means that the husband is required to
be in possession of the highest moral qualities. As the feelings of
man in respect of all his wives usually are not the same,
observation of justice and abstinence from unequal treatment is one
of his most onerous duties.

We all know that the Holy Prophet (saws), during the last ten years
of his life, that is, during the period of his stay in Medina, married
several women. This was a period of Islamic wars and at that time
the number of women, who had nobody to look after them, was
quite large. Most of the wives of the Prophet (saws) were widowed
and aged. Several of them had children by their former husbands.

The only maiden he married was Aisha, who often proudly said
that she was the only woman whom no husband, other than the
Prophet (saws), had ever touched.

The Holy Prophet always gave strict equal treatment to all his
wives and never discriminated between them. Urwah bin Zubayr
was a nephew (sister's son) of Aisha. He enquired of his aunt as to
how the Holy Prophet (saws) treated his wives. Aisha said that he
treated them with justice and complete equality. He never gave
preference to anyone over anyone else. Almost daily he called on
every wife and enquired after her health and how she was in
general. He passed the night with one wife, turn by turn.

If by chance he wanted to pass a night with another wife, he
formally came to the wife whose turn it was and took her
permission. If the permission was given he would go, otherwise he
would not. Aisha said that she personally declined to give
permission as and when he asked for it.

Even during his last illness which led to his death and when he was
too weak to move, the Holy Prophet (saws) scrupulously adhered

to the principle of equality in his treatment with his wives. His bed was shifted from one room to another, daily. At last, one day he called all his wives and asked them to permit him to stay in one room. With their permission he stayed in the room of Aisha.

At the time when he had two wives, Imam Ali (as) was so particular that he performed even ablution before prayer *(wudhu)* in the house of the wife whose turn was there.

Islam attaches so much importance to the principle of justice and equality in treatment that it does not allow the husband and the second wife to enter into a stipulation at the time of their marriage, by which the second wife agrees to live on unequal terms with the first wife. This means that it is an obligatory duty of the husband to treat each wife on terms strictly equal, and that he cannot renounce this responsibility by entering into a prior agreement with anyone of his wives. All that the second wife can do is to forego some of her rights for practical purposes. But no such condition can be stipulated, nor is it possible that she should not have equal rights. Similarly, the first wife also can voluntarily forego some of her rights for practical purposes, but she cannot formally renounce them.

Once Imam Baqir (as) was asked whether by mutual consent it could be stipulated that the husband would visit one of his wives only once a week or once a month, or that the maintenance allowance of one wife would not be equal to that of another wife. The Imam (as) said that such stipulations were not valid even with the consent of any wife. By virtue of marriage, every wife was entitled to full marital rights. All that she could do was to forego some or all of her rights after marriage, either to please her husband or for some other reason.

With all these strict moral conditions, polygamy becomes a duty instead of being a means of pursuit of pleasure. Pursuit of pleasure and licentiousness are possible only in an atmosphere of complete freedom to pursue one's desires. But where there is a question of discipline, justice and duty, there can be no room for lewdness.

Those who indulge in licentiousness under the pretext of polygamy misuse an Islamic law and the society has every right to call them to account and punish them.

10.32.3 Other Conditions

Besides the condition of justice and equality of treatment, there are also other conditions, which a husband has to fulfil. We all know that a wife has a number of financial and other rights, which the husband has to discharge. A husband has the right of having more than one wife, provided his financial condition allows him to do so. Financial soundness is a prerequisite to monogamy also. Anyhow, we skip over further discussion of this question. Physical and sexual potentialities are another prerequisite.

It is reported in *Al-Kafi* and *Al-Wasail* that Imam Sadiq (as) has said that in case somebody collects several women, while he is not fit to satisfy them all, he will bear full responsibility if any of them takes to sin.

The historical accounts of the harems narrate many stories of young women, who, forced by the pressure of their sexual urges, had recourse to sin and occasionally became the cause of crimes and murders.

By now our readers should have become aware of the causes for polygamy and why Islam has not abolished this system. They should also have become aware of the conditions and limits prescribed by Islam in this respect. Islam has not disparaged women by allowing this system, but has rendered a great service to them. If polygamy is not allowed even where women of marriageable age outnumber men, women may become worthless toys in the hands of men. They may be treated worse than slave-girls, for man recognises the child of a slave-girl as his own, but he makes no such commitment in respect of his mistresses and concubines.

10.33   Apprehension of not doing Justice

To be fair, it must be admitted that the number of those, who observe all the conditions laid down by the laws of Islam in respect of polygamy, is very small. According to the Islamic law, if a man apprehends that the use of water may be harmful to him he should not perform ablution for prayers, and if he apprehends that fasting may be harmful to him he should not keep fast. You come across many people who inquire of you whether they should or should not perform ablution, or whether they should or should not keep fast, for they apprehend that performing ablution or keeping fast might be harmful to them. Such inquiries are in order. Such people should not perform ablution and should not keep fast.

But the Holy Qur'an specifically says that if you fear that you will not treat your wives equally, you must have only one wife. Still you do not come across a single person who may say that he apprehends that he might not be able to treat two wives equally, and may inquire whether in his circumstances he should or should not have a second wife. It is evident that some people knowing well that they will not be able to do justice still have several wives. They do so under the cloak of Islamic law. These are the people who bring a bad name to Islam by their unworthy action.

10.34   Harems

Another reason why Islam is criticised for polygamy is because of the system of harems adopted by the former caliphs and sultans. Some Christian writers and missionaries have described polygamy in Islam as equivalent to the system of harems with all its shameful and cruel aspects.

Unfortunately, some of our own writers, who parrot the ideas expressed by Europeans, unnecessarily associate polygamy with harems. They are not endowed with enough independence of thought to be able to distinguish between the two.

10.35   Modern Man and Polygamy

Modern man is averse to polygamy, not because he wants to be content with one wife, but because he wants to satisfy his sense of variety by indulging in unlimited adultery, for which ample facilities are available. Sin and not fidelity has taken the place of polygamy. That is why modern man is opposed to the plurality of wives, which commits him to many duties and responsibilities, financial and otherwise. In the past, even for a licentious man, opportunities of sin were limited. That is why he had to take recourse to polygamy, and, in spite of evading many duties, he still had to shoulder certain responsibilities in respect of his wives and children. Modern man, who has ample opportunity for enjoyment, does not see any necessity of making the least commitment. Hence he is averse to polygamy.

The modern man employs women as secretaries, typists etc. for his enjoyment, and credits the expense to the account of the government, his firm or any other organization in which he may be working, without having to pay a single penny from his own pocket.

The modern man changes his mistress after every few days without undergoing any formalities of dower, maintenance and divorce. A certain successful businessman was vehemently opposed to polygamy, but he, himself, always kept a young, beautiful secretary at his side whom he upgraded every year. With such possibilities, there is evidently no need to countenance polygamy.

We read in the life account of Bertrand Russell, who was a severe opponent to polygamy, that two women, besides his grandmother, played an important role in his life. One was his wife, Alice, and the other was his sweetheart, Morrel. Morrel, who was one of the most prominent women of that period, was on friendly terms with a number of the writers of the early 20th century. Evidently, such a man could not support polygamy.

Apparently it was Russell's extra-marital love which put an end to his relationship with Alice. He, himself, writes that one afternoon, while he was going on a bicycle to a summer resort in the suburbs, he suddenly felt that he no longer loved Alice.

Conclusion

Having examined and criticised the various forms of "plurality of partners", it becomes clear that polygamy, whereby a man can marry more than one wife, is the only form that is acceptable and beneficial to all parties involved. It is a custom which has been practised since the ancient times and by civilised societies, and is grossly misunderstood and hypocritically condemned by the West.

Polygamy preceded the advent of Islam, which came only to restrict and control the way it was being used, setting in place rules and regulations to ensure the protection of those concerned.

It has been shown that polygamy serves the society in terms of protecting the moral structure as compared to the West, where in reality, polygamy is apparent, but through deception and without moral or legal responsibility.

The causes for the emergence of polygamy have been discussed, classified and justified accordingly. Most importantly, it has been shown through rational and statistical analysis that due to the numerical disproportion of the sexes, polygamy under certain conditions becomes a necessity and social responsibility.

Article 11

Flexible Marriage (Al-Mut'ah)

Ali Hussain Al-Hakim

Abstract

Flexible marriage or Mut'ah has always been a controversial issue both within the differing schools of Islamic Jurisprudence and amongst the laity. The aim of this paper is to rediscover the wisdom behind such a Divine law. After explaining the reason behind rejecting the typical term used for this kind of marriage, we will attempt to show firstly through an examination of Qur'anic verses and historical narrations that the permissibility of this law is well-founded. We will then demonstrate the reason why it is considered as an institutional marriage and we will present a comparison between both the flexible and permanent marriages. This is followed by a justification for our adoption of a modern term for this marriage, i.e. "The Flexible Marriage". We then present a brief elaboration of the family life and sexual satisfaction in the West, which manifests the parallel ideas of both cultures. We will then aim to highlight the purpose this law serves within the community and how it can be viewed as a wise solution for mankind's need for sexual satisfaction and as a mercy from God. Lastly we will show how people's opposition to and disapproval of this Divine law is in fact based on the way it is misused and abused within society.

Introduction

If we look at the texts of the *Shari'ah* law, dating back to the early periods of Islam, we are able to discover regulations concerning a form of marriage termed as *Al-Mut'ah*. The root of the Arabic term *Al-Mut'ah,* signifies to 'carry or take away'. Within this marriage, stipulating the dowry and time of its duration is a requisite for the validation of its contract. The aforementioned term -*Al-Mut'ah*- is the most commonly employed word amongst the Muslim jurisprudents when relating to this type of marriage. References to it and its derivatives can also be discovered in the Qur'an and Islamic narrations. This form of marriage has also been referred to as the 'temporary marriage', and was referred to as such during the lifetime of the Prophet (saws) and during the successive generations. The Shi'ah Imams (as), their contemporaries, as well as the proponents and opponents of this marriage have equally implemented both terms. The books of jurisprudence have used the following terms: *Mut'ah, al-nikah al-munqati'* (discontinued marriage) and finally *al-nikah al muwaqqat* (temporary marriage).

The author is of the firm belief that this term was badly translated into English after being wrongly understood in the original Arabic. Firstly, the word *muwaqqat* does not mean: 'temporary' in this context, rather it means: fixed-time. Secondly, the word is wrongly understood in Arabic, because it misleads everyone into assuming that it can never continue for a long period of time. I have no doubt that every woman will categorically reject a proposal of 'temporary marriage', nor give it a second thought, if it is introduced in this way. Obviously, it is absurd for any woman to give her heart, and base her love on an unreliable provisional agreement. Thus this technical term 'temporary marriage' encapsulates all negative thoughts that a word can ever bear within such a human being's complicated relationship. Therefore this paper has adopted another term, which even if not employed by other jurisprudents, yet captures and relates its positive fundamental nature.

All Muslims agree that this marriage was institutionalised by *Shari'ah* Law directly through the blessing of the Prophet (saws) of Islam, and that it was extensively practised within the Muslim community. Every jurisprudent -regardless of his sectarian background- unequivocally claims that, that which has been permitted and made lawful in *Shari'ah* Law, maintains its legality providing that place and time conditions do not affect the underlying philosophy of its legislation.

11.1   The Islamic Theory regarding Sexual Satisfaction

In Islamic *Shari'ah* Law the only structure in which sexual satisfaction is permitted is when it fulfils two requirements: 1) It is heterosexual 2) Both parties involved mutually agree and form a contractual "marriage". An exemption to this was in the past, when the institution of slavery was widely adopted and thus relationships with slave-girls were permissible. Obviously, nowadays such an institution does not exist and therefore it is an irrelevant matter for discussion. The Qur'an has explicitly declared this Islamic theory in the following verses:

> Successful indeed are the believers... and those who guard their chastity (i.e. their private parts, from illegal acts), except from their wives or (the slaves) that their right hand possess. (Qur'an, 23:1,5-7)

All these forms of lawful relationship are accepted amongst Muslims, however there are certain disagreements regarding the various forms of marriage. Hypothetically, marriage can be shaped firstly, into the ordinary, permanent type; whereby both sides agree to live together indefinitely, fulfilling certain duties and responsibilities incumbent on them, or secondly; a marriage whereby there are fewer responsibilities and fewer mutual duties.[1]

Within *Shari'ah* Law all Muslim scholars also firmly agree that there are two kinds of marriage: The ordinary one, i.e. permanent, and the second; the fixed-time marriage, which amongst jurisprudents has more often been called *Al-Mut'ah*. Among Muslims there are some who believe that the flexible marriage is no longer lawful, whilst others believe that it is still lawful and in fact very beneficial.

Those who believe that it is unlawful believe that the Prophet of Islam (saws), through Allah's command, allowed it for a very short period and thereafter disallowed it.[2] Those who believe it is lawful believe that the Prophet of Islam (saws) never prohibited it but rather it was the second Caliph -after the demise of the Prophet (saws) (at which time the Islamic *Shari'ah* Law cannot be changed)- who made it illegal. Thus, we may initially discuss the legality of this marriage, and then clarify its nature and qualities.

---

[1] Nowadays within Western countries one may recall a similar practice, i.e. the institution of (boy-girlfriend) as a typical manifestation of such a flexible relationship, however within Islamic *Shari'ah* Law it is not accepted that a Muslim virgin chooses a flexible marriage.

[2] Ibn Qudamah, *Al-Mughni,* Beirut, Lebanon, Third edition, vol. 6, p. 644.

11.2   The Legality and the Islamic Historical Roots of Mut'ah

Those who find *Mut'ah* lawful, support their claim from a verse in the Qur'an in which they believe it (flexible marriage) is mentioned. Obviously, if something was proclaimed lawful in the Qur'an, and has not been made unlawful elsewhere in the Qur'an, then it should remain permissible. The matter of dispute is rooted in the Qur'anic verse 4:24, which is here presented as in Mirza Puya's translation and *tafsir* (explanatory notes) of the Holy Qur'an:

> As to those whom you married for a fixed time (mut'ah), give them their agreed dowries; and there is no sin for you in what you mutually agree together after what has been settled. (Qur'an, 4:24)

The corresponding explanatory note follows: "فما استمتعتم به"
"Famastamta-tum bihi"

> And those women engaged in Mut'ah - a timed alliance with a woman - after the Mut'ah is null and void the parties are not entitled to inherit each other. This timed alliance or a temporary marriage or wedding was current during the time of the Holy Prophet, during the caliphate of Abu Bakr and also for some time during the regime of Umar, or later at his own choice against the sanction of the Holy Qur'an which is always and in all matters irrevocable and in which position was respected by Abu Bakr and even by himself. (The Holy Qur'an, translation and exegesis by Mirza Mahdi Puya, p.370)

If we now look at a different translation, we find that there is no clear mention of the flexible marriage referred to as being temporary in nature. Let us examine M. Pickhall's and T. B. Irving's translations:

And those of whom ye seek content (by marrying them), give unto them their portions as a duty. And there is no sin for you in what you do by mutual agreement after the duty (hath been done). (Pickthall)

Since you have thereby sought enjoyment with them, give them their marriage portions as is stipulated. Yet it will not be held against you should you come to other terms about it even after what has been stipulated. (Irving)

Thus, for the one who is not an expert in Qur'anic Arabic, it is difficult to determine whether *"famastamta-tum bihi"* in the Arabic version refers to *Mut'ah*, because although it is correctly asserted that the verb is derived from the same root, the literal meaning could, though, be referring to the other kind of marriage as well. One is then obliged to follow the narrations surrounding this verse in order to clarify the matter.

Both historians and jurisprudents have stated that the Prophet (saws) allowed Muslims to practise *Mut'ah* during their journeys and/or on long trips. It is mentioned in a narration, that the Prophet (saws) permitted flexible marriage after the Battle of Hunain. Thus we cannot say that people practised it because they did not know that it was forbidden. The narrations also confirm that flexible marriage was carried out with the direct order of the Prophet (saws). However, Sunni scholars also claim that he prohibited it on the Day of Khaibar. If the Prophet (saws) forbade the flexible marriage outright on the Day of Khaibar (1/7 AH), why was it then practised after the battle of Hunain (after 10/8 AH) once it had already been prohibited by direct order of the Prophet (saws)?

In other words: How is it possible that flexible marriage is forbidden perpetually and at two different points in time, once on the Day of Khaibar (1/7 AH) and again on the victory of Mecca (9/8 AH). People were practising it between these two occurrences of time, and indeed afterwards, with the explicit permission of the Prophet (saws).

Two Sunni scholars, Al-Qurtubi (in his commentary of the Qur'an) and Al-Nawawi (in his commentary of Sahih Muslim), are of the opinion that different narrations concerning the ban of *Mut'ah* specify seven different dates! Ibn Qudamah insisted, in his book *(Al-mughni),* that the Prophet (saws) revoked *Mut'ah.* The fact is that in Sahih Muslim one can read the following authentic narration:

> The Companions of the Prophet (saws) performed Mut'ah during his lifetime and during the reign of Abu Bakr and 'Umar.

Thus, during the first years of 'Umar's Caliphate this form of marriage was accepted. Any other such narrations tend to be spurious and contradictory. If the narrations are so contradictory and amongst such differing opinions, one cannot doubt that Imam Ali (as) was the most knowledgeable of all the companions. Concerning *Mut'ah,* he (as) said:

> Mut'ah is a mercy from Allah to his servants. If it were not for 'Umar forbidding it, no one would commit (the sin) fornication except the wretched (Shaqi).

Nearly all Muslims agree that the Prophet (saws) made the marriage of *Mut'ah* lawful; certain unconfirmed reports state that it was made unlawful following the demise of the Prophet (saws), and once the religion of Allah (swt) had been completed. It is also largely agreed that, after the Prophet (saws), no one has the authority to override his rulings.

Several years after the passing away of the Prophet (saws), 'Umar the second Caliph, for no just reason and with no legitimate authority to amend a law dictated by the Prophet (saws), suddenly declared from the pulpit:

> Two mut'ahs (referring to temporary marriage, and the combining of hajj and 'umra with having the right to sexual intercourse) were in force during the time of the Holy Prophet, but now I decree both of

them as unlawful; and I will punish those who practice them. (Tafsir Kabir's Fakhr Al-razi, Durr al Manthur's Souytti, Kashshaf's Zamakhshari, Mustadrak's An-nissabouri and others)

According to Tirmidhi, many Muslims, including the second Caliph's son, Ibn 'Umar, refused to agree with this decree, because it was made lawful by Allah (swt) and His Prophet (saws), whose pronouncements could never be revoked by anyone after him.

Thus the ruling issued by the second Caliph does not carry any authority and cannot affect the permissibility of the flexible marriage today; therefore one can deduce that such a practice is Islamically legal. There are a minority of Sunni Muslims – as we saw before - who turn to different narrations that indicate that the Prophet (saws), himself, forbade flexible marriage, but those narrations contradict each other – as we witnessed - and do not stand up to close scrutiny, and thus we are left with the same conclusion - that flexible marriage is permitted. However, to address this issue, we now quote from the Shi'ah Encyclopaedia:

> Sabra al-Juhanni reported on the authority of his father that, while he was with Allah's Messenger (saws), he said: O people, I had permitted you to contract temporary marriage with women, but Allah has forbidden it (now) until the Day of Resurrection. So he who has any (woman with this type of marriage contract) he should let her off, and do not take back anything you have given to them (as dower).[3]

A side comment of import is that in this narration the word *"Istimta'a"* has been used when referring to flexible marriage; this is the exact word employed which the Qur'an has used.

In the narration which follows after the above narration in Sahih Muslim, the same narrator (*Sabra*) has narrated the same narration

---

[3] Sunni references: *Sahih Muslim*, English version, vol. 2, chapter DXLI (Temporary Marriage), Tradition 3255; *Sahih Muslim*, Arabic version, Saudi Arabia, 1980, vol. 2, p. 1025, Tradition 21, Kitab al-Nikah, Bab Nikah al-Mut'ah.

with the addition that:

> I saw Allah's Messenger standing between the pillar and the gate of
> Ka'bah when saying the Narration.[4]

The following narration, however, indicates that the Prophet (saws)
allowed flexible marriage after the Battle of Hunain (after 10/8
AH), which was after the conquest of Mecca:

> Narrated Iyas Ibn Salama, on the authority of his father, that Allah's
> Messenger (saws) gave sanction for contracting temporary marriage
> for three nights in the year of Autas (this was after the Battle of
> Hunain in 8H), and then forbade it.[5]

Therefore, the Ahlul-Bayt (as) school of jurisprudence holds that
Mut'ah is lawful. Imam Ali ibn abi Talib (as) reversed the
uncalled-for innovation of the second Caliph, and thereafter it was
never again prohibited.

Finally, it is obvious that it is pointless arguing the legality of this
marriage with those who are not willing to accept it, for no reason
other than disliking it, or being pre-judgemental. The 'anti-*mut'ah*'
party may also claim that one ought to adhere to the law according
to the Islamic school of thought that he has chosen to follow, but
this is not a truly satisfactory answer for the inquisitive minds that
have not yet adopted a jurisprudence school.

---

[4] Sunni references: *Sahih Muslim*, English version, vol. 2, chapter DXLI
(Temporary Marriage), Tradition 3256; *Sahih Muslim*, Arabic version, Saudi
Arabia, 1980, vol. 2, p. 1025, Tradition 21, Kitab al-Nikah, Bab Nikah al-Mut'ah.
[5] Sunni references: *Sahih Muslim*, English version, vol. 2, chapter DXLI
(Temporary Marriage), Tradition 3251; *Sahih Muslim*, Arabic version, Saudi
Arabia, 1980, vol. 2, p. 1023, Tradition 18, Kitab al-Nikah, Bab Nikah al-Mut'ah.
{Note: The sentence inside parentheses is the Saudi translator's footnote, and is
not mine.}

11.3   Why is *Mut'ah* Considered as Marriage? What are the Differences?

The *Shari'ah* Law allows no provision for indecent acts, and only permits the intimate relationship between a man and a woman within the sanctity of marriage, whatever its form. It has further provided a severe punishment for those who violate these regulations of chastity. If *Mut'ah* is viewed bearing this in mind, we may conclude it is actually a great mercy from Allah (swt).

If we probe into the reasons as to why a person would want to contract such a form of marriage, and as to what purpose its serves, we may discover and understand the wisdom underlying the Divine permission of the flexible marriage. Indeed it is not intended as an alternative to permanent marriage, but rather as an option for those who have needs, and which permanent marriage does not cater for. To claim that permanent marriage meets all the requirements of each and every individual is foolish on close examination of society's different members. Thus flexible marriage was legislated in order to function alongside permanent marriage, and to fulfil the needs of those who cannot afford the heavy responsibilities necessitated by the permanent marriage. Imam Ali (as) is quoted on this issue as saying:

> It [temporary marriage] is permitted and absolutely allowed for the one whom Allah has not provided with the means of permanent marriage so that he may be chaste by performing mut'ah [temporary marriage].[6]

Mut'ah is a perfect example of marriage, therefore Shi'ah scholars have - for example - made it clear that the husband is obliged to pay the bride her dowry[7], and after being involved with her, is not allowed to avoid having sexual intercourse with his wife for more

---

[6] Al-Hur Al-'ameli, *Wasa'il*, Tehran: Al-Islamiyyah, 1984, vol. 14, pp. 449-450.
[7] M. J. Mughniyyah, *The Five Schools of Islamic Law*, Qum: Ansarian publication, 1995, p. 337.

than four months.[8] She has to preserve the waiting period *('Iddah)*, during which the husband has no right to marry her sister, unless the period *('Iddah)* during which the wife should wait, has expired. Furthermore the children are considered as fully legitimate and cannot be deprived the rights of heritage from both sides, i.e. their mother and father's side, and they should be treated equally as children from a permanent marriage.[9]

However, it is considered as 'flexible' because of the fact that *Mut'ah* differs from ordinary marriage chiefly in a key point that a fixed period of time functions as a central element within the mutual agreement, while there is no time limitation in the permanent marriage. Shi'ah scholars have emphasised that it is compulsory that the stipulated period of time should be mentioned. If, in a flexible marriage, the time period is not mentioned, the contract will either be void or be transformed unwittingly into a permanent marriage. However, the length of time is not specified; it is flexible.

Duties, which may be incumbent upon the husband in a permanent marriage, are not necessarily so in a flexible marriage. An apparent example is that of the right of subsistence, i.e. living, clothing and housing costs. For within a permanent marriage it is an obligation for a man to pay his wife's costs; however, a woman is not entitled to such rights within a flexible marriage. Ayatullah Sistani says:

> A woman with whom temporary marriage is contracted is not entitled to subsistence even if she becomes pregnant.[10]

> The woman within temporary marriage is not entitled to share the conjugal bed of her husband.[11]

---

[8] Ayatullah As-Sistani, *Islamic Laws*, London: The World Federation of Khoja Shi'ah Ithna 'Asharia, 1994, p. 448, article 2433.
[9] M. J. Mughniyyah, *The Five Schools of Islamic Law*, Qum: Ansarian publication, 1995, p. 337.
[10] Ayatullah As-Sistani, *Islamic Laws*, London: The World Federation of Khoja Shi'ah Ithna 'Asharia, 1994, p. 448, article 2433.

The partners within temporary marriage are not entitled to inherit each other, unless they put it as a condition in their contract.[12]

All these differences between permanent marriage and *Mut'ah*, some of which have been highlighted, reflect the very fact that *Mut'ah,* by its nature, provides room for negotiation, and leaves many things optional, thus an accurate term to describe such a marriage is hence 'Flexible Marriage'. Although this technical term has not been implemented by the early Muslims, or by the jurisprudents, it is, however, unavoidable for each rational human being to accept that this expression reflects the very nature of the *Mut'ah* marriage.

Western philosophers of ethics have suggested a similar form of marriage. This shall follow in the subsequent paragraphs.

11.4   Family Life and Sexual Satisfaction in the West

Sexual life in Europe has undergone different periods, ranging from the Victorian institutional marriage to the modern companionate marriage. However, this latter form of marriage was sporadically practised in the late 18th century. Historian Lawrence Stone describes late 18th century marriages as 'companionate.' He characterises companionate marriage as one of increased gender equality within marital unions. Prior to the companionate marriage, power roles in marriages were clearly defined and dominated solely by the husband, whose ability to work and own land far exceeded the political and social abilities of women. The wife, often chosen for the size of her dowry, was expected to submit to her husband in every aspect of their marriage. She was completely dependent on him for finances, accommodation, and protection. However, with the rise of the companionate marriage, unions became less contractual than in prior times. Essentially, more emotional connections existed between man and wife, yet the hearth-bound woman still depended on her husband for financial

---

[11] *Ibid.*, article 2431.
[12] *Ibid.*, article 2434.

support. Stone argued that women and men in the 18th century began to put the prospects of emotional satisfaction before the ambition for increased income or status. This in turn also had its effect in equalising relationships between husband and wife (Stone, p. 217). Yet most women lacked the freedom and capital to support themselves, and thus still depended entirely on men, regardless of the increased emotional satisfaction in the marriage. However there are other theories claiming that Lawrence Stone's theory about 'companionate marriage' in the 17th and 18th century could be detected to the Medieval Ages too. Professor Brooke argues -in his new book *Imagination and History*- against Lawrence Stone's central doctrine of "the growth of affective individualism, freedom of choice and marriage for love", which situates 'companionate marriage' in the 17th and 18th centuries. He suggests instead that there is too much evidence for 'marriage for love' during the 12th to 16th centuries, to support Stone's theory. Christopher Brooke added this information as a supplement to his former book, *The Medieval Idea of Marriage* (1989).

In contrast to the pre-industrial society, when marriage was commonly based on economic calculation and arranged by parents, the pattern in the 19th century was the companionate marriage, with participants exercising free choice based on mutual love, subject only to parental veto. The romantic ideal of Victorian marriage was not based on equality. It assumed that sharply distinguished roles could be deeply satisfying to both parties: to the husband on account of the emotional support he received from his wife; and to the wife because of the window on the wider world which his education and experience made available to her. Romantic love was therefore conceived solely as the attraction of opposites.

Nevertheless, family life within Western societies has undergone severe changes in the post-war era. One of the main changes is the shift to the 'companionate' marriage (Rodger, 1996). Rodger argues that a fundamental shift, which is often alluded to in popular as well as academic literature, is from the 'Institutional' marriage to the 'Companionate' relationship.[13]

Traditionally, marriage was considered as an institution whereby economic prosperity was to be secured and psychological needs were to be fulfilled. Since the pre-Christian period, family ethics were structured in such a way as to safeguard the female virtues and male patriarchal dominance. In his book *Marriage and Morals* Bertrand Russell has referred to this fact. He sates:

> The primary motive of sexual ethics as they have existed in Western civilization since pre-Christian times has been to secure that degree of female virtue without which the patriarchal family becomes impossible, since paternity is uncertain. What has been added to this in the way of insistence on male virtue by Christianity had its psychological source in asceticism, although in quite recent times this motive has been reinforced by female jealousy, which became potent with the emancipation by the female.[14]

While observing the social changes in the post war era, Bertrand Russell discussed the matter from a liberal philosophical angle. He analysed, initially, the ethical reason for marriage within Western societies:

> In a rational ethic, marriage would not count as much as the absence of children. A sterile marriage should be easily dissoluble, for it is through children alone that sexual relations become of importance to society, and worthy to be taken cognisance of by a legal institution. This, of course, is not the view of the Church, which under the influence of St. Paul, still views marriage as rather the alternative to fornication than as the means for the procreation of children. In recent years, however, even clergymen have become aware that neither

---

[13] John J. Rodger, *Family Life & Social Control*, London: MacMillan, 1996, p. 69.
[14] Bertrand Russell, *Marriage and Morals,* London: Unwin Books, 1961, p. 9.

men nor women invariably wait for marriage before experiencing sexual intercourse.[15]

During the early decades of the 20th century, a social revolution took place within sexual relationships in America. Premarital relations became more common, and this contributed to changing ideas about the classical relationship between men and women. A new 'companionate marriage' promised individual fulfilment, with couples bound together by mutual love and sexual attraction, not concepts of duty. This was essentially a middle-class ideal. These social changes are fairly studied in Elaine Tyler May's *Homeward Bound: American Families in the Cold War Era* (1988) and in Steven Mintz's, *Domestic Revolutions: A Social History of American Family Life* (1988).

That is why Russell has drawn attention to this fact that in America, England, Germany and Scandinavia, a great change has taken place since the war... and that young men, instead of finding an outlet with prostitutes, have had affairs with girls of the kind whom, if they were richer, they would wish to marry. He has also stated that this process has gone further in the United States than it has in England.[16] These social changes mentioned called for a deeper reflection to provide a wise and accepted social structure that could embrace such relationships without trivialising its natural and serious consequences.

Other Western thinkers, who have analysed the social conditions of their Western societies, have reached a result similar to that solution provided by Islamic *Shari'ah* Law more than a thousand years ago. They spoke about a comparable suggestion to flexible marriage, i.e. 'Companionate Marriage'. We will now deal with the term itself, which has been repeatedly used throughout our prior discussion.

---

[15] *Ibid.*, p. 81.
[16] *Ibid.*

The *American Heritage Dictionary of the English Language* (Fourth Edition 2000) has given a modern definition for this marriage as:

> A marriage in which the partners agree not to have children and may divorce by mutual consent, with neither partner responsible for the financial welfare of the other.

Thus if we summarise this phenomenon, we may conclude that companionate marriage is an institution in which motives of passion, romantic affection and emotional intimacy predominate. And it is Western culture that has taken it to the furthest reach of the pendulum's swing in the last few decades. Bertrand Russell has elaborated on the history of the Modern era's adoption of this type of marriage:

> Judge Ben B. Lindsey, who was for many years in charge of the Juvenile court at Denver, and in that position had unrivalled opportunities for ascertaining the facts, proposed a new institution which he calls 'companionate marriage'. Unfortunately he has lost his official position, for when it became known that he used it rather to promote the happiness of the young, rather than to give them a consciousness of sin, the Ku Klux Klan and the Catholics combined to oust him. Companionate marriage is the proposal of a wise conservative. It is an attempt to introduce some stability into the sexual relations of the young, in place of the present promiscuity. He points out the obvious fact that what prevents the young is lack of money, and that money is required in marriage partly on account of children, but partly also because it is not the thing for the wife to earn her own living. His view is that young people should be able to enter upon a new kind of marriage, distinguished from ordinary marriage by three characteristics. First, that there should be for the time being no intention of having children, and that accordingly the best available birth-control information should be given to the young people. Second, that so long as there are no children and the wife is not pregnant, divorce should be possible by mutual consent. And third,

that in the event of divorce, the wife should be entitled to alimony. He holds, and I think rightly, that if such an institution were established by law, a very great many young people, for example students at universities, would enter upon comparatively permanent partnerships, involving a common life, and free from Dionysiac characteristics of their present sexual relations. He brings evidence to bear that young students who are married do better work than such as who are unmarried. It is indeed obvious that work and sex are more easily combined in a quasi-permanent relation than in the scramble and excitement of parties and alcoholic stimulation.[17]

Russell has described this proposal about a 'Companionate Marriage' as a proposal from a wise conservative. Again he emphasised after only a few pages:

For my part, while I am quite convinced that companionate marriage would be a step in the right direction, and would do a great deal of good, I do not think it goes far enough.[18]

However, seen from an objective angle and to compare between these two ideas; *Shari'ah* Law's *Mut'ah,* and the Western thinkers' Companionate marriage, one can straightforwardly conclude that Western thinkers used their capacity of reflection in order to find a suitable solution after having been faced with the specific societal problem, whilst the Islamic *Shari'ah* had foreseen the natural needs of the human being before the occurrence of the problem itself.

Thus, one does not need to detect premarital sexual relationships in order to realise the necessity of legislation for flexible marriage. Also, Islam has never promoted sexual relationships in an environment of fiesta combined with alcoholic intoxication or wild parties; rather it calls for sexual gratification through a natural mutual enjoyment, where responsibility and the awareness of the

---

[17] *Ibid.*, p. 84.
[18] *Ibid.*, p. 85.

consequences are fully clarified for both sides. Another option within Islamic flexible marriage is left open for the couple to decide, i.e. the procreation of children. However, in the 'companionate marriage' this issue is nonexistent because the reason given was that a sterile marriage is easily dissoluble. While not denying this very psychological fact, one could claim that establishing this option - within the *Shari'ah* Law - could have paved the way for many couples and led to a permanent relationship upon realising their compatibility, whereupon they would have been able to have a child and ultimately agree that they were the perfect match for each other.

In conclusion, we understand the similarity and the advantages resulting from these two –different, but very much alike– solutions; however one can, without difficulty, settle the positive points one has over the other parallel act.

Vivien Green Fryd's book, *Art and the Crisis of Marriage*, has presented the 'companionate marriage' from a totally different angle. She claims that marriage - as an institution - is in crisis. Therefore, this classical permanent marriage shall be exclusively practised within limited circles. She introduced companionate marriage as an arrangement that emphasised mutual sexual gratification and greater freedom for women. Companionate marriage is accordingly recognised through a wider emancipated development throughout the Western world.

After what has been discussed at the beginning of this subtitle - that this phenomenon can be traced back to the 17th century or even to the 12th century - one can hardly agree on this groundless statement. If we furthermore take into consideration the *Shari'ah* Law's institutionalisation of the flexible marriage, one is left with no choice but to reject it completely.

Also, Rodger's understanding of the shift from the 'institutional marriage' to the 'companionate marriage' cannot be approved. It is probably clear that within Western milieu this phenomenon could be well perceived in this direction. However, we are not willing to accept that this is the correct way of analysing this phenomenon. An astute sociologist can certainly put this form of relationship under the same category of marriage without any reluctance, as this marriage is an 'institution' too, where all the fundamental characteristics of marriage are found. Therefore, the Islamic legislator did not find any problem to consider it an institutional marriage. Also, the assumed paradox between marriage and intimate relationship is nothing but an unsubstantiated allegation. Islamic moral values and family ethics speak definitively for the opposite.

Compared to English Law one can easily claim that Islamic *Shari'ah* laws outlined above are fairly straightforward, but clearly, there is considerable potential for a conflict of laws when flexible marriage is not wisely practiced in England and Wales. According to Halsbury, 'English Law does not acknowledge the concept of a trial or temporary marriage'.[19] The case cited to illustrate this is *Dalrymple v Dalrymple* (1811) 2 Hag Con 54 at 105. From 1936 onwards, the only mention of temporary marriage in the 'All England Law Reports' was in a case of obscene publications in which an advertisement had been placed for such a union: "Guy requires turned on chick for temporary marriage. (R. V. Anderson and others)" It is clear that great efforts would have to be made to distinguish *Mut'ah* marriage from such tawdry case law should the matter come before the English judiciary. Due to the flexibility of this marriage, a dispute will normally be over the upbringing of children, particularly after the flexible marriage's fixed-time expires. The father of any children born of a cohabitation relationship will become a parent without parental responsibility under the children Act 1989 s.2(2)(b) unless he obtains parental responsibility agreement s.4(1)(b), or through a court order s.4(1)(a). Therefore, it is very much desirable to give future possible conditions a considerable time and comprehensive discussion before getting involved in any flexible marriage.

---

[19] Lord Mackay of Clashfern, Halsbury's Laws of England, Butterworths, 2001, 4th Edition Reissue, vol. 29 (3), p. 39.

Finally, whatever the conditions were within Western societies, and regardless of how it will be in the future, a statement has been predicted and moderately summed up by a matrimonial lawyer who said:

> Because people will be living longer and will be healthy to an older age, there will be an enormous turnover in marriage. It will not be unusual for a person to be married five or six times. There will also be two forms of marriage -a permanent one and a "companionate marriage". The latter, by its very nature, will be a relationship terminable at will, but still conferring legitimacy upon offspring. The "permanent" marriage will be governed by the more conventional and usual rules. The companionate marriage will be a lot more fun.

11.5   Unfair Accusations

There are many unfair accusations and allegations directed against the flexible marriage, from both Orientalists as well as from different Muslims. We will now examine and answer a few of these arguments:

1- *Mut'ah* is often referred to as a pleasure marriage and is compared to prostitution. The man pays the woman a dowry and they enjoy each other and then move on. Thus, it is a covert form of prostitution.

In reality, the flexible marriage is nothing like prostitution, as it is a union before Allah (swt), and any children resulting will be legitimate. It is, in all senses of the word, a sacred marriage. Just as in permanent marriage, the woman has a waiting period after the end of the marriage before she can take another spouse. The waiting period serves many purposes including making sure of any paternity, avoidance of embarking upon another relationship too soon, and giving the couple time to reconcile. A woman is unlikely to be able to 'make a living' from flexible marriage, because she could legally have less than half a dozen partners in a year. In this way, it is clearly unlike prostitution. Payment of a dowry does take place in flexible marriage, but it is unlike prostitution because the payment is not for sex, but rather it is identical in purpose to the dowry given in permanent marriage. It is further unlike prostitution because a man is not supposed to marry a woman with lax morals or a woman who is known for indecent behaviour.

Flexible marriage probably more often occurs without any sex than it does solely for the purpose of sexual gratification. Flexible marriage, unlike permanent marriage, may have conditions stipulated into it, such as the most common one, which is that no sexual intercourse shall take place. Western philosophers -such as Bertrand Russell in his book *Morals and Marriage*- were not in favour of prostitution, but had no reservations in adopting this form of companionate marriage.

2- Many consider this marriage as a cover for their unfounded lust or unlawful wild desires. Therefore, this marriage is usually associated with the natural consequences of any immoral act. Unfortunately, one-third of the time the wife – of marriages I have witnessed – has been secret from family, friends, and/or community because of the stigma and judgement that would result. Thus, when someone made an inquiry one remained silent until the inquiry could be handled in another way. Also, the children were kept in secret as if they were born illegitimately.

Every intelligent Muslim perceives this institution as a form of decent relationship, and as an established marriage. But it should be used only whenever it is needed, and whenever conditions make it viable. Imam Ali Al-Ridha (as) says:

> It is permitted and absolutely allowed for the one whom Allah has not provided with the means of permanent marriage so that he may be chaste by performing mut'ah.[20]

In *Marriage and Morals in Islam*, contemporary writer's, S. Mohammed Razawi states that flexible marriage must be

---

[20] Al-Hurr Ameli, *Wasa'il*, Beirut, Lebanon, vol. 14, p. 449-450.

considered within a need-only aspect, and therefore flexible marriage is strongly emphasised under those circumstances. Thus he claims that he cannot over-emphasise the temporary nature of mut'ah. He argues that the message of Islam is quite clear: marry on a permanent basis; if that is not possible, then adopt temporary abstinence; if that is not possible, only then use the mut'ah marriage.

Although we may disagree with his conclusion, insofar as deeming it the final message of Islam, the essence and philosophy behind it is indisputable; that this marriage should correspond solely to the conditions or circumstances that require it.

3- If one were to discuss this form of marriage with many Orientalists and Muslims, we are likely to hear responses suggesting that this form of legal relationship could lead to extreme conditions which would inevitably become misused within society. Flexible marriage would allow Muslim men to indulge in sensuality, and girls could be manipulated or seduced in such a way as to loose their virginity with no security in return.

The fact is that no laws exist, which cannot be misused, whether within Islamic *Shari'ah* Law or within secular laws. This fact is undeniable amongst all legislators.

It has also been advised that Muslim men who are already married, and not in need of it, should refrain from chasing women and girls for further sexual satisfaction. It has been emphasised by many narrations that the nature of this marriage should not be transformed to this level of misuse. The following saying of Imam Ridha (as) is clear. Once 'Ali bin Yaqtin, a prominent Shi'ah, who held a high post in the Abbasid government, came to Imam 'Ali Ar-Ridha (as) to ask about *Mut'ah*. The Imam (as) said:

> What have you to do with it because Allah has made you free from its need.[21]

Furthermore, according to Ayatullah Sistani, it is forbidden to marry any non-Muslim woman in flexible marriage if he is already married to a Muslim woman, with or without his wife's consent.[22]

It has been emphasised that the *Mut'ah* marriage should not be contracted with a virgin girl; furthermore Ayatullah Sistani states:

> In marrying a virgin girl, whether Muslim or from Ahlul-kitab, it is necessary to get the consent of her father or paternal grandfather. [23]

11.6   Practical Benefits

In modern society, the flexible marriage may meet the needs of someone who is travelling for a long time and in need of companionship, or someone who cannot find a permanent spouse.

Additionally it may serve the needs of someone without the financial means to have a wedding and then to support his wife financially. (The requirement that he maintain his spouse according to his means, and according to what she is accustomed to does not have to apply in flexible marriage.)

Elderly widows who have little realistic chance of finding another permanent spouse can more easily find temporary spouses to serve the need for companionship.

Arab feminists nowadays support this form of marriage, and believe it is a wise institution. Contemporary Anthropologist and New York University Professor Lila Abu Lughod is a lecturer in Middle East studies. Having obtained a Ph.D. from Harvard, she

---

[21] *Ibid.*, p. 449.
[22] Abdul Hadi Al-Hakim, *A Code of Practice for Muslims in the West*, London: Imam Ali Foundation, 1999, p. 213, Answer to Question: 421.
[23] *Ibid.*, p. 204, Act 391.

has spent the last twenty years working on topics of gender, class, marriage and modernity. Her essay, *The Marriage of Feminism and Islamism in Egypt: Selective Repudiation as a Dynamic of Postcolonial Cultural Politics,* despite the extensive title, develops an interesting argument which is in favour of 'Companionate Marriage'. The celebrated Qasim Amin -amongst other nationalist-feminist writers- also advocates the concept of companionate marriage around the turn of the 19th century. Within the not-so-limited circles there are many who think that youths, who are too young for the responsibilities of permanent marriage, but in danger of being seduced and consequently fail to keep their chastity, may lawfully meet in a flexible marriage. However it is worth emphasising that this last case does not grant freedom for the youth to freely mingle with the opposite sex, which may create a false image that Shi'ah Muslims promote liberal or casual sex. A condition - as it was highlighted before - that militates against this abuse is the requirement that a virgin female have the permission of her father to enter any into any marital relationship, including flexible marriage, unless the father is found to be one who is unreasonable in that regard. It is also further commonly required, as mentioned earlier, that a condition of the marriage, is that it shall not take place with a prostitute or a woman of bad repute.

Flexible marriage can furthermore be used for formality purposes. Ayatullah Sistani states in his *Islamic Laws* the following:

> Contracting a temporary marriage with a woman is in order, even if it may not be for the sake of any sexual pleasure.[24]

In conclusion, this marriage's function and purpose can be sheer formality, or even pure companionship for the sake of getting to know the other party without any form of sexual pleasure. Therefore, there can be huge legal benefits following a formal-

---

[24] As-Sistani, *Islamic Laws*, London: The World Federation of Khoja Shi'ah Ithna 'Asharia, 1994, p. 448, article 2430.

contract of flexible marriage.[25]

11.7   Cases under Study

I have known more than a handful of couples, whom I have either helped into marriage, or who were already involved in a flexible marriage, who have embraced Islam. The rumours of blatant misuse of this marriage are not to be found with those I have known, and this fact reflects what we already mentioned, i.e. that this institution functions as a sophisticated marriage for civilised people.

The majority of problems that occur within the flexible marriage arise because the partners did not allow ample time for thought and thorough consideration. Flexible marriage is supposed to suit various cases, but in the cases of which I have personal knowledge, any problems arose due to initial lack of adequate dialogue. Aside

---

[25] The practical benefits are as follows:

- Engagement is not marriage, yet couples often involve themselves in the kind of behaviour that should only take place within marriage. The logical alternative to avoid sin is simply to have a temporary marriage prior to the permanent marriage so that the couple can make sure they are suited to each other. Flexible marriage is the way to avoid sin when permanent marriage is not possible. Some Muslims today commit sin prior to their marriage with the person that they are engaged to. Islam is clear that between men and women, touching, viewing private parts of each other's bodies that should be covered and visiting while unescorted are sins unless they are married.

- While searching for a compatible partner, a pure way in order to know each other would be to contract the flexible marriage initially, and once the couple know and like each other they could then make a permanent marriage.

- A man marrying a daughter of a family, but his biological mother-in-law is not the contemporary wife of his actual father-in-law. This fact would necessitate this women always being in constant Hijab whenever he is present. Obviously this is not a comfortable request for her, and in this case the whole family will encounter hardship. However if the wife has a daughter from the same father or from another, by simply making the formality of the flexible marriage between the man and the other daughter, before the original marriage takes place, a great deal of hardship will be saved. Once the fixed-time marriage expires, the daughter will not be his wife, but the mother will still be considered as *na-mahram*. Therefore she does not need to perform Hijab while in his presence.

from the remarks made in the previous points, one of the main obstacles that I witnessed throughout the studied samples, was that the wife was not aware that this form of relationship might not necessarily terminate in a varying and permanent marriage. These marriages appear to have been entered into in such a way that the men provided unrealistic hopes of a consequent permanent marriage, resulting in the women waiting, only to be disappointed by offers of yet more fixed-time marriages over the course of time. In public, the women had to frequently claim to other people that they were unmarried because temporary marriage was not welcomed, or dismissed.

Ultimately, by being a temporary as opposed to a permanent spouse, the women felt partially rejected by their husbands, even if there was no reason for this. The women required more from the relationship than the men were willing to give, as the latter were unable to do more because it contradicted the mutual agreement at the outset of the marriage.

One does not wish to paint men who choose flexible marriage, even for prolonged periods in a bad light, nor hold a negative view of those fixed-time brides, merely stereo-typing them or pre-judging them on hearsay. In most cases, the majority of couples are trying to act correctly and do love their partners.

Their dilemma often stems from the rejection they find or anticipate from their family and society because of the race, social class, economic condition, cultural background or nationality of their partners. Sometimes they find each other without the traditional blessing and the time-honoured arrangements made by their family, or they feel they are violating the classical norms they may ultimately have been brought up to preserve. Or often, they were initially only able to pursue a flexible marriage and not a permanent one, and had to hide their marriage because of the very negative reactions and rejection they would receive from people, especially family, if it were made public. I sympathise with the desire to want both family and partner, but in the end, these partners often have to choose one or the other.

However, one can see the case in another light, for rightfully, they should not have to choose amongst these difficult options. People should accept an individual's choice in spouse regardless of his/her race, cultural and economic background or nationality, especially if s/he is a pious person. People should not allow stigma to be thrust upon those who find the need for flexible marriage. This stigma has no place on something that was made lawful by Allah (swt) and the Prophet (saws); it should even be encouraged or mandated when sin is the likely alternative. Flexible marriage has a place in society and the need for it is not altogether uncommon. It is uncivilised to accept fornication, homosexuality, masturbation and other forms of inhuman sexual satisfaction more easily than flexible marriage.

People suffer because of the prejudices held by others. Just as in a monogamous permanent marriage, polygamous and flexible marriages can contain abuse and bad outcomes. It is the abuse that should be stigmatised, and not the institutions themselves. In fact, stigmatising the marriages causes abuse within them to be more likely due to the consequent likelihood of the marriages being done in secret. Therefore, if one is concerned about the misuse of the fixed-time and polygamous marriages, then let them come out of the closet into the public domain. One can only remove a stigma through conscious and deliberate effort within oneself. Although previous damage cannot be fully repaired, future damage can be prevented if more people, perhaps starting with the reader him/herself, become active and audible in their support of polygamous and flexible marriage, and those individuals who pursue them lawfully.

Conclusion

Flexible marriage is one of the Divine laws permissible until the Day of Judgement. Misunderstandings over its legality arise due to a lack of research carried out over the authentication of relevant narrations, and a lack of knowledge concerning the Arabic language.

Islam is a religion that provides laws which are suited to human nature, and which conform confidently to human needs. Allah (swt) - our Creator - in His wisdom has provided laws suitable for differing circumstances and situations. Permanent marriage is not always possible; therefore flexible marriage provides an alternative method for certain people, and allows them to find an intimate relationship and romantic companionship, which is their basic human right.

Ignorant people wrongly liken this form of marriage to prostitution; however, apart from being a legal marriage, whereby the rights of all parties are protected, it saves the society from such social ills as fornication and adultery, and functions as an appropriate alternative for those who can not afford to marry permanently.

Like any law, the law allowing flexible marriage is open to abuse. It has to be realised that any misconduct witnessed, results from the lack of responsibility by both women and men and thus does not reflect on the law itself. If used correctly and when necessary, flexible marriage is no less than a mercy from God for individuals, including those who are in urgent need of sexual satisfaction and this through a legal and civilised course.

Article 12

Divorce: An Islamic Institution

Adeela Shabaz

Abstract

This paper sets out to discuss divorce as an Islamic institution given to mankind as a Mercy from Allah. According to the teachings of Islam there is equality among the sexes as to who may institute divorce proceedings. The process is something clearly delineated, involving attempts at mediation and reconciliation, arranging separation, establishing financial arrangements, and arranging for care and development of children. This paper will explore the reasons and consequences of divorce. Comparisons will be made with other systems where divorce is not permitted due to a system defined by an ecclesiastical hierarchy, where unhappy couples are forced to either survive in a melancholy marriage, or opt out for an alternative, but immoral, relationship with others.

Introduction

The Islamic Institution -Divorce- is given by Allah (swt) as a mercy to mankind. Although permitted, it is one of the most disliked actions allowed.

Contrary to popular belief, divorce is not intended to be a quick fix left to the whims and fancies of men. As with marriage, there are set rules and guidelines. According to the teachings of Islam, there is equality among the sexes, as to who may institute divorce proceedings. The process is clearly defined i.e. mediation, reconciliation, separation, financial arrangements, care and development of children etc.

This paper will aim to expound some of the reasons for divorce and the consequences thereof. A comparison will be made with other systems where divorce is not permitted. This may be due to systems put in place by the clerical upper echelons and the conditions of the lives of couples that are forced to survive in a melancholy relationship or opt out for an immoral one if they feel the need to do so.

12.1   Divorce: An Islamic Perspective

To discuss this paper, Divorce, as an Islamic institution, we will need for the sake of clarity of understanding, to look firstly at marriage as an Islamic institution for it would be illogical for divorce to take place without there first being a marriage.

Marriage is a contract between two persons (male and female). It is a solemn contract to which God is the primary witness. It is carried out in God's name and according to his divine dictates: furthermore it imbues such attributes as spiritual elevation, morality, social integrity, peace, love and more. It is used as a means of permanent relationship, as in the main those who commit to marriage hope that it would be a lasting affair.

Islam takes a realistic view on life and makes allowances for unpredictable events. Human behaviour can sometimes be volatile and unpredictable and although Islam encourages the marital status as much as possible, Allah (swt) out of His Mercy for His creatures has allowed divorce as a solution in cases where life has become so unbearable and there is outright animosity towards each other. It is unacceptable for a marriage to continue in a hostile, destructive manner; destructive to partners, children, families etc. Although permitted, it is the most disliked of permissible actions allowed by God. It is therefore allowed in case of need and is accompanied by strict instructions on how it is to be carried out. Such as is clearly stated in the Holy Qur'an:

> Parties should hold together in kindness or separate in kindness.
> (Quran, 2:229)

> Either take them back in kindness or set them free on equitable terms.
> (Quran, 2:231)

These being supported by another verse, which says Allah (swt) has not created hardship for you in matters of religion, and the Prophet Muhammad (saws) has said that he was sent with a true and tolerant religion.

As mentioned previously, marriage is based on many virtues. Divorce likewise is based on similar attributes though, I must stress, that that is when it is carried out according to the advice given regarding this issue. It is quite common to see acrimonious divorces amongst both Muslim and non-Muslims, where the aim is to totally destroy each other.

Before the advent of Islam, as taught by Muhammad (saws), there was behaviour among the pagan Arabs and other social groups, which was grossly unfair to women. Marriage was no exception. Islam abolished such unjust practices and replaced them with more wholesome and just rules. For example, there used to be the practice whereby a man in a fit of anger, would swear an oath in God's name that he would have nothing to do with his wife, thereby depriving her of all sexual enjoyment, conjugal activities and the benefits, which can be derived from such relationships. In the meantime she was unconditionally tied to him yet at the same time he had the right to remarry or remain with other wives. Such a husband, when questioned about his behaviour towards his wife would cite his oath, which he said bound him to his behaviour. Not only did Islam disapprove of such thoughtless oaths, it insisted on intentional, solemn oaths and that they should be scrupulously observed, for Allah (swt) judges by intention and not mere thoughtless words.

> And make not Allah's name an excuse in your oaths against doing good or acting rightly or making peace between persons for Allah is the one who hears and knows all things. (Quran, 2:224)

So divorce although disliked, is allowed in Islam so long as the prescribed guidelines are adhered to. There are systems other than Islam, both pre and post Islam, which have no clearly defined guidelines on this subject. Either they were so restrictive and narrow, allowing no divorce, no remarriage and variant combinations, or they were so lax that the sanctity of marriage was made a mockery of. In cases even after the death of a husband a wife had no right to life, she had to die with him (Hindu practice of sati) by throwing herself on the funeral pyre.

12.2   Judaic Law (Incorporating the Law of Moses)

Evidence exists to show that marriage contracts and matters relating to marriage and divorce existed at least five centuries before the birth of the Christian era. Findings unearthed at Elephantine in Ancient Africa (Egypt) revealed the existence of betrothal contracts, marriage contracts and payment of divorce settlements. From such historical findings we learn that equality existed between the sexes, the only difference being in matters to do with finance.

The dowry (a financial gift given to the bride) or purchase price as it was known, is evident in most of the contracts found. In cases of divorce the dowry went to the woman, as was since that time considered the woman's property. Again, it is evidenced in the Greco-roman period about two centuries before the Christian era that women were almost equal to men in matrimonial matters except in matters of reproductive function, and women had rights that allowed them to obtain divorce. Rules seem to have been changed throughout the ages to the extent that today we find Jewish women having to fight their way through secular courts and soliciting the aid of prominent politicians to help them gain some degree of respectability and compensation regarding divorce issues. What has gone wrong? Have man made laws been allowed to supersede Divine laws?

In the Pentateuch (the first five books of the Old Testament), divorce was allowed and so was remarriage. Remarriage was based on the production of the divorce certificate (similar to today's decree absolute). Equality of the sexes was encouraged within the Law of Moses; nevertheless it was the responsibility of the man to write the divorce certificate. Rabbinic courts had the authority to force a man to grant a divorce when a wife was justified in seeking one. These edicts were culminated in the 11th century decree of Rabbi Gershon of Mayence, which decreed an end to the theoretical right of the husband to divorce his wife when he pleased. If either party could show just cause, the guilty party could be forced to divorce (Meshnaic law, based on the Talmud,

Jewish religious law). The changes in the decree were not an innovation of the Rabbi, for they were based on what was already in the law and used in a way similar in the Islamic system (*Ijtihad,* scholarly consensus based on what is already enshrined in the law).

12.3   Christian Views

It is a traditionally held belief that Jesus (as) forbade all divorce except in the case of adultery. It is also believed that he forbade remarriage. Around the year 70 AD, those claiming to follow the teachings of Jesus (as) had discarded most of the teachings of the Old Testament and replaced them with a string of statutes, based on their own ideas and values when it came to the matter of marriage and divorce. There were such reformers/church fathers as Justin Martyr 139 AD, Athenagoras 177 AD, Clement of Alexandria, on through to Calvin and Luther in the reign of Elizabeth I. Two earlier reformers, Ireaeus and Ptolomalus, went as far as asserting that the Law of Moses (as) was inferior to the law of Jesus (as) and furthermore that Moses (as) was merely expressing his own opinions. Moses (as), we must remember is a prophet who was sent with a Divine message, the same being the basis for the upright and moral conduct in the Christian way of life: "The Ten Commandments".

It was the consensually held view that marriage was indissoluble except by death, adultery, or desertion.   Luther followed this theological trend but allowed remarriage in the lifetime of the ex-spouse, with the justification that an adulterer was spiritually dead. He also allowed divorce in cases of impotence and, as is in the Mosaic Law, refusing to fulfil conjugal rights. At this time the same conditions were enshrined in the Islamic Shari'ah law.

Today, as we see, the laws of divorce are mainly left for the secular courts to deal with. Such laws having roots in the conflict which arose during the reign of Henry VIII, when in the 15th century, he engineered his own strategy to procure his divorce from Catherine of Aragon, to enable him to marry Anne Boleyn, thereafter breaking away from the doctrines of the mainstream church.

Statutes were henceforth put in place which cited more reasons why divorce could be allowed i.e. dislike, cruelty, prolonged absence etc. Thereafter the Anglican Synod allowed the annulment of marriage which in each case required an act or parliament, it was extremely expensive and within a period of 160 years only 300 marriages were annulled, an average two per year. It is easy to deduce that with such rigid laws coupled with the cost of obtaining a legal divorce, couples who could no longer live together and did not have the means of obtaining a divorce, would involve themselves in relationships which were adulterous, that resulted in the security of the family and the status of marriage becoming gradually eroded.

Luther being one of the most progressive thinkers of his time summed up the behaviour of men and women in this part of his sermon:

> God has given every man a spouse to keep for his sake to put up with the difficulties involved in married life. They tire of it too quickly and if it does not go the way they would like, they immediately want a divorce and a change. Daily there have to be many troubles and trials in every house, city and country. No station in life is free of suffering and pains, both from your own, like your wife or children, household help, subjects and from the outside, from neighbours and all sorts of accidental trouble. When a person sees and feels all this, he quickly becomes dissatisfied and he tires of his way of life. This is what the Jews found out too, as they changed their marriage partners. The best way to prevent divorce and other discord is for everyone to learn patience in putting up with common faults and troubles of his station in life and put up with them in his wife as well knowing that we can never have everything just right, the way we would like to have it.

This piece of writing, though thoughtful and commendable, seems a little bit unjust as it fails to also address the trials and tribulations which a wife has to go through in her many roles.

12.4   Islamic Perspective

It is advisable when choosing spouses to try as much as possible to ascertain their character and their practicality in observing the dictates of the Holy Qur'an and the Prophetic narrations.

The need for divorce can be categorised by the four following headings:

Obligatory- Where there seems to be no chance of reconciliation

Compulsory- In the case of desertion and neglect

Permissible- With good reason and where it is the best solution

Forbidden- Where partners behave in such a bad way that the other is forced to seek divorce

Within the above mentioned categories are several reasons why marital discord may take place e.g. Cruelty, intense dislike, non fulfilment of terms of marriage contract, insanity, impotence, desertion without reason, forced marriage, marriage under false pretences, abuse of polygamy, customs contrary to Islamic beliefs.

We will look at three examples: *(a) Polygamy (b) Deception in marriage (c) Cruelty*

12.4.1   Polygamy (Plurality of Partners)

Included here are polygyny, polyandry and communal marriage. Polygyny is the only type of polygamy allowed in Islam and was commonly accepted and practiced from ancient times. Prophets including Abraham, David and Solomon (as), all had more than one wife at the same time. It is widely practised today under many guises and without responsibility in most cases; leading to unwanted and neglected children, divorce, infidelity and other social ills. The Islamic system is practical and above board where all are meant to benefit justly.

The abuse of this system is sometimes cited as a case for divorce. Due to men not observing the edicts, women are sometimes seen as dispensable objects. If they disagree to plurality of wives, such as when the husband cannot finance the upkeep of another wife, they are viewed as bad wives. Nonetheless, in his pursuit of flesh matters, he contracts another wife bringing untold misery to the primary wife or wives. Physical and psychological abuse, neglect and other factors can lead to the wife opting for a divorce if such oppression continues.

12.4.2 Deception in Marriage

Partners may discover that they have been deceived into marriage or that the prenuptial agreements are broken, they would then be within their rights to seek for a divorce. We need only to take the case of some sisters who live in affluent countries. Sadly, it is a common occurrence whereby women can be deceived into a marriage with a man of seemingly good intentions, only to later discover that he had ulterior motives, namely gaining permission to reside legally within the country. Many men unfortunately having sought to find an Islamically practising wife fail to uphold such values themselves and slip away into the Western lifestyle. In such cases divorce is permitted.

12.4.3 Cruelty to Women (vice versa)

As touched on earlier, cruelty takes on different forms. Women may suffer from broken bones, bruised and battered bodies and there are known cases whereby husbands encourage young sons to hit their mothers as perhaps their fathers encouraged them as little boys, thus continuing the cycle of violence. Women's self esteem can become so low that they will suffer in silence fearing to seek help as the same oppressor will quote selective verses about what a good woman is and what will take a woman to hell. So she continues to endure hell on earth, or -if lucky- she may find the strength to put an end to such misery and regain her self worth and dignity as Islam intended.

The three examples mentioned above do not mean that men do not encounter difficulties due to women's behaviour. They surely do, but the bulk of the known cases of cruelty find that it is the men who are the perpetrators of domestic violence. Muslim communities, mosque directors, Imams and those who can do so, should be more helpful in redressing this injustice. Finding better ways can do this, as well as implementing social care programmes for those within their communities. Some are already doing this, may God continue to bless and guide them.

12.5   Discord *(Nushuz)* in Marriage

The Arabic word *nushuz* has no direct translation in the English language, but it is understood to mean, rebellion, and lack of harmony, unresponsive to reasoning.

There are minor differences between the different schools of Islamic thought; the overall view being that discord can emanate from either of the parties and each party has equal right to redress. Most of the published literature sadly seems to focus more on the discord when it emanates form the female side and stresses what the husband is supposed to do to return harmony. They give little credit to women who by virtue of their God-fearing nature and understanding, help to nip discord in the bud by advising and reminding the husbands of right conduct and by so doing keep the family together. This of course is in a situation where wives are treated with respect as shown in the behaviour on our Prophet Muhammad (saws) who gave the best example by consulting with his womenfolk before making certain decisions regarding women.

However matrimonial discord seems to be more widespread now than in times gone by. Is it because people have become less patient, or is it that divorce is more easily accessible, or perhaps that the pressure of living in some societies brings to bear its own difficulties which puts an unbearable strain on a marriage leading to marital breakdown? The Islamic process for dealing with marital discord is as follows:

12.5.1 Discord Emanating from the Wife

Examples whereby the wife could be guilty of creating discord is where she leaves the house without the legal right to do so, visits unacceptable places and places disliked by her husband, elevates herself above what God has ordained, refuses the husband intimate relations, abuses and slanders the husband, announces his shortcomings that are better left private. It could be that she is ignorant of her role and responsibilities of a wife or that she in influenced by misguided persons. Correct advice will suffice, if she means to learn and change her ways. Some of the above apply to husbands also.

12.5.2 Discord Emanating from the Husband

For example the husband refuses the wife intimate relations, mistreats and otherwise abuses her, does not fulfil her mandatory rights over him, commits sexual acts which are forbidden, does not involve her in decision making relevant to family matters, stays out late at night without informing the wife what time he might be expected back and displays aggression when he returns through sheer arrogance, and orders her to do acts which surely conflict with the teachings of Islam ...etc.

12.6   Remedy

To remedy discord which emanates from the wife:

The husband is advised to:

1- *Admonish and guide* (Qur'an, 4:34)

At this stage the couple take the time to discuss one's or each other's behaviour and how it is affecting the other and how it is affecting the tranquillity of the home. They are reminded of what is right in the sight of God. If this fails to bring an end to the troubles, the next phase is avoidance.

2- *Avoidance*

When admonition and guidance do not improve the situation, the husband is advised to avoid the wife in certain ways. This is personal between them both without involving others; he can avoid speaking with the wife for a maximum of three days and he can also avoid intimate relations although they share the same sleeping place.

This action has its own psychological message. Avoidance must take no longer than four months. In most cases the first phase and if necessary the second will suffice, this is also a means of testing the relationship (how might life be if a divorce should occur?) Prophet Muhammad (saws) avoided his wives for no longer that one month. Avoidance though is only a suggestion and not a hard and fast rule, and the husband must look at the pros and cons of the situation. Will avoidance stop the bad behaviour or will it lead to agitation on the wife's part causing her to be more entrenched in her position. After a period of four months and if the discord still continues, the third phase (symbolic chastisement) will be employed.

3- Symbolic chastisement (striking in a non violent way)
This is the stage of physical intervention; it is also a stage where more serious talking takes place.

The Islamic stance is that a man should never wrong or oppress his wife; as it is narrated from the Prophet (saws):

> Be gentle with women, the best among you are those who are kindest to their wives.

Given all this, what exactly does this physical intervention entail; and what is it meant to achieve? Some jurists say that it is befitting to hit with a handkerchief, or something equivalent to a lock of hair, or a *miswak* (a piece of stick used for cleaning the teeth, the size of a toothbrush) yet others say that the hit is no hit at all, so don't bother. Trying to understand this I looked at the analogy of children at play. When as an adult you observe what you believe is aggression and you bring to account the "aggressor", both children would point out to you that they were playing and that it was an accident. On another occasion, when they have a falling out, one only needs brush past the other for a serious complaint to be made, a complaint which the complainant expects will incur the maximum punishment. Striking then although non-violent serves its purpose psychologically.

After the three steps, admonition, avoidance and symbolic striking have taken place and the discord still continues, the next step will be arbitration. The wife would have a representative who would represent her, presenting any wrong doing that she alleges. Likewise the husband will have a representative. The arbitrators should be trustworthy and knowledgeable, should have insight into understanding why the discord is occurring, who is to blame and what could be done to rectify the situation. An errant wife may think it best to wait until this stage as she may feel that the husband is treating her unjustly while at the same time trying to apply the rules to his benefit. Arbitrators would advise them both to amend their ways so that the situation does not occur again.

4- Arbitration

Arbitration is put in place to stop further deterioration of the marriage. It is for reconciliation and that is the arbitrators primary concern.

> If you fear separation between two married partners, then send an arbitrator from his family and an arbitrator from her family if the two want reconciliation. God will cause such an agreement between them for God is all knowing, well informed. (Qura'n, 4:5)

There is more than one opinion regarding the role of the arbitrators:

-Arbitrators are appointed for reconciliation only.

-Arbitrators are only to give testimony regarding injustice and therefore the matter of separation is not in their remit.

-Arbitrators have a quasi-judicial role. It is their responsibility to keep partners together but if in their opinion it is better for them to separate, then they can separate them.

12.7   Divorce (*Al-Talaq*)

If after arbitration there seems to be no hope for reconciliation, the last option sadly is divorce.

O Prophet, when you divorce women divorce them in accordance with the prescribed waiting period. Keep to the completion of the waiting period and fear God your Lord. Do not expel them from their homes, but do so only if they commit a clear act of adultery. These are the limits set by God and whoever transgresses the limits set by God has surely wronged his own soul. You do not know if God might afterwards bring forth a new situation. (Qura'n, 65:1)

Dissolution is done through one of three ways:

a)   Judicial decree

b)   *Al-Talaq* (by the husband)

c)   *Al-Kula'* (by the wife)

Antagonists have tried to decry this Islamic system claiming that it degrades women, allows for physical abuse and that divorce could be executed thoughtlessly and unjustly. Not only are such claims spurious, they are anathema to Islamic thought. To date, such antagonists have been unable to produce a better system or at best a comparable one. Although we must note that the secular courts have realised that family mediation is a useful tool for helping families, especially where children are concerned, as hostile divorce can have lasting negative effects on children.

12.7.1 Procedure

The husband makes one verbal declaration of divorce after the wife has purified herself from menses and before having intimate relations with her. He then avoids further intimate relations with her. At this stage they are not divorced and must wait until the waiting period is completed. During this time the wife remains in the matrimonial home and is entitled to all benefits due to a wife. The husband has the right to return to his wife, there is no need to consult her guardian for permission nor is a new dowry to be given.

Talaq is pronounced three times during a prescribed period. A husband abuses the right of *talaq* if he pronounces it three times simultaneously, the divorce then being incomplete. It is also forbidden for a man to divorce his wife during the monthly period or after intimate relations took place during the fresh purity.

The space must be observed between the three *talaq*s, as in the case of three simultaneous *talaq*s, there is no space for reconciliation which is what the time suggested (four months) is meant to achieve. During menstruation, intimate relations are naturally forbidden besides that, at this time, the woman has to deal with fatigue, stress and other psychological/physiological factors. The extra burden of a divorce pronouncement at this time and the inability to get close to the husband is counter-productive to reconciliation.

12.7.2 Fresh Purity

If, after the purification from menses, intimate relations take place, the first pronouncement would be invalid and the husband must wait until the next fresh purity to make another pronouncement. During this time the wife could have become pregnant. This new situation has two dimensions:

1. The waiting period is delayed until after the birth of the child.

2. The expectation of a new offspring could turn the situation around for the better

It is unacceptable for a man to pronounce divorce when he is intoxicated or angry, as he may make a declaration while he does not have the capacity to fully appreciate what he is doing, only to regret his actions later and seek forgiveness for his behaviour.

12.7.2.1 *'Iddah* (Waiting Period)

The waiting period varies according to circumstances:

- A woman who never had intimate relations with the husband has no waiting period.

- A woman whose husband died before there was a chance for intimate relations waits four months and ten days.

- A woman who was living in normal circumstances when the husband died waits for four months and ten days.

- A pregnant woman must wait until the birth of the child.

- A menstruating woman waits for three menstrual cycles.

- A non- menstruating woman waits for three lunar months.

The period of *'iddah* brings benefit to both partners. It gives the husband a period of time to rethink and overview the whole situation. The wife benefits from the security of a home and financial support; *'iddah* fosters clarity of lineage. If one of the partners dies during this time, the situation and inheritance would be the same as for married partners.

After the *'iddah* is completed, he is advised to leave her in kindness and beneficence. Should he desire to remarry her and she agrees, this will be a new marriage consistent with Islamic requirements. If she requires marrying someone else she should not be hindered from doing so. A couple has the chance of remarriage twice, that is they can be married to each other for up to three times after which it is not lawful for them to remarry to each other unless the woman is genuinely married to someone else. Some husbands who desire reunion with their wives after they have divorced three times have been known to set up bogus marriages by arranging for a man to marry his ex-wife and pretend to live as married partners without consummation of the marriage, thereafter they will be divorced and the two former partners will be "free" to remarry. This behaviour is condemned. The bogus husband is in Arabic known as a *"muhallil"*.

Prophet Muhammad (saws) said:

> Allah curses the muhallil and the one who uses the muhallil.

He further said:

> Shall I inform you about a borrowed stud goat? He is a muhallil, may God curse him and those who use him.

12.8   Al-Khula'

The wife institutes this form of divorce. She gives something in compensation to be freed from the matrimonial situation. Nowadays, however, wives who work or contribute to the financial upkeep of the house and family are more inclined to seek judicial decree so as to assist them in having some degree of security after divorce. Women are advised to divorce purely for sincere reasons and husbands are advised not to treat wives badly so that the wives are forced to ask for divorce and husbands take the dowry back.

> Do not treat them harshly so that you can take back part of what you have given them. (Qur'an, 4:19)

A wife can also seek an annulment of marriage when the husband fails to provide for her, if he is impotent, abusive, has an incurable disease, if he is sentenced to a long period of imprisonment, also on other grounds such as desertion, deception, dislike. She can also divorce even if there is no fault in the husband, perhaps just that they are incompatible and she detests living with someone in such circumstances. An example of such an incident is given regarding Thabit Ibn Qays. The wife of Thabit approached the Prophet (saws) and said: "Oh messenger, as for Thabit Ibn Qays, I find no fault in him concerning religion or behaviour, but I dislike that the ingratitude of a wife for her husband might ruin her Islam". The Prophet (saw) asked her "Will you return his garden to him?" "Yes" she replied. The messenger then said to Thabit "Take back the garden and divorce her one time".

Al-Khula' is valid if a woman calls for divorce from her husband and goes before one just witness where he agrees to her request. If he refuses to testify, his action is used in support of the wife's claim and the marriage is annulled.

The system of *Al-Khula'* is in place to avoid wrongdoing and injustice. For example, if a woman were to marry, ask for a substantial dowry and then divorce, keeping the dowry, this would lead to unscrupulous, mercenary behaviour and at the same time such behaviour would belittle the status of marriage and promote injustice.

Conclusion

As shown in this paper, divorce as an Islamic institution is based on the teachings of the Holy Qur'an and the Prophetic narrations. It is a truly unique system, unequalled in its upholding of the sanctity of marriage and likewise unequivocal in matters of divorce. The rules are plain and straightforward and therein lay the basis for solutions to matrimonial discord. It is therefore extremely important that those who are entrusted with the task of dealing with such matters fear God and acknowledge it as a form of *'ibadah* (worship). After all, who would like to be accountable on the Day of Judgement for causing pain and suffering to others who trusted them and had been betrayed in the name of God?

It is to be noted that a national helpline set up by Muslim women to support Muslim women in the United Kingdom reports that 80% of calls received are to do with marital discord and abuse of women. None of the large established Muslim organisations have any effective system or broad based framework to deal with crucial social issues. While we are good at rivalling each other in constructing impressive structures and self promotion, we fail to address some basic needs within our communities; needs such as domestic violence, mental health, rehabilitation after incarceration or addiction, counselling and advice giving.

One helpline support worker told me recently of a call she received from a client. She was impressed when the client told her that she and her husband had gone to see a counsellor regarding their 'rocky' marriage. "Alhamdulillah (God be praised), your husband is one in a million" "Yes indeed" replied the client "nothing he agreed to at the session was done on our return home".

Article 13

Rights of Custody in Islam

Turan Jamshidian

Abstract
The aim of this paper is to clarify the rights and roles of mothers in terms of custody. Custody means supporting and treating the child in a humane manner or taking care of him or her in terms of food, shelter, and education. The principle of custody originates from human nature and is based on a close relation between the child and his or her parents. There is a close relationship between custody and breastfeeding (*rida'a*). As such, different aspects and views about breastfeeding (with regards to custody issues) will be discussed in this paper. It will be revealed that Islam seeks to take into consideration the welfare of both the parents, but ultimately it is the well-being of the child which is paramount.

Introduction

In this article, we aim firstly to present a general view of the woman in Islam. This view is presented in order to establish a principle that human beings regardless of their gender are equal in Qur'anic terminology; however this introduction will be classified and discussed briefly. This will be followed by a thorough discussion on the rights of custody in Islam, which is the main subject of this paper.

13.1   Viewpoints regarding "Mankind" in the Holy Qur'an, and Authentic Narrations

Throughout the Holy Qur'an, Allah (swt) has addressed mankind in differing terms:

- *Adam* (man): the personal name of the first man created by Allah (swt).

- *Naas* (group of people): Refers to man collectively.

- *Insan* (human being): This refers to man as a species, and tends to be a general term although it can be used on an individual basis.

The Holy Qur'an uses the term *Insan* to signify a human being's exaggerated behaviour, for example, "*insan* is impatient" or "*insan* is frightened". Both men and women are considered to be human beings, and when praising or blaming, no distinction is made.

In the Holy Qur'an there are many verses that refer to man. They are categorised as follows:

- 65 verses about *Insan*

- 18 verses about *Ens*

- 5 verses about *Onas*

- 1 verse about *Onasia* (many people)

- 1 verse about *Insan* (human)

From among the above verses, we cite the example of verse 4 of surah Teen:

Certainly We created man in the best mould. (Quran, 95:4)

From the apparent view of the above verse, it can be perceived that Allah (swt) has created man in two different ways:

1. Independent creations, as in the case of Adam (as) and Eve (as), who were created independently; i.e. "*Nafsen Vahida*".

2. Creation to continue the race or the creation to produce new generations, in the likeness of the parents.

The Holy Qur'an indicates directly that generally speaking, the human being as he is human, is responsible and is bound by religious obligations; and in this context, being a man or a woman makes no difference. Responsibility is the unique feature of being human.

It can be discerned from the Qur'an and Islamic narrations that Allah (swt) in His commandments addresses both men and women collectively and hence there is no gender discrimination. This is evident from the phrase: "O you who believe....", which is a general address, irrespective of gender.

There is a consensus among all Muslim scholars that the Qur'anic verses are directed towards all people irrespective of whether they are male or female, but that relevant verses carry with them special conditions that are applicable to each gender.

In the language of the Qur'an, men and women are defined as being 'a sign of Allah (swt)'. In fact, they need each other in order to be complete and attain perfection, without knowing the other part they would be deficient. Thus by the two parts existing and knowing their own status, perfection, so loved by Allah (swt), can take shape. In Surah Rum, there are several verses regarding this point:

> And one of His signs is that He created mates for you from yourselves that you may find rest in them, and He put between you love and compassion; most surely there are signs in this for a people who reflect. (Quran, 30:21)

The word "calmness" (*sukun*) is used almost synonymously with the word "compassion". In the language of the mystics the word "proximity" (*ons*) is commonly used, which implies "rest and comfort".

Man and woman have been described as being the essence of rest for each other. Creation has provided one with the other in order that they find peace therein and gain real happiness.

We can now raise the point as to whether the Holy Qur'an recommends a proposed way by which the human being can reach perfection. The answer of course is yes, and that through faith and righteous deeds both men and women respectively can attain the highest levels of spirituality. The Qur'an says:

> So their Lord accepted their prayer; that I will not waste the work of a worker among you, neither male nor female. (Quran, 3:195)

And:

> Whoever does good whether male or female and he is a believer, We will most certainly make him live a happy life. (Quran, 16:97)

It also states:

> O you men! Surely, We have created you of a male and a female, and made you tribes and families that you may know each other; surely the most honourable of you with Allah is one among you most careful (of his duty); surely, Allah is Knowing, Aware. (Quran, 45:49)

And:

> And that He created pairs, the male and the female. (Quran, 53:45)

Woman without man and man without woman do not exist in the system of creation. They are created together and together they reach a pleasing perfection in a natural way.

In the Holy Qur'an, this point appears in numerous places. Sometimes the human being is referred to in general terms and at other times each gender is addressed distinctly. In the latter case, each gender has different responsibilities and so different commandments are prescribed in order to suit each of them.

13.2   Section One - Shared Responsibilities

Men and women are granted some common capabilities and some common responsibilities, and even in case of *wilayat*, that is, when the human being reaches the status of Divine vicegerency, no gender distinction is made. A man is capable of manifesting the attributes of knowledge, power and wisdom of Allah (swt), as is a woman. Maryam (as) is the best example in this regard.

Islam has revealed its commandments according to *fitrah* or nature. Islamic laws and regulations are not against nature. They are like water from a fountain that moves according to natural processes. There is no obligation in this regard, and again, between man and woman no difference exists.

Let us here take a look at the creation of the human being. *Insan* has been created in two different patterns. He/she is created as a couple because he/she is not meant to live alone and to last eternally. According to religion, *insan* should live in pairs, in groups, and inhabit the world. They should marry and procreate.

When human beings live together, they make up the society and society needs safety. When considering the safety of the society, some factors are necessary. An important factor is the *hijab* (modest dressing), this is obligatory for both men and women, the outer dressing should indeed reflect an inner quality that leads to respect for the human being and helps to deter him from sin. The basis for *hijab* is a natural phenomenon. If we want a kernel to ripen to its full bloom, it has to have the protection of the outer shell otherwise it will spoil without reaching its maturity. Living creatures also need protection. Islam for both men and women proposes the *hijab* according to their natures. Owing to the fact that Allah has given more importance to the protection of the woman, He has proposed a more elaborate and special *hijab* for her.

The woman has a special status and special goals. In order for her to succeed on her divinely ordained path, she must present herself in such a way so that she is not misused or abused by men.

The Holy Qur'an in this regard says:

> Say to the believing men that they cast down their looks and guard
> their private parts; that is purer for them; surely Allah is Aware of
> what they do. (Quran, 24:30)

> And say to the believing women that they cast down their looks and
> guard their private parts... (Quran, 24:31)

Regarding the above point we can perceive that Allah has given the human being an elevated status, and likes them to not make mistakes in their relationships and daily lives. The woman especially is also advised in her daily interactions with others not to speak in such a way that 'one who is sick in his heart' would be unduly distracted. The woman should act in a manner that deserves the status granted to her by Allah, not forgetting the fact that Islam regards both man and woman as equal.

The inner *hijab* is known as *"Hijab-an-Noor"*, it is a Divine *hijab* and both men and women should strive to attain it. Hazrat Fatima Zahra (as) held this quality in the highest level, and we should endeavour to follow her example.

According to Islam, not only does there exist no discrimination on the issue of the spiritual progress of a man and woman, but also they are also encouraged to compete in a healthy manner towards this goal. As regards this matter, Imam Khomeini (ra) says:

> If Allah had so willed that there would come another prophet after
> Prophet Muhammad (saws) there would be none to fit the bill except
> Hazrat Fatima az-Zahra (as) and the Tradition of Allah would alter so
> that women would become prophets. Hazrat Fatima az-Zahra was
> capable of (the responsibility of) prophethood. Imam Hassan (as) says:
> "We are Allah's Proof for mankind and our mother, Zahra (as), is a
> (Divine) Proof for us".

Allah (swt) has created man as a social being, so He has prescribed laws and regulations for him. To facilitate the observance of these regulations, testimony and judgement are provided.

As regards social life, Islam insists on two principles; some factors are individualised while there are other factors that are common among all. As for the common factors, there are special laws just as some special laws are provided for individualised matters. There is a legal argument that claims that a human being is always changing; thus, how can a fixed set of laws be applicable to his life. If we take for example the daily prayers, which are an obligation on all human beings, there are prescribed methods, which we must follow. However, there are some concessions that have been allowed in this regard, such as for the old or sick, who are allowed to pray in sitting or lying-down positions. There are also some physiological differences between a man and woman like the period of pregnancy and delivery, which women go through exclusively, thus, they have to observe certain special laws. For example, the *iddah* (a prescribed period of waiting which a woman has to observe after divorce or her husband's demise, before she is permitted to remarry) is obligatory for all women except for infertile ones.

13.3   Section Two: Different Responsibilities

Different laws originate from different natures. In the acts of devotion there are some differences in the obligations for each gender, whereas there are no differences between them in the transactional acts. It is due to the fact that Allah (swt) desires to show that the status of prayer is high, that during the menstruation cycle, women are exempted from obligatory prayers; and instead, in this period they are asked to "worship" Allah. This difference does not mean that the woman is weak, but it means that the prayer has a very high status. This is the same as the mosque, whereby it is forbidden for one who is ritually impure to enter, whether male or female. We need to accentuate here that the differing obligations in devotional acts of the genders is not because of discrimination, but because of the innate differences between a man and woman. As far as the issue of maturity is concerned, a girl reaches the maturity of wisdom earlier than a boy; and thus is given responsibility sooner. It is owing to the fact that a girl reaches the age of puberty earlier than a boy and because she is capable of accepting responsibility much earlier than a boy that she is bound by certain obligatory devotional acts, earlier than her male counterpart.

However when looking at responsibilities, there is one responsibility which would never apply to a man, and that is the responsibility of motherhood. If man is the axis of social activities, woman is the axis of housework and domestic responsibilities. She is the "mother" of the family. The success in the lives of great men is due to their initial training on their mothers' pious laps.

In the system of religion, the selection of a good mate is considered very important. But in the case of the wife, the one who will mother the children in the future is considered the most important choice. In this regard, it has been said directly that you should be very careful about choosing the mother of your children.

13.4   Custody

Considering the above discussion about gender differences in Islam, I will talk specifically about custody and particularly on the woman's custodial rights in Islam.

In this section I will discuss and analyse eight subjects related to custody from point of view of the Holy Qur'anic verses and the narrations:

- What is custody?

- What does custody mean in the Arabic language?

- What is custody according to Islamic jurisprudence?

- Is there any gender discrimination concerning the child?

- What is the philosophy behind custody in Islam?

- How long is the duration of custody?

- Custody in the Shi'ah jurisprudence.

- What is the relation between custody and breast-feeding?

- If there is a child who has lost both parents who has the right to his/her custody?

13.4.1   What is Custody?

Custody in Islamic jurisprudence is the subject of this article. Custody means the protection and support of the child, or nurturing and taking care of him/her. All living creatures need protection, human or animal. Both, or at least one of the parents, must ideally provide this protection.

The principle of custody has its origin in the nature (*fitrah*) of the human being, and his/her natural relation with his/her parents. For this reason, it is said that custody is a natural phenomenon, and it becomes meaningful when a child is in need of it. So, when a child reaches adulthood and does not need protection anymore, the issue of custody dissolves by itself. This is the reason for the difference between the custodial laws for male and female children. The age of custody going to the father is younger in boys than in girls. The girl stays longer with the mother due to her different tendencies and requirements.

13.5   What is Custody according to the Qur'an and in Islamic Narrations?

There are four sources from which the custodian laws can be derived from in Islamic law:

- The Holy Qur'an

- Narrations

- Scholarly consensus

- Wisdom

In the Holy Qur'an, it says:

> Neither shall a mother be made to suffer harm on account of her child.
> (Quran, 2:233)

A mother should never allow her child to encounter difficultly or suffering. If a mother severs her relationship with her child when he/she needs her love and care, she could inflict great damage and suffering on the child.

Among the Holy Narrations, Ave Sabah Kan'ani quotes from Imam as-Sadiq (as):

> And she has the right of the custody of her child until she breastfeeds
> him/her irrespective of whether it is a girl or a boy.

13.6   Is there any Gender Discrimination in the Laws of Custody?

When the child needs her/his mother's milk, the mother has the right to custody, regardless of whether the child is a boy or a girl. At the end of the two years (duration of breast-feeding), the boy will be given to his father and the girl to her mother until she reaches seven years. But if the mother remarries then she loses the custodial rights of the daughter.

13.7   What is the Philosophy behind the Custody in Islam?

Custody is dependent on the child's need for protection. This protection is material, in terms of food, clothing, shelter, and education as well as emotional in terms of giving affection and love.

13.8   How long is the Duration of Custody?

Sayyid Khadim Al-Yazdi in *Al-'Orwatul Wothq'* writes:

> A mother deserves the right to custody and the training of her child
> more than anyone else.

Obviously this opinion is based on a narration from one of the Shi'ah Imams. [1]

Regardless of the gender of the child, and irrespective of whether the child is being breastfed or not, he/she is given to the mother for two years. Then the girl lives with her mother up to seven years of age.

The reason behind the girl being given to the mother for seven years can be understood from a narration of Imam Sadiq (as):

The girl is given to the mother until seven years, but if she is not trained such that she can live independently, then she will be left with the mother for more time. In this case the mother deserves to retain the right of custody.

The Holy Prophet (saws) says:

You have the right to custody excepting when you remarry.[2]

13.9   Custody in Shi'ah Jurisprudence

In the system of Shi'ah jurisprudence, the condition for custody is that the mother must be a Muslim, because Allah (swt) has created a child monotheistic by nature and He does not permit non-Muslims to raise a Muslim child.

13.10   What is the Relationship between Custody and Breast-Feeding?

There are several narrations in this regard. For example, a mentally sick or retarded mother is not permitted to breast-feed her child because the process of breastfeeding has deep physical and psychological effects. In this same manner a mentally unwell or retarded mother is not granted the right to custody.

---

[1] *Wasa'il ash-Shi'ah*, vol. 14, Book of Marriage, chapter 81, narration 6.
[2] *Ibid.*

13.11   Who has the Right to Custody of the Child whose Parents are not Present?

In Islam the issue of custody has important educational implications and the Islamic government is responsible for providing a suitable environment for the child. This matter should be organised and systematised. Custody of the child is given to the mother but the father is responsible for the child's expenses. If the father is poor, the government should provide his/her expenses.

In case the child is rich enough (by way of inheritance) to pay his/her expenses, then he/she has to pay. If the mother has the right to custody, it is not obligatory on her to manage everything on her own. She can use help but it is important for her to organise and supervise the healthy upbringing of her child in a suitable manner.

In case of the father's demise, the custody of the child that had earlier been given to the father will return to the mother, even if she has remarried. She is given priority over all others excepting for the paternal grandfather of the child. In case the mother does not accept the custody of the child, it is then transferred to the father. If both of them do not accept it, then the government should compel them to take on their responsibility. This is because custody is an obligation; in fact, custody is a right. As regards whether the parents can forsake the responsibility of custody: The late Sabzevari says: "Yes". But we say "No". The reason is that the philosophy of custody is not based on personal choice, but it is based on the (natural) need of the child to be protected.

Another question that arises is whether the parents have the right to delegate the custodial rights to each other. In this case the jurisprudents say: 'There is no problem in this, provided that the child is not neglected'. In case the man claims that the woman does not have the necessary means for the healthy upbringing of the child, and, if the woman claims otherwise, the jurisprudents are obliged to accept the mother's claim. The mother's word should not be doubted and when she claims that she has the necessary means to take care of her child, it should be accepted.

According to Islam, in case both parents who are responsible for the child do not deliver their responsibilities as they are expected to, the government is responsible for the child's custody. In case of divorce or conflict between a couple the right of custody is given to the woman and nothing nullifies this right. If a child is the result of an unlawful marriage or is born out of wedlock, then the mother has the right to the custody of the child.

In case a woman is pregnant and if her husband dies before the birth of the child, and if the paternal grandfather is not available to take over the custody, the right of custody belongs to the mother, regardless of the child's gender.

The custody of the child continues until the time that the child reaches puberty, along with a certain level of maturity; merely considering the age of puberty is not enough. This is because a human child needs a certain level of mental development in order to analyse and handle his/her problems; thus, until that time he/she is in need of protection and custody.

13.12   What Needs Fall under the Issue of Custody?

Custody means taking care of the need for food, clothing, shelter, and health and other emotional, psychological, and educational needs.

Conclusion

Laws are needed to protect and ensure the efficient running of a society. As human beings we have been placed on earth with the unique feature of responsibility. Mankind bears responsibility on an individual and collective level. Islam as a complete system provides laws to ensure the protection of the needs of people; such needs become the responsibility of individuals and society.

In the event of divorce it is the need for protection of the child or children involved which is of paramount importance. Islam takes into consideration the affect such a situation could impose on other parties involved, and wishes to place no undue burden or hardship on individuals. The child has a basic right to nurturing, and thus it is the right of the mother and child, that the child remains with the mother for the two years of breastfeeding, unless otherwise mutually agreed. Islamic law takes into consideration the emotional well-being as well as economic security of the child, and thus the differences in custodial ages arises between girls and boys.

Custodial laws in Islam ensure the basic rights and needs of the child and places responsibility on the parents at an individual level. Failing this, such responsibility then becomes the obligation of the state and society.

Article 14

The Islamic Modest Dress- A Shortened Version of Mutahari's Book "The Islamic Modest Dress"

Ali Hussain Al-Hakim

Abstract
The philosophy of Islamic Hijab depends on several factors; some are psychological and relate to the home and family. Others have socio-logical roots, and others relate to raising the dignity of a woman and preventing her debasement. Our aim in this paper is to explore each of the above-mentioned issues as well as analysing different arguments exerted for the appearance of the modest dress in history and whether or not such reasons hold true for Islam as well.

14.1 The Meaning of the Word 'Hijab' (Modest Dress)

Before we begin our discussion, it is necessary to look at the meaning of the word *hijab*, which is used in our age to refer to a woman's covering. This word gives the sense of 'covering' because it refers to a veil. That 'covering' which is referred to as a *hijab* is that which appears behind a curtain. The Holy Qur'an describes the setting of the sun in the story of the Prophet Solomon (as),

> ...until the sun was covered (bilhijab) and time for the afternoon ritual
> prayer was over. (Qur'an, 38:32)

The diaphragm separating the heart from the stomach is also called '*hijab*'.

The use of the word *satr* in the sense of 'covering' became common instead of *hijab*, especially by the religious jurisprudents. It would have been better if the word had not been changed and we had continued to use the word *satr* because, as we have said, the prevalent meaning of the word *hijab* is a veil. If it is to be used in the sense of 'covering', it gives the idea of a woman being placed behind a curtain. This very thing has caused a great number of people to think that Islam wants women to always remain behind a curtain, to be imprisoned in the house and not to leave it. The duty for covering, which has been established for women in Islam, does not necessarily mean that they should not leave their homes. It is not the intention of Islam to imprison women. We may find such ideas in the ancient, pre-Islamic past of some countries like Iran or India but no such thing exists in Islam.

The philosophy behind the *hijab* for the woman in Islam is that she should cover her body in her associations with men 'whom she is not related to according to the Divine Law *(na-mahram)*' and that she does not flaunt and display herself. The verses of the Holy Qur'an, which refer to this issue, affirm this and the edicts of the religious jurisprudents confirm it.

14.2   The Real Visage of the Modest Dress

The fact is that the *hijab* is not concerned with whether or not it is good for a woman to appear in society covered or uncovered. The point is whether or not a woman and a man's need of her should be a limitless, free association or not. Should a man have the right to satisfy his needs with every woman and in every place short of committing adultery? Islam, which looks at the spirit of the problem, answers: No.

Men are only allowed to satisfy their sexual desires with their legal wives within a marital situation based upon the laws of marriage, which establish a series of heavy commitments. It is forbidden for men to have any physical relations with women they are not related to by marriage.

Should the seeking of sexual pleasure be limited to the family environment and legal wives, or is the freedom of seeking sexual fulfilment something that should be satisfied in society at large? Islam defends the first theory. According to Islamic precepts, limiting sexual desires to the family environment and legal wives helps to maintain the mental health of the society. It strengthens the relationships between the members of the family and fosters the development of a perfect harmony between a husband and wife. As far as society is concerned, it keeps and preserves energies to be then used for social activities and it causes a woman to attain a higher position in the eyes of man.

That is, Islamic precepts aim at limiting all kinds of sexual enjoyment to the family and the marital environment within the bounds of marriage, so that society is only a place for work and activity. It is opposite to the Western system of the present era, which mixes work with sexual enjoyment. Islam separates these two environments completely.

14.3   Psychological Tranquillity

Without limits being established for relations between men and women or with unlimited free associations, sexual excitement and stimulation increase, and demands become unquenchable and insatiable. The sexual instinct is a powerful, deep-rooted instinct, which resembles the fathomless ocean. Although one thinks that by obeying it, one will have tamed it, its rebellious nature continues to show forth. It is like a fire: the more fuel added to it the more intense the flame.

History recalls those who coveted wealth, who were continuously seeking to add to what they already had; however much they gained, they were still hungry for more. It also mentions, and applies to those who were covetous of sexual pleasure. In no way did possessing beautiful women and dominating them satisfy men's desires. This was the situation of all of those who had harems and, in truth, all those who had the power to possess women.

At any rate, Islam has placed a special emphasis upon the amazing power of this fiery instinct. There are traditions which speak of the danger of a look, the danger of a man and woman being alone together and, finally, the danger of the instinct which unites a man and a woman.

Islam has established ways of controlling, balancing and taming the instinct. Duties have been given to both men and women in this area. One duty, which is the responsibility of both men and women, relates to looking at each other.

> Say to the believing men to cast down their glance and guard their private parts. (Quran, 24:30) Say to the believing women to cast down their glance and guard their private parts. (Quran, 24:31)

In summary, the command is that a man and a woman should not fix their eyes upon each other; they should not flirt with each other; they should not look at each other with lust or with the intention of seeking sexual pleasure (unless it is within the sacred bounds of marriage).

Islam has established a particular command for a woman which is that she covers her body from a man with whom she is not *mahram* and that she should not flaunt herself or put her body on display in society. She is asked not to stimulate the attention of men by any means.

The reason why the Islamic command to cover is exclusive to women is because the desire to show off and display one's self is a particular trait of women. She is the hunter for the domination of the hearts of men, and man is the prey, whereas man is the hunter for the domination of the body of women and she is the prey. A woman's desire to display herself comes from this essence of the hunter. It is the female instinct which, because of its particular nature, wishes to capture hearts and imprison the male. Thus, the deviation begins with the female instinct and therefore the command for her to cover was issued.

14.4   Solidifying the Roots of the Family

There is no doubt that anything which confirms the roots of the family, and increases the perception of marital relations is good for the family unit. The greatest efforts must be made to have this happen. The opposite is also true. Anything which causes the relationship between a husband and wife to grow cold is detrimental to a family and must be struggled against.

Finding the fulfilment of sexual desires within the family environment and within the framework of a legal marriage will strengthen the relationship between a husband and wife, causing their union to become more stable.

The philosophy of the modest dress and the control of sexual desires other than with a legal wife, from the point of view of the family unit, is so that one legal partner will be the cause for the well being of the other.

The difference between the society which limits sexual relations to the family environment and a legal marriage, and a society which promotes free relationships is that marriage, in the first society, is the end to the anticipation and deprivation, whereas in the latter it is the beginning of deprivation and limitation. In the system of free sexual relationships, the marriage contract ends the free period of boys and girls and it obliges them to learn to be loyal to each other whereas, in the Islamic system, their deprivation and anticipation is met.

14.5   Preserving the Society

Taking sexual desires from the bounds of the family environment to society has weakened society's capacity for work and activity. Contrary to the opinion that 'the modest dress results in paralysing half of the energy potential of the individuals of society', the lack of the modest dress and the gradual development of free relationships has caused the social force to fail.

That which has caused the paralysis of women's power and that which has imprisoned her talents, is the lack of the modest dress. In Islam, there is no question of the modest dress prohibiting a woman from participating in cultural, social or economic activities. Islam neither says that a woman cannot leave her home nor does it say that she cannot seek knowledge and learning. Rather, men and women must both learn and seek knowledge. There is no objection to women's economic activities in Islam. Islam has never wanted women to be useless and unoccupied. It has never desired that women bring up useless and indifferent children. The covering of the body, except for the face and hands, is not to prevent any kind of cultural or social or economic activity. That which paralyses the working force is the corruption of the work environment by the element of seeking the satisfaction of sexual pleasures.

14.6   The Reasons for *Hijab*

It seems that throughout history there were many reasons for which *Hijab* as a social phenomenon existed. Within the next few pages we will examine those reasons.

14.6.1 The Philosophical Reason

Social commentators have often presented their reasons for the appearance of the modest dress centred on the idea that, even in the first principles of nature, no covering or veil has been made to come between males and females. They say that there is no instance in nature where a curtain or veil appears between the male and female sex, or for the female sex to be set aside behind a curtain and to wear a covering.

The philosophical reason Centres on the tendency towards asceticism and struggling with pleasures in an effort to subdue the ego. The main source for this thought is perhaps India where a barrier was created between men and women through the pursuance of asceticism because a woman was considered to be the highest form for receiving lustful pleasure. If men were to mix freely with women, according to this idea, a man would mainly pursue this and his society would remain underdeveloped in other areas. Therefore, he had to struggle to conquer his own soul by denying it the enjoyment of sexual pleasures. Thus they began to seek celibacy and asceticism.

The second reason given for the appearance of the desire for asceticism is the opposite of the first. Persons who were very extreme in their sexual practices, to such an extent, that even exceeded the limits of nature, would develop an aversion and suddenly turn away from sex.

As to these two reasons, we do not say that they did not exist in the world. They could have been and these causes might have had these effects, but Islam established the modest dress. It did not exist during the Age of Ignorance in Arabia. We have to see whether or not these causes have been mentioned in Islam and have been given as proof or whether other reasons have been given for it. Does this precept conform to other Islamic precepts? Does the Islamic spirit of asceticism conform to the concept of asceticism, which we have mentioned? We will see that Islam has never presented this point of view and, as matter of fact, Islam has struggled greatly against this view. Even non-Muslims agree that Islam never promoted asceticism and ascetic practices. The concept that began among Hindus and extended to Christianity did not exist in Islam.

The Holy Qur'an says that the creation of the means of embellishment is among the mercies that God has shown His creatures, and it severely criticises those who deny themselves the beauties of this world. The Holy Qur'an says:

> Who has forbidden the beautiful (gifts) of God which He has produced for His servants and the things, clean and pure, (which He has provided) for sustenance? (Quran, 7:32)

Islamic traditions say that the pure Imams (as) consistently debated with the Sufis and referring to this very verse of the Holy Qur'an, invalidated their deeds.

The legitimate pleasures, which spouses receive from each other, are considered to be blessings in Islam, among the Divine rewards; it is perhaps difficult for foreigners to understand this concept and perhaps they wonder to themselves, "How strange that they call this filthy act a blessing, a spiritual reward!" It is surprising for a Hindu or a Christian to realise how much spiritual reward there is in performing the ritual bath (*ghusl*) after sexual intercourse and washing away the sweat, which has been created by this act.

Islam has placed many limitations on such issues, but within the area that has been limited, not only does it not forbid it, but rather it encourages it.

Therefore, it is clear that the above-mentioned philosophy of asceticism cannot be attributed to Islam. This philosophy might have existed in some places in the world but it does not conform to Islam.

14.6.2   The Social Reason

Another cause, which has been given for the observance of the modest dress, is the sense of insecurity. They say that the modest dress appeared due to a lack of security, which had developed. Lack of security was very extensive in the past. Just as there was no security in relation to wealth and property, there was no security in relation to women either. Just as men were obliged to hide their money and their wealth, they were also obliged to hide their women.

History records that in Sassanid Iran, the high priests and princes would seek out and take any beautiful girl that they heard about. The idea of the modest dress then was to hide women so that no other man would come to know about her.

It could now be argued that since security exists, there is presently no need for the modest dress. We have to compare this with the philosophy of Islam. Was the reason Islam introduced the modest dress because of this question of security? When we look at the issue, we see that neither in Islamic analyses has such an issue appeared nor does it conform to history. The modest dress did not exist among the Arab Bedouins during the Age of Ignorance and, at the same time, security existed. That is, at the same time that individual insecurity and aggression against women had attained the greatest extent possible in Iran and women covered themselves, this type of aggression did not exist among individuals in the tribes in Arabia. The very tribal character protected the women.

The security, which, did not exist among the tribes, was social or group security and covering does not solve this kind of problem.

When two tribes fought, they not only took the men, but the women, their children and everything else as well. Covering would not have protected the women.

In spite of the obvious differences, which the Arab Bedouins had with our industrialised life, it resembled our life in the sense that adultery, in particular, by married women, was rampant. But because of a certain type of democracy and lack of tyranny, no one would forcibly take the wife of another man. Yet the individual insecurity, which a person in the industrialised West sensed, was lacking among the Bedouins.

The covering prevents the aggression of a person who lives in one place. This kind of aggression does not exist among tribes. Therefore, we cannot say that Islamic precepts established the modest dress simply to provide security.

Our discussion will now Centre on the issue of the modest dress (*hijab*) in Islam but we must first hold a more general discussion because the modest dress is not exclusive to Islam. That is, it is not the idea that the modest dress appeared for the first time in the world with Islam. It existed before Islam among ancient peoples other than the Arab nations. It existed in ancient India and in ancient Iran, as well. The modest dress which ancient India and Iran had was much stricter than that which Islam brought. Of course, if we take the Arabian Peninsula into consideration, Islamic modest dress was established, not imitated. That is, Islam imported the modest dress into the Arabian Peninsula but it existed in non-Arab lands throughout the world.

It is a phenomenon, which existed during non-Islamic times. Philosophical, social, economic, ethical and psychological reasons have been given as the cause for the development of this phenomenon and as to how it happened that the modest dress came to appear in history among people. It is necessary to mention these reasons because they have said that these are the causes for the appearance of the modest dress and that it first appeared because of certain very particular conditions, which existed in those times.

Conditions whereby it was, perhaps, necessary for it to be but now that those conditions no longer exist, there is no reason for the modest dress.

Thus, we have to see what the reasons mentioned are, whether or not they are the real causes or is it, as some people say, that which caused the modest dress to come into being was unjust.

14.6.3   The Economic Reason

Some claim that the modest dress developed because of economics, and of course, to exploit women. They claim that history shows that there have been four eras in the relationship between men and women including the present age.

The first age of humanity, according to this view, was a communal age with reference to sex. That is, essentially no family life existed. The second era was when men dominated women and women were seen as their slaves and a means to serve men. The second era, then, was the era of ownership by man. The third era was the age when women arose in objection to men and the fourth era is the era of equality of rights between men and women. These four stages expressed in this manner are all erroneous. There are no facts regarding the first era, which they mention as being communal. There is no evidence that family life did not exist from the very beginning.

We do not intend to go into detail about these eras but will simply refer to the fact that they say the modest dress relates to the era when men dominated women. Men saw that it would be to their advantage to put women behind a curtain and prevent their comings and goings so that they would better undertake the work of the house, which had been allocated to them. Thus, men did this in order for them to have hired women from the economic point of view; otherwise there was no reason to do such a thing. Wherever the modest dress appeared, it was accompanied by such a situation of the employment of women to work in the houses of men.

Is it true that this reason existed in those places in the world where the modest dress appeared? We do not deny that perhaps in some corners of the world this situation existed. However, we are discussing Islam. Islam, on the one hand, established and brought the modest dress and, on the other, very directly stated something which is among the very clear aspects of Islam, which is that a man has absolutely no right to gain, economically, from a woman. A woman has a right to work outside the home as long as it does not harm the family environment. Whatever she earns belongs to her alone, no matter what legitimate work she performs.

It must be clearly recognized then, that Islamic precepts do not intend for the modest dress be a means to economically exploit women. If this had been the intention, the ruling would have reflected this. For instance, the precepts would have stated that a man has the right to employ his wife in his home and a woman must wear the modest dress. A system, which states that a man has no right to exploit a woman, but on the other hand has established the modest dress clearly then did not establish the modest dress to exploit women.

14.6.4 The Ethical Reason

Another reason given for the appearance of the modest dress has an ethical aspect, and relates to the character and nature of an individual. It stems from the selfishness of men and men's jealousy. A man dominated a woman so that he could enjoy her exclusively. This is a type of excessive greed, which existed in men, and caused them to impose the modest dress.

Bertrand Russell says that human beings have been able, to a certain extent, to dominate over their greed for wealth in such a way that they later encouraged charity and sharing the table with others because these things related to wealth. They came to regard excessive greed as something disagreeable in human beings, but they were not able to control their greed for sex in the same way. Thus, they came and changed the name of this attitude to 'manliness' or 'zeal'.

Imam Ali (as) said, "A noble, zealous person never commits adultery". He did not say 'a jealous person never commits adultery' but rather a zealous one. The reason for this is because manliness is a noble and human virtue. It is a human virtue, which relates to society and its purity. Just as a zealous man does not allow corruption of the women he is related to, neither is he content to see the women of society being corrupted. This is because zeal is other than jealousy. Jealousy is a personal and individual affair and stems from a series of spiritual beliefs but zeal is an emotion and a sensitivity, which relates to the human species as a whole.

Human beings have been given an instinct, which is the basis for the preservation of society, and that instinct is that: Women are desirous of preserving their generations and so are men, but women are protected as a result. When a child is born, it is clear who its mother is and the mother knows her child. Even if she were to have intercourse with a thousand men, she would know that the future generations are assured, but men are not reassured in this way unless they have guarded that woman and created some precautions whereby they are assured of their paternity.

Can a person say that we must eliminate this instinct called 'zeal', which exists within human beings? And that this is the same thing as jealousy? Even those who live in a communal way, concerning property, have not claimed the above in relation to women.

14.6.5   The Psychological Reason

Some people believe that the modest dress and staying at home are based on psychological reasons and that women have developed an inferiority complex towards men since the beginning. A woman's monthly period was considered to be a kind of deficiency in ancient times, which led to the isolation of women during their prescribed courses, and their avoidance by those around them. Islam changed this, the Prophet (saws) forbidding such isolation saying: 'Nothing is forbidden except sexual intercourse'.

Many ideas have further been expressed regarding the fact that women have a sort of emotional deficiency and subsequently both men and women came to believe that woman was abased.

Whether they are correct or not, there is no relation between this and the philosophy of Islam about women and the modest dress or 'covering'. Islamic precepts neither refer to menstruation nor the modest dress as a reason to consider women as lowly or abased.

14.7   The Modest Dress Brings Dignity to a Woman

One of the criticisms which have been attributed to the modest dress is that it deprives the woman of honour and respect. We know that human dignity has become one of the important goals of humanity since the development of charters concerning human rights. Human dignity is respected and it must be preserved; all human beings share in this whether man or woman, black or white, or whatever nation or creed.

It has been claimed that the Islamic modest dress opposes a woman's dignity. We accept the right of human dignity. The discussion is whether or not the modest dress, i.e. the modest dress which Islamic precepts mention, is disrespectful to women, and an insult to her dignity. This idea came into being from the idea that the modest dress imprisons and enslaves a woman, and enslavement opposes human dignity. It is further asserted that because men, to enable them to exploit women, introduced the modest dress, they thus wanted to captivate woman and imprison her in a corner of her home. Therefore, her human dignity is insulted and hence the respect, honour and nobility of a woman, call for her not to adorn herself with the modest dress.

As we observe, if a man leaves his house naked, he is rebuked and reproached and possibly arrested by the police. Even if a man leaves his house in his night clothes, or in his underpants, everyone will stop him, because it opposes social dignity. Law or custom rules that when a man leaves the house, he should be covered and fully dressed. Does it oppose human dignity to tell him to cover himself before leaving the house? Similarly, if a woman leaves her house, covered within the prescribed limits, it causes greater respect for her. That is, it prevents the interference of men who lack morality and ethics. If a woman leaves her house covered, not only does it not detract from her human dignity, but it adds to it. She should be dressed so that she does not distract a man and turn his attention from what he is doing. Does this oppose a woman's dignity? Or does it oppose the dignity of society? If a person says something which applied to non-Islamic societies -i.e. that the purpose of modest dress was to restrict women, or that a woman must be imprisoned in the home with no right to associate with anyone outside- this has absolutely no basis or relation with the teachings of Islam.

However, a woman must not do anything that could disrupt family life. She should not, for example, leave to spend a week with her sister if her sister is corrupt, or visit her mother if her absence from home would lead to chaos. The tranquillity of the family must not be disturbed. A second condition is that leaving the house, according to the Holy Qur'an, must not be a pretext in order for someone to flaunt herself, to disturb the peace and tranquillity of others, or to prevent the work of others. If these afore-mentioned circumstances are not going to arise, then there is no problem in her leaving the house.

14.8   Is 'Looking' Permissible For Men?

If we say that it is not obligatory for women to cover their face and hands, does this agree with the saying that it is advisable for men to lower their gaze? Is it something which needs to be discussed separately? We know from the lifestyle of the Holy Prophet (saws) that it is not obligatory for men to cover their head, hands, face or neck. Does this mean that it is also not advisable that men lower their gaze, if they are walking down the street and women are passing? These are two different issues and must be discussed separately.

Another point is that the face and the hands are among the absolute necessities of Islam whereby covering everything but them is obligatory for women. Of course, this, itself, has an exception, which is that when women reach beyond a certain age, it is no longer obligatory for them. But in general, covering the hair of a woman is among the compulsory precepts of Islam. Covering the neck, chest, the arms above the wrists, the feet (which is debated), from the ankles above, are all among the obligatory aspects of Islam. There is no controversy here.

Another point is whether or not lowering the gaze is advisable. If the look is of a flirting nature, looking with the anticipation of pleasure, this is another clear issue, which is among those, which are forbidden. Not only is it forbidden to look at strangers or persons to whom one is not *mahram*, it is also forbidden to look at those who are *mahram* in this way as well. In Islam, lust is allowed exclusively between marital partners. It is not permissible in any form anywhere else between anyone else.

But this should be distinguished from *riba'* which means to look but not with the intention of lust nor to really see or view the other person. It is a special state, which could be dangerous. That is, the fear exists that the look will cause a person to deviate to a forbidden state. This, then, is also forbidden and there is no difference of opinion on this.

We have said that there are two issues involved here. First, what is obligatory upon women and what is permissible for men. Those points which are clear are that it is obligatory upon women to cover themselves except for their face and hands. It is neither compulsory, nor mentioned in the Holy Qur'an, nor can we find any reason, in the traditions, to believe that it is obligatory for women to cover their face and hands.

Thus there are only these two questions. Is it obligatory upon a woman to cover her face and hands, and secondly is it permissible or not for a man to look without lust or fear of deviation?

14.9   From the View Point of Muslims Narrations

From the point of view of the traditions, it is more or less certain that it is not necessary for women to cover the face and hands and it is not forbidden for men to look at a woman's face or hands if his look is not one of lust or fear of deviation. The traditions are numerous; one is from Imam Ridha (as) who is asked:

> Is it permissible for a man to look at the hair of his wife's sister? He replied: No. It is not permissible unless she is a woman who is past childbearing age. A wife's sister is just like any other woman that you are not related to according to the Divine Law and you can only look at her and her hair if she is beyond child-bearing age.

Whenever the Imams (as) were asked if it is permissible to look at a woman's hair, etc., they were never asked if it is permissible to look at a woman's face when the look is not one of lust or fear of deviation.

There is another tradition from Imam Ridha (as) about a young boy. "Must a seven-year old boy be encouraged to recite the ritual prayer?" He said, "It is not obligatory but to encourage it is a good thing." It is not necessary that a woman hide her hair from him until he reaches puberty. We see that again it is covering the hair, which is referred to, and not covering the face.

14.10   Hearing the Voice of a Non-*Mahram* Woman

Another issue is that of hearing the voice of a non-*mahram* woman. Is this forbidden or not? It is clear from the edicts that it is not forbidden as long as it is not for lust or in fear of deviating. However, it is forbidden for a woman to make her voice pleasant and attractive so as to attract a man whereby a man who has a sickness in his heart hears her voice, and becomes attracted to it through lust.

14.11   Muslim Customs

If we assume that Muslims have acquired a custom from the beginning of Islam, and it is discovered to have been from the customs of the Holy Prophet (saws) and the Imams (as), it should be preserved. However, a custom of the people is not proof in itself, except when it is discovered to be from among the customs of the Holy Prophet (saws), as then it becomes proof and must be observed.

The modest dress did not exist among the pre-Islamic Arabs. Islam brought the covering of the head, neck, and chest, etc. and the forbidding of looking with lust. But a part of that which Islam brought existed in non-Arab areas. It was a very strong influence in Iran, in particular, among the Jews and people were influenced by their way of thinking.

Islam did not make uncovering the face obligatory. It said it is obligatory to cover the hair, not to display the face. Clearly, those nations which came to accept Islam were following their own customs because Islamic precepts did not say it was obligatory to display the face, except in the harem. Nor did they say it was forbidden to cover the face - it gave a choice and left it up to the various nations to practice their own customs of the modest dress if they so desired.

History shows that non-Arabs felt it was obligatory to cover the face. Thus, this custom of covering the face, as we find it now, is not a custom from the Holy Prophet and the Imams (as).

Conclusion

If a person were to look at Islam with an open mind, he or she would confirm that the way of Islam is the way of moderation. At the same time that Islamic precepts have exerted the greatest extent of precaution to protect the purity and sanctity of sexual relations, in no way do they prevent the human talents of women from blossoming. As a matter of fact, these precepts provide for both the spirit to remain healthy and for family relations to be more intimate and serious as well as better preparing men and women for a healthy social environment, far from any extremes.

Only by respecting the nature that God has given them, and by protecting the beauty of their gender, will women rediscover their

real personality and the possibility that they will no longer be a
tool, a toy and a means to men's lust, in the name of freedom and
equality.

Glossary

Alamu l'ghayb	The unseen world
Amirul mu'minin	Prince of believers
(as)	Alayhi salam- peace be upon him
Awliya Allah	Leaders of Allah
Ayah/t	Sign of Allah (also refers to Qur'anic verse)
Batul, al-	Free from menstruation and postnatal bleeding
Bid'a	Innovation
Darajah	Degree of authority
Da'awah	The call to Islam, usually the process of propagating Islam to non-Muslims
Eid ul Adha	Islamic festival, marking the end of Hajj
Fatwa	Islamic legal opinion based on sound evidence from Islamic texts
Fitna	Evil clash or corruption
Fitrah	Inherent nature of man
Fuqaha (faqih sing.)	Islamic jurisprudent
Hadeeth qudsi	A sacred narration which is said

	by Almighty God (swt), however it is not a part of Qur'an
Hazrat	His/her honourable
Hijab	Islamic modest clothes
Hijab an Nur	Covering of light, refers to inner spiritual quality
Hijrah	Islamic Calendar
Hukm	Legal ruling
Ibadah	Act of worship
Ibadou (pl. Of abd)	Servant
'iddah	Waiting period following dissolution of marriage
Ifrath	Exaggeration
Ijtihad	Lit. 'exertion', and technically the effort a jurist makes in order to deduce the law, which is not self-evident from its sources
Insan	Human being
Jabr	Predestination, a belief which states that everything is fixed by God
Jahilliyah	Era of pre-Islamic ignorance
Jamaa'	In congregation
Jihad	Holy war or struggle

Jilbaab	Article of clothing, usually long, covering the entire body
Jubn	Cowardice, regardless of situation
Khaira ummatin	Best of people
Khilafah	Caliph, the Islamic Leadership after the Prophet's (saws) demise
Khula	Divorce, usually instigated by wife
Madhahib (pl. Of Madhhab)	Religious faction or school of jurisprudence
Madrasa	School
Mahram	Person who one is forbidden to marry (e.g. Father, brother etc.)
Marabout	Religious leader/intermediary in context of the Sufi *turuq:* plural of *tariqah* meaning path or way within mystical teaching
Masjid	Mosque
Masjid ul jaama'	Friday mosque
Muhallil	Bogus husband
Mut'ah	Flexible marriage
Nushuz	Rebellion, lack of harmony, discord in a marriage
Osveh hassaneh	Righteous example

Owrat	Area of body requiring covering
Ramadan	Holy Islamic month, of fasting
Riba'	To look at the other sex without lust
Rida'ah	Breastfeeding
Salaat	Prayer
Satr	Covering
(saws)	Salallahu alayhi wa'alihiwa salam - peace and blessings be upon him & his household
Shari'ah Law	Islamic Law
Shuhud	Gnostic knowledge
Sunnah	Teachings of the Prophet (saws)
Tafrit	Insufficiency
Tafsir	Qur'anic exegesis
Tahawwur	Fearless, regardless of situation
Tajwid	Art of reciting the Qur'an
Talaq	Divorce (instigated by the husband)
Taqwa	Piety
Turuq	Adherents to the Sufi path
Ulema	Religious scholars

Ummah	Islamic community
Wilayat	Guardianship
Wudhu	Ablution

Index

A

Abbasid
    Caliphs, 284
Abbasids, 228
Abduh, 198, 211
Abduh, sheikh Muhammad, 150, 151, 153, 161, 165, 166, 174, 198, 214
Abdullah, Jabir, 227
Abraham
    Wife of, 112, 120
Abraham, Prophet (as), 25, 110, 111, 112, 113, 120, 135, 331
Abu Bakr, 209, 300, 302
Abu Hanifa, 195, 198
Abu Lahab, 112, 121
    Wife of, 112, 121
Abu Rafi, 202
Abu Yusuf, 195, 198
Abyssinia, 136
Afghani, sayyid Jamaluddin Al-, 198
Afghanistan, 143
Africa, 20, 41, 84, 141, 220, 221, 222, 223, 226, 234, 235, 264, 328
Age of Ignorance. See pre-Islamic society
Agriculture, 249
Aisha, 149, 157, 176, 205, 208, 216, 240, 290, 291
Aleppo, 140
Alfonso I, 246
Algeria, 143
Amazon feminism. See Feminism
America, 84, 263, 277, 310
American Revolution, 31, 55
Amin, 60, 319
Amin, Qasim, 319
Amoli, Javadi, 113, 117, 118
Anas, Malik ibn, 195, 198
Andalusia, 253
Angelic world, 154
Angels, 169
Anglican Synod, 330
Anthropology, 220, 221, 222, 230, 231, 235
    Islamic, 220, 222, 235
Antino, 247
Anushirwan, Persian/Iranian king, 251
Aquinas St. Thomas, 88
Arab feminists. See Feminists

B

C

D

E

F